# STALIN

# STALIN

## A Time for Judgement

JONATHAN LEWIS
and
PHILLIP WHITEHEAD

Thames Methuen

First published in Great Britain 1990
by Methuen London
Michelin House, 81 Fulham Road, London SW3 6RB
In association with Thames Television International Ltd
149 Tottenham Court Road, London WIP 9LL

A CIP catalogue record for this book is
available from the British Library.

ISBN 0 413 63360 8

Typeset by Rowland Phototypesetting Ltd,
Bury St. Edmunds, Suffolk
Printed in Great Britain by
BPCC Hazell Books Ltd
Member of BPCC Ltd
Aylesbury, Bucks, England

*To those who suffered*

## AUTHORS' NOTE

Many of the quotes in this book are drawn from the interviews filmed for the Thames Television series *Stalin*. They can be identified, and distinguished from the other quotations, because they do not have a footnote reference number. A full list of the people we interviewed is given in an appendix at the end of the text.

*A note on transliteration of proper names*

In our use of Russian proper names we have generally followed the familiar western usage for well-known personalities (eg. Joseph rather than Iosif Stalin) and have used the i-ending for first names, and y for surnames, where the two are often interchangeable.

# CONTENTS

# ILLUSTRATIONS

*Maps*

The publishers are grateful to the following for permission to reproduce the illustrations. All possible care has been taken to trace and acknowledge the sources of illustrations. If any errors have accidentally occurred, however, we shall be happy upon notification to correct them in any future editions of this book.

*Black and white illustrations*: Tofik Shakhverdiev, Moscow: 1, 107, 110; Stalin Museum, Gori: 2, 3; David King Collection, London: 4, 6, 8, 10, 15, 20, 21, 26, 31, 35, 37, 45, 56, 58, 63, 68, 69, 75, 77, 78, 82, 86, 88, 90, 92, 93, 94, 97, 99; Young Pioneers' Hall, formerly Gori School: 5; Ushangi Davitashvili, Private Collection, Tbilisi: 7, 9, 11, 28, 40, 41, 42, 85; Novosti Press Agency, London: 12, 14, 16, 19, 25, 30, 71, 104, 108, 109; Popperfoto, London: 13, 76, 80, 81, 84, 95, 96, 100, 106; Lenin Museum, Alliluyev apartment, Leningrad: 17, 18; Hoover Institution Archives, Stanford University: 44; HIA, Russian Pictorial Collection: 22, 23; HIA, Charles Hall Collection: 24; HIA, Poland: Ministry of Information Collection: 62; HIA, Karski Collection: 70; The International Historical Press Photo Collection, SVT, Stockholm: 27, 29, 34, 43, 65; Second World Center, Amsterdam: 33, 61; Marina Goldovskaya Collection, Moscow: 36; Karelian State Regional Museum, Petrozavodsk: 38, 39; Jonathan Lewis: 46, 47, 48, 49, 50, 51, 52, 89; Anna Larina, Private Collection, Moscow: 53, 54; Julien Bryan, International Film Foundation, New York: 55; Zenon Pozniak Collection, Minsk: 57; National Archives, Washington DC: 59, 60, 64; Evgenii Ryabko-Minkin, Moscow: 66, 67, 73; Imperial War Museum, London: 72, 74; School of Slavonic and East European Studies, University of London: 83, 91; United Nations, New York: 87; Hulton-Deutsch Collection, London: 98, 101, 102; Countess Hélène Zamoyska, St Clar-de-Rivière, France: 103; Mikhail Chiaureli, Private Collection, Tbilisi: 111.

*Colour illustrations*: Hoover Institution Archives, Stanford University (RU/SU 2317.5): 1; HIA (RU/SU 1855): 2; HIA (RU/SU 628): 4; School of Slavonic and East European Studies, University of London (reprinted from *Ogonyok*): 3; Archives of the West German Foreign Ministry, Bonn: 5; Pyotr Belov, courtesy of his widow, Marianna Belova (photo by Albert Lekhmus): 6, 7; David King Collection, London: 8, 9.

*Maps*: The maps were drawn by Neil Hyslop. The maps on pages 127 and 142 are based on maps in Martin Gilbert's *Soviet History Atlas* (Routledge Kegan Paul, 1979).

# ACKNOWLEDGEMENTS

This book is the work of many hands, but the final responsibility for its contents is ours alone. We would like to single out Isobel Hinshelwood for her unstinting dedication to the picture research, and to the assembly of the book. It could not have been produced without her, and her name should properly join ours in its creation. Our other colleagues on the Thames Television series, Tony Cash, Teresa Cherfas, Raye Farr, Mary Horwood, Karen Snare and Adrian Wood have all put in much extra work to supplement our efforts and to protect us from error. We have benefited from the advice and guidance of the publishers, and from the personal support of Ann Mansbridge and Alex Bennion at Thames Methuen and Sara Drake at Thames Publishing, as they steered us towards deadlines so different from those of television.

The consultants to the series were always helpful, and open to our queries, however detailed or tedious. Our first thanks must go to Professor Alec Nove, who has also found time in a life of extraordinary industry to write the foreword. Anton Antonov-Ovseyenko and Professors Stephen Cohen, Alexander Chubaryan, John Erickson, Yuri Polyakov and Oleg Rzheshevsky were present at all or most of our seminars, and otherwise generous with their time. So, throughout, has been our friend and colleague Dr Gregory Guroff, the senior consultant to WGBH TV, Boston. We also owe a debt to Professors Robert Tucker, Moshe Lewin, Leszek Kolakowski, Robert Conquest and Warren Kimball, and to Dr Robert Service, who helped us with many difficult points of interpretation.

All those who were interviewed for the series are named and briefly described in the Appendix. Over one hundred interviews in Russian, Georgian, Ukrainian, Byelorussian, Serbo-Croat and English were conducted by our colleagues Tony Cash, Teresa Cherfas, Isobel Hinshelwood and ourselves, and by Yevgen Sverstiuk, Marina Levashov-Tumanishvili, Yuri Mechitov, Tanya Kosinova, Angelina Grasso and Zenon Pozniak on our behalf. We record our thanks to the interviewees, and our satisfaction that this is one of the first books on this subject in which no source has had to seek the refuge of anonymity.

We have other debts to pay. Much of the pictorial material for this book comes from the voluminous David King Collection in London and we both thank him and salute his industry in preserving records which, for a dark period, those in power in the Soviet Union would have preferred to destroy. The additional material owes much to the help we received in the field from our devoted television crew, Jim Howlett, Eric Brazier, Dennis Fordham and John Baker, and its embellishment back at Thames to our designer Morgan Sendall, and to Jack Frogell and Carl Fuss of Thames Visual Services. We were greatly assisted in the Soviet Union by Vladimir Savitsky and the staff of the American-Soviet Kino Initiative, especially Lyudmila Sotkovskaya and Irina Antonyan, and by many friends, some of whom were also interviewed. We should particularly mention the Alliluyev family, Yuri Aichenwald, Yevgenia Albats, Pavel Butyagin and Maryanna Tovrog, Ivan Chukhin, Viktor Glukhov, Marina Goldovskaya, Alexander Khersonsky, Yuli Kim, Maxim Korobochkin, Lydia Kovalenko, Georgi Levashov-Tumanishvili, Misha and Flora Litvinov, Albert Lekhmus, Vladimir Maniak, Sergei Mendelevich, Stepan Mikhalkov, Arseni Roginsky and Alexander Daniel of Memorial, Nina Savenko, Tofik Shakhverdiev, Tanya Shur, Nina Soboleva, Lyudmila Zaprageyeva, Galina Kusminskaya, Roman Konbrandt and Gorky Film Studios, *Pyatoe Koleso* (Fifth Wheel) Television Programme of Leningrad, and the Bukharin Club of Naberezhnye Chelny.

Outside the Soviet Union we received invaluable assistance from Anatoli Danilitski of the Soviet embassy in London, a new kind of diplomat, and from Svetlana Alliluyeva, Tanya Ablakat and Jessy Kaner, Luciano Camprincoli, Tanya Chambers, Ludmilla Matthews, Pat Montgomery, Bengt von zur Mühlen, Igor Pomerantsev, Graham Roberts, Natalya Rubinstein, Masha Slonim, Cecilia Toddeschini, Robert van Voren, Gary Waxmonsky, Beryl Williams, the Ukrainian Press Agency, the Lesley Howard Language Service, the National Archives and the Jamestown Foundation (Washington DC), the Hoover Institution Archives (Stanford University, California), Theodor Gehling and the archives of the West German Foreign Ministry (Bonn), and the Imperial War Museum (London). In the United States our way, as always, has been made easier by our colleagues at WGBH, led by Peter McGhee, and the hospitality and resources so ably marshalled there by Sheila Brass, Marcia Storkerson and Joshua B. Saul of the Russian Research Center, Harvard University.

Lastly we should thank our wives and children for their support and forbearance when the absences of filming seemed varied only by the 'internal exile' of long hours of writing at home.

Jonathan Lewis
Phillip Whitehead

London, December 1989

# FOREWORD

by Professor ALEC NOVE

Was Stalin one of the principal villains of Russian or any other history, or was he a modern Peter the Great, dragging a backward country kicking and screaming into the eighteenth or twentieth century? What does his career tell us of the role of great men in history? How did it happen that a revolution inspired by the principles of liberty and of socialism spawned a totalitarian tyranny? How much of Stalinism is explicable by the political traditions of Russian autocracy, by the terrible experiences of revolution and civil war, by some aspects of Marxism and Leninism? Can he be seen as the executor of Lenin's will, or the executioner of Lenin's comrades? How was he able to defeat with apparent ease a whole number of men who seemed to be his intellectual superiors, such as Trotsky, Kamenev, Bukharin? Was there an alternative path, which could have saved much suffering, to the one Stalin took at the end of the 1920s, when he abandoned the mixed economy of the New Economic Policy and launched the policies of forcible collectivisation and crash-programme industrialisation? To cite the title of one of my own early articles, 'Was Stalin really necessary?' What was the scale of human losses involved in his war against the peasants and in the Great Terror that followed it? Was Stalin psychologically abnormal, and was this an explanation for the scale and viciousness of the Terror?

Such questions as these have long been asked by western scholars. In the most recent years, thanks to *glasnost*, we have been joined by Soviet scholars, and discussion there too has raged with a degree of openness and vigour which we can only welcome. There are hardly any views and interpretations which do not have their supporters (and opponents) in the USSR.

Among the key questions is one about Stalin and the war. He had a large proportion of senior officers killed; he refused to allow precautionary measures. Yet once he recovered from the initial shock he became a symbol of resistance, the Generalissimo, and the dearly bought victory gave him real popularity, so that many wept sincerely when he finally died in 1953. His last years, however, were disfigured by a new purge (the 'Leningrad affair' cost many lives), the attacks on literature, the 'anti-cosmopolitan' campaign, anti-semitism, the forced isolation of Soviet science, the ludicrous claims to have invented everything from the steam engine to radio. This, and the imposition of terror on Eastern Europe, was no doubt linked with the Cold War, and another topic of discussion is the role of Stalin as a progenitor of the Cold War. Then – how much of his system outlived him? A Soviet historian (Gefter) published in 1988 an article entitled 'Stalin died yesterday'. Brezhnev's long reign could be seen as Stalinism minus mass terror. Only now, under Gorbachev, can we see vigorous steps to destroy the Stalin legacy. But there are those, inside as well as outside the Soviet Union, who see the need for a 'firm hand', a strong man who can impose order on a society which would otherwise disintegrate. Few will speculate confidently about a highly uncertain future.

Jonathan Lewis and Phillip Whitehead have written a valuable and vivid introduction to a complex and fascinating subject. It deserves wide readership.

ALEC NOVE

November 1989

# INTRODUCTION

The Soviet Union is now engaged in a complex and potentially dangerous act of surgery. It is trying to remove the cancer of Stalin. But the surgeons – politicians, journalists, writers, film-makers, historians and a host of eloquent survivors – have to distinguish between the malignant and the benign in Stalin's part in their country's past. The two are not always easy to identify and are often entwined. In his speech on the Seventieth Anniversary of the October Revolution, Mikhail Gorbachev recognised this problem of delineation: 'We must see both Stalin's indisputable contribution to the struggle for socialism and the defense of its gains and the flagrant political mistakes and arbitrary actions committed by him and his entourage, for which our people paid a great price and which had grave consequences for the life of our society.'[1]

This was a system which enslaved one in ten of its inhabitants, not just for some aberrant period of exceptional crisis or trauma, but for decades. It outlived Stalin himself. Its side-effects became bred in the bone of Soviet society.

It is now believed that the death toll under Stalin, apart from losses in the Second World War, is certainly in excess of 20 million and may well be in excess of 30 million people. These harsh losses have not been softened by the passing years. There are countless people in the Soviet Union today who simply do not know what happened to their father, mother, children, neighbour, best friend. They do not know how they died, why they died or where their remains are. Some do not even know for sure *if* they are dead. There is a tidal wave of grief which has no outlet. A woman plants flowers in a forest where she thinks her father was shot. A man prays in a cemetery where his mother's ashes may have been scattered. A group of old villagers recall their school-mates who died swollen-bellied from hunger while grain was guarded by soldiers down the road. A wife last saw her

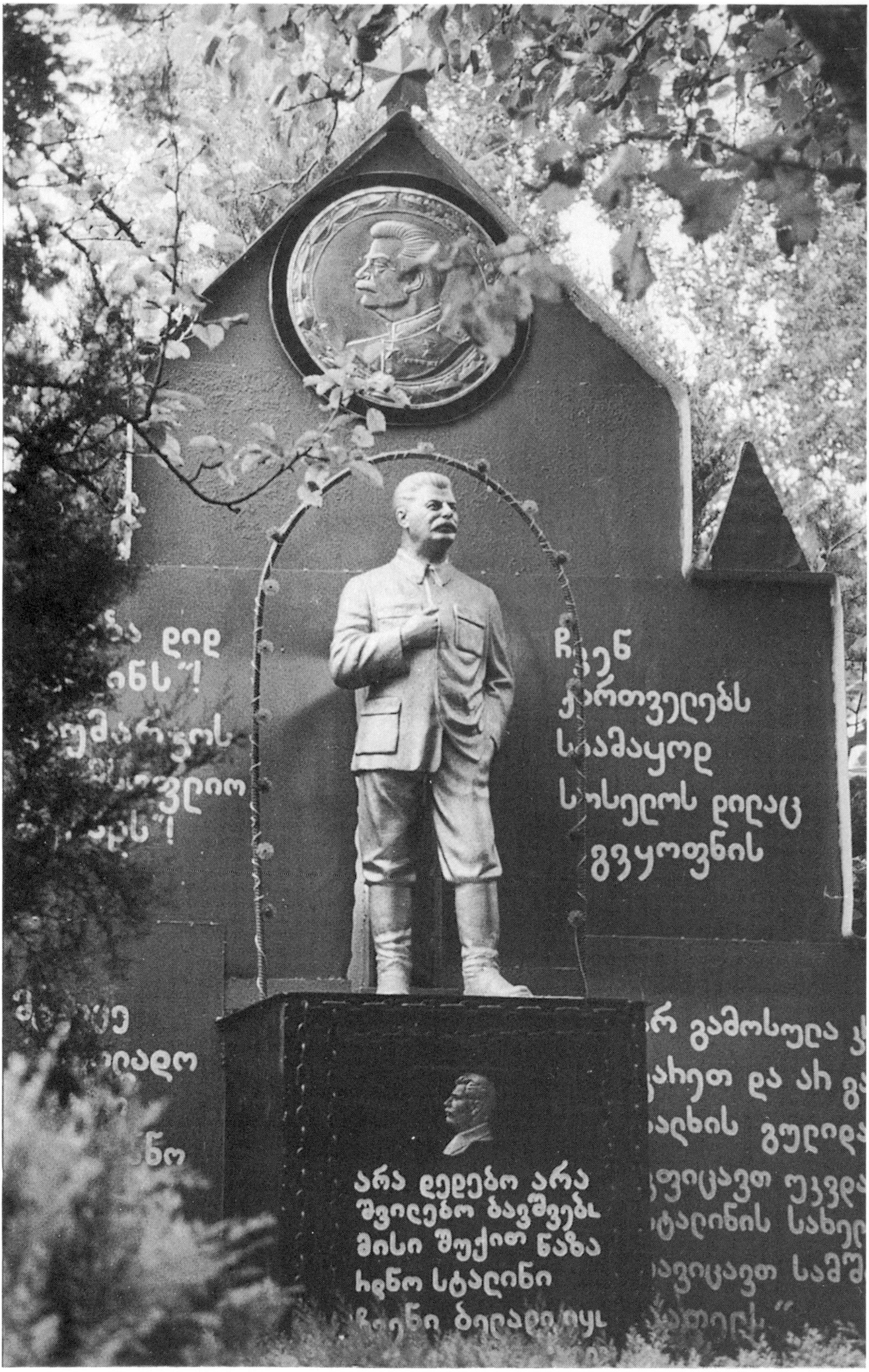
ჩვენ
ქართველებს
გვყოფნის
არა დედებო არა

husband being taken away at night sixty years ago, and still dreams about him.

And yet the difficulty of cutting out the malignant cancer of Stalin is enormous, because many people in the Soviet Union look back on his time as one of great achievement. Stalin is remembered as the leader who gave them pride in their country, in its progress from wooden ploughs to nuclear power, in its victory in the Second World War, and in themselves as both instruments and beneficiaries of these achievements.

And these things were done despite the isolation in which Russians have habitually felt themselves. If it meant literacy without liberty, military strength at the expense of consumer satisfaction, the collective rather than the individual, there are still many who look back to that time of sacrifice with nostalgia. Seen through the wrong end of the telescope of time, Stalin, like the ruthless tsars Ivan and Peter, has still a terrifying presence.

'Why do the intelligentsia harp on his crimes?' ask some who are more preoccupied by the social flux and economic uncertainties of the present. But Gorbachev has made it clear that surgery is essential, that the past has to be faced for the sake of the future. 'A truthful analysis should help us solve our current problems of democratization, legality, openness and the overcoming of bureaucratism – in short, the vital problems of restructuring. For this reason, here, too, we must have complete clarity, accuracy and consistency.'[2]

There is, though, another risk in all this. The surgeons searching out the cancer of Stalin in the body and life of the country do not know exactly how far it extends. The danger is that opening up the past might reveal that the source of the cancer lies at the very heart of the Soviet Union: Marxism, the dictatorship of the proletariat, the October Revolution, Lenin himself. How to cut out Stalin, without undermining the legitimacy of communist rule? The danger is faced differently by different people in the Soviet Union. Some, spotting the threat to the status quo and to their own positions, simply batten down the hatches, ignore the horrors of the past and try to keep the archives firmly locked. Others see some hope in Lenin's last programme, which rescues them from the Stalin–Lenin quandary: the New Economic Policy, the emphasis on co-operatives, education and

1 Stalin lives on in his native Georgia.

culture, the criticisms of both bureaucracy and nationalism, the recommendation that Stalin be removed from the post of General Secretary. With all this as a lifeline for the Party, Stalin can float away on the tide of history; the revolution is intact because Lenin turned out to have the right answers in the end. Faced with similar problems, Gorbachev can follow in Lenin's final footsteps all the way from nudging Stalin aside to letting in a little capitalism: 'We are now turning with increasing frequency to Ilyich's last works, to Lenin's ideas of the New Economic Policy, seeking to take from that experience everything that is valuable and necessary for us today.'[3]

There is another group. It is the most challenging to the system and therefore the most vulnerable. It is a mixed bag of journalists, survivors from Stalin's camps, historians and academics from within the Party itself. They are not afraid to look at the past critically, even if it calls into question the role and responsibility of Lenin. Their work is an encouragement to others to study the *whole* history of the Soviet Union without blinkers or hobby horses. It was this group that historian Moshe Lewin had in mind when he commented: 'There will now be no consensus. Things will be tougher for Marx and Lenin. But people should use their heads, and not brooms.'[4]

There is much to learn from all shades of opinion in the Soviet Union today, not least from those who wish we would all go away and leave Stalin and the past in peace. They often, tantalisingly, seem to hold missing pieces of this enormous jigsaw puzzle. And despite a flood of books, articles and films under the banner of *glasnost*, there are many gaps – gaps which can only be filled in by the Soviet people themselves reclaiming their past from archives and their own memories. It is a time for great optimism, and a time to keep one's fingers crossed as well.

The interesting thing about the past, Soviet historians say, is that you never know what will happen there. This book, and the television series on which it was based, have the advantage that we could travel one stage of the journey into the past with Russians, Byelorussians, Ukrainians and Georgians, who know that what they learn happened there will hold the clue to their present. We have travelled from Stalin's birthplace in Georgia to the remote death camps in the Arctic Circle, where, they say, a body lies under every railway sleeper. We have seen farms collectivised by force during the terrible famine in the Ukraine, the killing fields of Kuropaty in Byelorussia, and the survivors of the great wartime siege of Leningrad, who found that after their three-year ordeal Stalin's hand was raised against them. We have followed the intellectual debate that now rages, from the new Congress meeting in Moscow and the writers' dachas of Peredelkino to the new Bukharin Club in Naberezhnye Chelny. Abroad we have talked to a wide range of exiles who knew Stalin and his works, or suffered from them. We have also talked to the senior surviving members of his family.

The questions both book and television series hope to answer are these: Who was Stalin? Where did he and his ideas come from? How did he come to power? What did he do with that power and why? What is the scale of the horrors perpetrated under him and where does the balance of responsibility for them lie? What is his legacy and what will the Soviet Union do with that legacy: shrug it off, come to terms with it, or come to be grateful for it?

We do not, of course, have all the answers. But we have seized with both hands the opportunity to put these questions to a wide range of people in the Soviet Union, as well as to those who have left it and those who have spent their adult lives studying it. We have spoken to Old Bolsheviks who remember seeing Lenin at the Finland Station, to Ukrainian peasants who lost their whole families in the man-made famine of 1932–3, to people who thrived under Stalin, and to those who cowered under him. In helping us to tell the story of Stalin, they have had to recall their own. This is their history too.

Jonathan Lewis
Phillip Whitehead

**2 & 3** Stalin's parents Yekaterina and Vissarion Djugashvili. As the only survivor past infancy, he was cosseted by his mother, but the father, a drunken and violent cobbler, remains a shadowy figure. These portraits now hang in his birthplace, but that of Vissarion may have been posthumously reconstructed to fill out Stalin's family history.

**4** The Djugashvili home in Gori, Stalin's birthplace. In 1936 it was reconstructed under an elaborate neo-classical structure, as a shrine for the Stalin cult.

# 1 THE MAKING OF A REVOLUTIONARY

Joseph Stalin's origins set him apart from most of the Bolshevik leaders who spearheaded the proletarian revolution. Trotsky's father was a farm-owner, Bukharin's parents were schoolteachers, Dzerzhinsky's family was Polish landed gentry and Lenin himself was the son of a provincial school inspector.

Stalin's mother Yekaterina was a twenty-year-old peasant girl. Her husband, Vissarion Djugashvili, was a cobbler. They rented a hovel on the edge of Gori, a small valley town in eastern Georgia. The simple two-room dwelling has been lovingly preserved and is sheltered beneath an elaborate pillared canopy, built in the 1930s. The whole edifice bears witness not only to the beatification of Stalin in his lifetime but also to the strong local feeling which continues to tend the shrine.

The living quarters reek of a studied, well-scrubbed homeliness when the accounts are of poverty, hardship and drunken violence. The bare room adjacent goes further: on the wall are photographs, amongst others of Stalin's mother and the only known one of his father. Yet the photograph looks too much like Stalin himself retouched and not, perhaps, enough like a turn-of-the-century photograph. Furthermore, it is a photograph found rarely indeed in Georgia but not at all elsewhere, even in official publications.

There are rumours that Stalin's real father was a tsarist official in whose house Yekaterina worked for a time – rumours which the picture of Djugashvili may have been concocted to silence. Certainly later accounts say Stalin referred to his mother, in the company of others, as an 'old whore'. There are rumours too about Djugashvili being a poor cobbler: they say that he was a boss with ten cobblers working under him. The mix of spite, truth and subsequent revision in Stalin's parentage defies unravelling without hard evidence.

Yekaterina and Vissarion Djugashvili had had three children who did not live before Joseph, nicknamed Soso, was born on 21 December 1879. He was small and wiry, surviving smallpox, being knocked over by a runaway cart and blood-poisoning which caused his left arm to stiffen at the elbow-joint and wither. Later in life he would conceal his infirm arm and photographers would take care to doctor the smallpox scars from his portraits. He used to talk to his daughter Svetlana about his childhood:

> It was a rather horrid childhood of poverty, with a father who was a drunk, who used to beat the rest of the household, his mother and himself. And the boy, when he grew up a little bit into a teenager, he used to protect his mother, and one time he even threw a knife at his father in protecting her. And then he had to run away and was hidden by the neighbours from his furious father. It was a pretty rough childhood. However, he used to say that he loved his mother always – who used to beat him too. He admitted that, but that didn't obviously make any difference. He kept a certain reverence and really very sincere admiration for her and her character until his late years. He liked to talk about her.

When the boy was about five, his father moved to Tbilisi about forty miles away to work in a shoe factory. His mother made ends meet by taking in washing. Young Soso worked hard at school, and played hard in the streets of Gori. He dropped bricks down a neighbour's chimney, filling the house with soot. He loved the countryside, climbed cliffs, fought in the school playground and knew his lessons by heart. Even then, he tended to be a loner to whom winning mattered a great deal. As his childhood friend Joseph Iremashvili remembered, 'To gain a victory and be feared was triumph for him. He was devoted to only one person – his mother. As a child and youth he was a good friend so long as one submitted to his imperious will.'[1]

In September 1888 he entered the elementary clerical school in Gori. His mother wanted him to become a priest, against the wishes of her husband. Nearly half a century later, Yekaterina remembered the arguments in an interview with *Pravda*: 'He studied extremely well, but his father – my deceased husband Vissarion – decided to take the boy out of school and train him in his shoemaking trade. I objected as strongly as I could and even quarrelled with my husband, but in vain, he insisted on having his way. A little later, however, I managed to put the boy back in school.' It may well be that what gave her the chance to do this was the death of her husband in the 1890s in a drunken brawl. Perhaps more protectively, local Gori wisdom has it that Djugashvili died peacefully in his bed of old age, and that he is buried in the town of Telavi where his grave is marked, they say, by a headstone. His body was wrapped in wool for better preservation.

Despite his mother's dedication and hard work, Stalin did not visit her often later in life. Svetlana only met her grandmother once, when she was eight, in 1934: 'We didn't speak Georgian, she didn't speak Russian . . . she was old, grey-haired, with bright light eyes, freckled, and she was crying and tears were streaming down her face because she was happy to see us, her grandchildren. And she was stretching on a plate some candies to us. And that was the only communication between us which was possible.'

The Djugashvili family spoke Georgian, but most of the lessons at the Gori parochial school were in Russian. Soso learned Russian quickly, speaking it till the end of his life with a thick Georgian accent. Another schoolfriend remembered his eagerness to achieve and his aptitude at doing so: 'He was always exceptionally well prepared and carried out assignments to the letter. He was considered the best pupil not only in his class but in the whole school. During class periods he would strain not to miss a single word or idea.'[2]

In 1894 he graduated from the Gori school at the top of the class, ahead of the children from better-off families. He took the next step towards fulfilling his mother's ambition for him by winning a scholarship to the Theological Seminary in Tbilisi.

Far from ensuring his adherence to a straight and narrow path of piety, sending young Stalin to the seminary in Tbilisi was to expose him to the heady mix of a repressive regime enforced by the staff, and subversive revolutionary politics rampant among the students. The seminary was a microcosm of the rebellious turbulence in Georgia itself, which for a hundred years had been living under, and bitterly resenting, tsarist Russian rule. There had always been a tradition in Georgia of strong resistance to the invader; occupation by the Mongols, then Turks, then Persians had ensured that. Throughout the nineteenth century, first in guerrilla fighting, then in intellectual and political activism, the idea of Georgian nationalism was nurtured.

5  **Joseph Djugashvili (*back row centre*) went to the parochial school in Gori from 1888 to 1894. Small but assertive and quarrelsome, 'Soso' was the school's star pupil.**

The connection between this and revolutionary anti-tsarism in Russia is explained by the historian Robert Tucker:

> A notable characteristic of the Georgian intelligentsia was its blending of the ideas of national liberation and social change. Influenced by the Russian populist revolutionary literature, and realizing, no doubt, that the yoke of tsarist autocracy could not be lifted from Georgia without deep changes in Russia itself, some Georgian intellectuals in the seventies and eighties made common cause with the Russian *narodniki*.[3]

The *narodniki* were a populist group who came to believe that Russia should be ruled by an organisation of revolutionaries acting for the people and transforming Russia from above on socialist principles. They were Russo-centrist without the Marxists' internationalism.

As Tucker says, '. . . it had an enduring effect upon history owing to the influence that it exerted upon the political thought of Lenin.'[4]

There were other, even more immediate connections which linked progressive Georgian thought to Marxism. Noi Zhordania was a Georgian who had been at the Tbilisi Seminary ten years before young Stalin. He had then gone abroad, studied the works of and met the German Social Democratic thinker Karl Kautsky and the Marxist Georgi Plekhanov. He returned to become the leading figure in the Georgian revolutionary group *Mesame Dasi* (Third Group). He was to find the theological seminary of the 1890s a receptive seedbed for the Marxist ideas of Georgian Social Democracy.

Young Stalin's character had undergone some change after entering the seminary, as his friend Vano Ketskhoveli recalled: 'He lost his love for games and childhood pastimes. He became reflective and, somehow, withdrawn. He gave up games but not books, and would go off in a corner and read assiduously.'[5] The authorities confiscated a host of forbidden books from him, including Victor Hugo's *Ninety-Three* about the French Revolution. Iremashvili recalled their furtive dedication to political self-improvement: 'Secretly, during classes, services and sermons we read "our" books. The Bible was open on the desk, but on our laps we held Darwin, Marx, Plekhanov or Lenin.'

In 1934 Stalin gave an interview to the German author Emil Ludwig in which he explained his politicisation forty years before.

> *Stalin*: 'I joined the revolutionary movement when fifteen years old, when I became connected with underground groups of Russian Marxists then living in Transcaucasia. These groups exerted great influence on me and instilled a taste for underground Marxist literature.'
> *Ludwig*: 'What impelled you to become an oppositionist? Was it, perhaps, bad treatment by your parents?'
> *Stalin*: 'No. My parents were uneducated, but they did not treat me badly by any means. But it was a different matter at the Orthodox theological seminary which I was then attending. In protest against the outrageous regime and the jesuitical methods prevalent at the seminary, I was ready to become, and actually did become, a revolutionary, a believer in Marxism as a really revolutionary teaching.'[6]

The 'jesuitical methods' involved spying, searching personal belongings and 'worming their way into people's souls' – an ironic critique of methods Stalin's secret police were to hone to perfection in later years.

Reading politics went hand in hand with talking politics in a succession of study groups. According to Iremashvili, Stalin had to be in charge and became violent with those who didn't agree with him. From study groups gathering in secret within the seminary it was a short step to attending meetings outside.

More and more, the people he was close to were committed to revolution. More and more, the life inside the seminary was encouraging rebellion in him. 'Djugashvili is rude and disrespectful towards persons in authority and systematically fails to bow to one of the teachers . . . reprimanded. Confined to the cell for five hours . . .' went a report on his behaviour. In 1898 he joined the Georgian revolutionary group *Mesame Dasi*. In 1899 he left the seminary.

Stalin's daughter Svetlana recalls her grandmother's response:

> She was distressed about it until her last days. She always wanted him to become a priest, and when he visited her the last time, and she had come to her last days, she still showed her character and she told him: 'What a pity that you have never become a priest.' That was something that he admired – that she didn't care what he had become: a head of state of a big country.

The twenty-year-old Stalin now entered an underground life of agitation, propaganda, covert printing-presses and secret meetings. The world outside was in a state of considerable change. Tbilisi was at the centre of a mini-industrial revolution as foreign capital poured in to develop the Baku and Batumi oil fields. There were factories going up and mines being dug down. *Mesame Dasi* located itself at the centre of a huge work region where conditions were poor and strikes and trade unionism illegal. The railway junction at Tbilisi was the nexus of industrial movement and the railway yards were a key focus of political activity. They became young Stalin's first 'posting'.

In 1926 he revisited them and made a speech acknowledging his debt to the workers in the railway workshops:

> Compared with these comrades, I was then quite a young man.
> I may have been a little better-read than many of them were,
> but as a practical worker I was unquestionably a novice in
> those days. . . . It was here, among these comrades, that I
> became an apprentice in the art of revolution.[7]

But what actually did he do, and what did he believe in? His
activities in the early years seem to have involved writing pamphlets
and articles, developing the political consciousness of the workers
through discussion, and later on organising demonstrations and
strikes; but he was willing, indeed determined, to go a lot further.
His natural inclination was towards the militant wing of *Mesame Dasi*
at a point when Marxism as a whole was split between 'legal
Marxism', which toned down its ideology to clear the tsarist censorship, and Marxism proper, which appeared moderate by renounc-
ing 'individual terror'. In fact Marxism held that the whole system
needed to be overthrown and that there was therefore no point in
killing individuals. Why, when the inclination of *Mesame Dasi* and
Georgian Social Democracy as a whole was towards comparative
moderation, did Stalin tend towards militancy?

The answer perhaps lies in his judgement, made early on and never
deviated from, that to be with Lenin and Marxism was to be on the
winning side. This decision may well have been conditioned by his
realisation that his was the very class Marxism sought to unshackle –
the unawakened, inert mass. He knew from first hand the need, and
the urgency. He didn't have to learn to feel the oppression of the tsar,
capitalist or landlord. The historian Isaac Deutscher points out:

> The class hatred felt and preached by the revolutionaries from
> the upper classes was a kind of secondary emotion that grew in
> them and was cultivated by them from theoretical conviction.
> In [Stalin] class hatred was not his second nature – it was his
> first. Socialist teachings appealed to him because they seemed
> to give moral sanction to his own emotion. There was no shred
> of sentimentalism in his outlook. His socialism was cold,
> sober, and rough.[8]

Young Stalin studied Lenin's writings avidly. He read the newspaper *Iskra* (The Spark), edited by Lenin, from cover to cover, and

in 1900 he got to know Viktor Kurnatovsky, a professional revolutionary who had met Lenin. When in 1903 the Russian Social Democratic Labour Party split into Bolsheviks under Lenin, and the more moderate Mensheviks, Stalin was an ardent Bolshevik. But what did that mean?

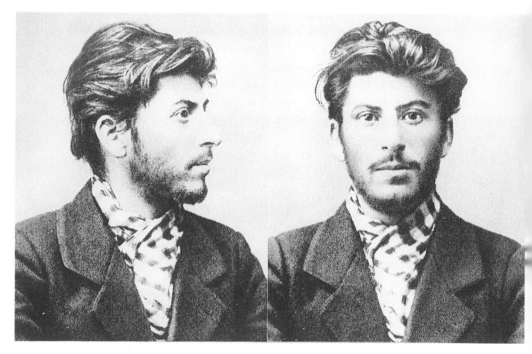

6 Stalin in 1902. Using the pseudonym 'Koba' he was arrested in Batumi in April at a committee meeting of the local Social Democratic (Marxist) Committee, photographed, for police files, and sent to Siberia.

Marx, so popular among Russian intellectuals in the late nineteenth century, in fact offered them no hope of working-class emancipation through revolution in the foreseeable future. The pre-conditions simply did not exist. Russia was not a capitalist country on the brink of proletarian revolution, but a huge semi-feudal peasant country on the brink of industrial revolution. The answer for Lenin was to make this transformation happen. Firstly, this required him to monopolise the interpretation of Marxism in order to allow the evolution of a doctrine which would provide the theory to underpin Russian revolution. Secondly, he had to create an organisation which could take that theory as its credo and make this revolution happen: the Party. In 1902, Lenin wrote a key treatise entitled 'What is to be Done?' in which he spelt out these two prerequisites:

> Without a revolutionary theory there can be no revolutionary
> movement. This thought cannot be insisted upon too strongly
> at a time when the fashionable preaching of opportunism goes
> hand in hand with an infatuation for the narrowest forms
> of practical activity. . . . Our Party is only in process of
> formation, its features are only just becoming outlined, and it
> is yet far from having settled accounts with other trends of
> revolutionary thought, which threaten to divert the movement
> from the correct path. . . . The national tasks of Russian
> Social-Democracy are such as have never confronted any other
> socialist party in the world. . . . *The role of vanguard fighter can*
> *be fulfilled only by a party that is guided by the most advanced*
> *theory.*[9]

The essence of the Party was that it was to be what the historian Robert Daniels has defined as 'a narrow organisation, not the mass of like-minded sympathizers, but the active and conscious minority, the professional revolutionaries'.[10]

Indeed that was what split the Mensheviks from the Bolsheviks: the former believed that Party membership involved co-operation; the latter insisted on participation. Membership, Lenin held, called for disciplined, committed work in the organisation.

This concept of a party was not new. There are some disturbing parallels with the ideas of a violent mid-nineteenth century Russian fanatic, Sergei Nechayev. In 'Catechism of a Revolutionary', Nechayev defined the real revolutionary as being 'absorbed by a single exclusive interest, a total concept, a total passion: revolution. . . . He knows only one science, the science of destruction.'[11] For Lyudmila Saraskina, one of the younger generation of Soviet political writers, these echoes are distinctly worrying.

> When Nechayev set up a group of underground revolutionaries
> . . . their methods were that for the sake of the ultimate
> aim you could do absolutely anything, anything was
> justifiable. . . . It seems to me the great sorrow of our country
> that the traditions of Nechayev fell on to well prepared, well

tended, well fertilised ground. They were most appropriate in the Russian revolutionary movement. They could be put to use extremely easily. . . . Lenin took advantage of them . . . and the party created by Lenin took advantage of them.

It is impossible to say whether Stalin shared Nechayev's view that the end justified the means. What is clear is that becoming part of Lenin's tightly knit party of dedicated revolutionaries suited him down to the ground. Stalin was not a great orator like Trotsky, he was not a great theoretician like Bukharin, but he was a natural practical revolutionary: secretive, tough and self-possessed. It is clear from his earliest writings that he subscribed to Lenin's view of the role of the party. 'It is *the technical guidance and organisational preparation of the all-Russian insurrection* that constitute the new tasks with which life has confronted the proletariat. And if our Party wishes to be the real political leader of the working class it cannot and must not repudiate these new tasks.'[12] The tasks were not confined to speaking on street corners and printing pamphlets. '. . . our committees must,' Stalin wrote in 1905, 'at once, forthwith, proceed to arm the people locally, to set up special groups to arrange this matter . . . to organize workshops for the manufacture of different kinds of explosives, to draw up plans for seizing state and private stores of arms and arsenals'.[13]

He had become increasingly involved in the organisation of strikes and demonstrations. According to the official Soviet biography, Stalin led a rally in Batumi in March 1902 in which 6,000 workers were fired on by police and 15 were killed, 54 injured and 500 arrested. He inevitably caught the attention of the Okhrana, the tsarist secret police. Their 'wanted' descriptions of him bear witness to his elusiveness and relative importance: '. . . active and very serious . . . very careful and could therefore be lost by an observer . . . it is impossible to count on favorable results from a search of him in Vologda, in view of the extremely conspiratorial nature of his actions'.[14]

Ever since those years, there has been a persistent trickle of allegations that Stalin was himself an undercover agent of the tsarist secret police. No hard evidence of this has ever emerged. It would be a very severe blow to those who admire Stalin were it to be proved that he had betrayed Bolshevism, and yet there are many who do not

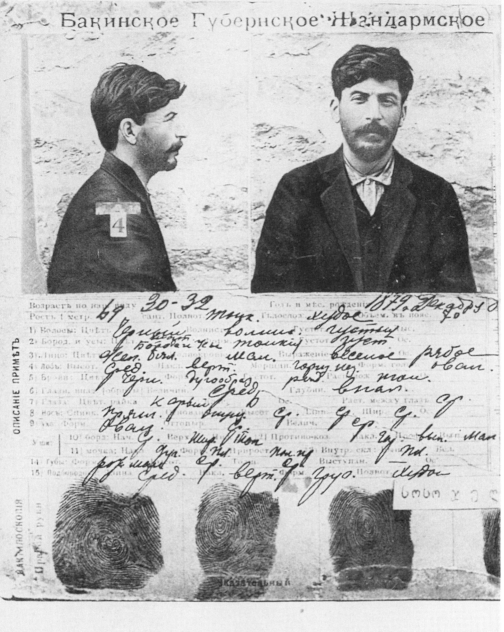

**8 & 9** Stalin in exile (*back row with broad-brimmed hat*), 1903. To his left is Kamenev and, beyond, Sverdlov in a white shirt. The doctored picture was re-issued in the 1930s after Kamenev and others depicted had been purged and shot.

admire Stalin who consider he betrayed it anyway by his subsequent despotism.

These years before the revolution throw up another test-case for those thinking about Stalin – and Lenin – today. This is the issue of the so-called 'expropriations' – bank robberies. Between 1905 and 1908, around 1,150 acts of terrorism were recorded in the Caucasus, some injuring or killing innocent bystanders. These were not actions of dissident, 'rogue' revolutionaries out of control. They were policy, as Robert Tucker says: 'Lenin approved and relied heavily upon them as a source of funds to finance political activity. . . . In an article of 1906 on "Partisan Warfare" Lenin declared that funds obtained through "expropriations" were used in part for the maintenance of the "expropriators" – the "persons waging" the revolutionary struggle.'[15] These operations came to light when Maxim Litvinov, the future Commissar for Foreign Affairs, and other important Bolsheviks were arrested trying to change stolen high-denomination notes in European banks. There was a storm in the press and when the Mensheviks called for a ban on such activities at the 1907 Congress, Lenin abstained.

For the Soviet writer Lyudmila Saraskina, it is another example of the amorality of Bolshevik revolutionary practice: 'It was a terrible omen that for the sake of their aims, they should have used really terrible methods. And under such circumstances the ultimate aim becomes suspect . . . because the aim doesn't justify the means. The aim determines the means.'

Stalin never discussed his role in these activities, although his name is closely associated with the planning at least of several large robberies. His daughter Svetlana comments: 'He was a practical revolutionary. These people were involved in all kinds of dangerous things and, yes, bank robberies, yes. Bank robberies, yes. I don't know [whether he was] personally or not, but that was part of getting means for revolution.'

Stalin paid a price for his involvement in the struggle. Between 1902 and 1913 he was arrested eight times, exiled seven times, and escaped every time save the last – only freed from exile in northern Siberia by the February Revolution. In 1902 Stalin married for the first time and had a son. His wife, Yekaterina Svanidze, died in 1908 or 1909. His old childhood friend Iremashvili was at the funeral and recalled Stalin's grief-stricken words: 'This creature softened my

**10 Stalin's first wife, Yekaterina Svanidze, who bore him a son, Yakov, in 1908.**

**11 Yekaterina's early death devastated Stalin, who said: 'This creature softened my heart of stone.' From now on all those closest to him would be equally dedicated to revolutionary activity.**

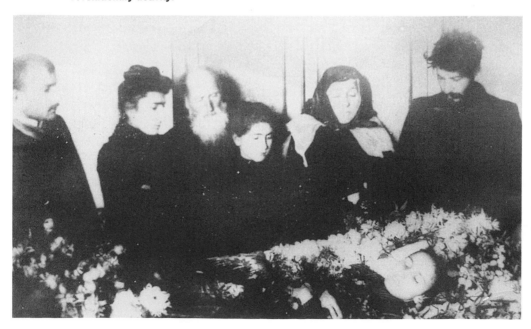

heart of stone. She died and with her died my last warm feelings for people.'[16] (His second wife, Nadezhda Alliluyeva, twenty-one years his junior, whom he married in 1919, was the daughter of an Old Bolshevik, Sergei Alliluyev, with whom he frequently lodged in the capital in those revolutionary days.)

It is certainly the case that Bolsheviks who met Stalin during his periods of exile found him cold, uncommunicative and even haughty, though that is how he had seemed to contemporaries ten years before at the Tbilisi Seminary. Exile offered him the chance to enjoy solitude and nature. Fishing, hunting and walking improved his health and perhaps conditioned him to feel that 'a good dose of exile in Siberia never hurt me', so casually was it meted out as punishment to millions later on.

Yet Stalin was not content to bide his time as 'a journeyman in the art of revolution' as he described himself looking back on those years in Baku, Batumi and Tbilisi. He was ambitious and impatient, both for the revolution itself and for achieving an important place in it. Two obstacles needed to be overcome. To rise up the hierarchy of the Bolshevik party he would need to travel abroad, since the leadership was in exile; and he would need to impress, not just with his feats of undercover work, but with Marxist erudition. By 1905 he had won Lenin's attention and approval for a sharply written pamphlet supporting Lenin himself. In December of that year he was on his way to the Bolshevik conference in Tammerfors, Finland, to meet Lenin for the first time.

Russia and its neighbours at the time
of Stalin's pre-revolutionary travels

*O c e a n*

*Bering Sea*

a

i

R. Lena

*Sea of Okhotsk*

Igarka
Kureika
Turukhansk

b

e

i

esi

arim

Achinsk

Novaya Uda

*Lake Baikal*

Krasnoyarsk

Manchuria

Irkutsk

WAY

R

E

*Mongolia*

Vladivostok

*Sea of Japan*

Korea

JAPAN

Sinkiang

C H I N A

*Pacific Ocean*

Miles

0    500    1000

# 2 LENIN, STALIN AND REVOLUTION

> I was hoping to see the mountain eagle of our Party, the great man, not only politically, but, if you will, physically, because in my imagination I had pictured Lenin as a giant, stately and imposing. What, then, was my disappointment to see a most ordinary-looking man, below average height, in no way, literally in no way, distinguishable from ordinary mortals.[1]

This was Stalin's first impression of Lenin. Vladimir Ilyich Lenin was then thirty-four years old. He was born in April 1870 in the town of Simbirsk on the Volga, one of six children of parents from the minor gentry. His family name was Ulyanov, but he set a pattern for the Bolshevik leadership by adopting the pseudonym Lenin. Following suit, the young Djugashvili took the name Stalin – man of steel. Lenin's political education was sudden and shattering. His older brother Alexander was a talented student who, resenting police repression of all political protests, joined a terrorist group which had broken away from the old populist organisation People's Will. They plotted to kill the Tsar, but before doing so, the group was arrested. Lenin's brother was found guilty with four others; he did not plead for mercy and was hanged on 5 May 1887. This had a traumatic effect on Lenin, and propelled him towards a life committed to revolution in Russia. He had a brilliant mind; he read and mastered the works of Marx and Engels, had a genius for understanding how to apply them to the Russian situation and an extraordinary flair for persuading others to his viewpoint. By the time Stalin met him, Lenin outshone all others in the revolutionary political firmament.

Stalin came to realise Lenin's extraordinary power as soon as he heard his speeches.

> I was captivated by that irresistible force of logic in them which, although somewhat terse, gained a firm hold of his

audience, gradually electrified it, and then, as one might say, completely overpowered it. I remember that many of the delegates said: 'The logic of Lenin's speeches is like a mighty tentacle which twines all round you and holds you as in a vice and from whose grip you are powerless to tear yourself away: you must either surrender or resign yourself to utter defeat.'[2]

This later account, delivered after Lenin's death, should not be allowed to obscure Stalin's own independence of mind from Lenin. There is a somewhat traditional view of Stalin in this period that he was a nobody, that he didn't have an original idea in his head, that he was dazzled by Lenin and clung to him with blindly loyal subservience. This version suited a wide range of people who wished to denigrate an unworthy usurper of Lenin's position. Aspects of it even suited Stalin himself, subsequently rewriting his own history to bring it as closely as possible into line with the Leninist orthodoxy. It is not, however, true. Stalin had always been, and remained, his own man. He stood apart from the Bolshevik leadership not simply because his personal style was that of the self-contained, secretive loner. He was literally cut off from the upper echelons of the party because most of them were in self-imposed exile in the capitals of Europe while he lived in the uncertain underground world of Russia itself. He had to write articles, letters and pamphlets to keep up both his connections with and status in the collegiate circle of emigré revolutionary intellectuals.

Attendance at party congresses abroad, such as Finland in 1905, Stockholm in 1906, London in 1907, entailed illegal and risky border crossings. It was a time when clever, loyal and fearless Bolshevik activists were thin on the ground, particularly on Russian ground. Hence Lenin's wife Krupskaya's comment in 1909: 'We have no people at all,' and Zinoviev's: 'At this unhappy period the party as a whole ceased to exist.' Stalin, having reached the congresses abroad and the company of Lenin and the other leaders, did not sell himself short in tacit obsequiousness. He took advantage of the climate of discussion which allowed dissent, as the historian Robert Service writes:

> Stalin was never a mere errand boy for Lenin. Before 1917
> there had been several clashes between the two Bolshevik
> leaders. In December 1905 Stalin, unlike Lenin, had opposed

Bolshevik participation in the electoral campaign for the First State Duma [elected democratic assembly]. Lenin lost the discussion. In 1906 Stalin had opposed Lenin's proposal at the Fourth Party Congress for an agrarian programme involving land nationalisation; he and the majority of the Bolshevik delegation argued, successfully, that peasants would be annoyed at the land becoming governmental property and would anyway seize it for themselves whatever the Bolsheviks or any other party might prefer.[3]

**12 The pleasures of exile. Lenin playing chess with fellow exiles on Capri on a visit to Gorky (*back row with hat*). Vladimir Ilyich Ulyanov (1870–1924) established an early ascendancy among the Marxist revolutionaries by sheer force of personality and intellect. Whereas Lenin spent most of his time abroad, Stalin made only brief foreign forays – to Finland, England, Sweden and Austria – between 1905 and 1913.**

In a complex theoretical argument between Lenin and a former colleague, Bogdanov, Stalin refused to take Lenin's part and dismissed
the row as 'a storm in a teacup'.

Lenin was offended by this jibe, as he told the Georgian Bolshevik,
Sergo Ordzhonikidze, who knew Stalin of old. 'You say, "Koba
[Stalin's cover name] is our comrade", as if to say, he's a Bolshevik
and won't let us down. But do you close your eyes to his inconsist-
ency? Nihilistic little jokes about a "tempest in a teacup" reveal
Koba's immaturity as a Marxist.'[4]

In other letters to colleagues, Stalin criticised Lenin, accorded
praise to Bogdanov for pointing out 'individual faults of Ilyich', and
took side-swipes at the Bolshevik leaders in general who sat around in
comfortable European capitals: 'in general the workers are beginning
to look upon the emigration with disdain: "Let them crawl on the
wall to their hearts' content." '[5] These disagreements were part and
parcel of Bolshevik politics; what they show is the normality of
Stalin's relationship with Lenin and the Party. Robert Service again:

> Attempts have been made to claim that it was mainly an
> Oedipal-style rivalry which existed between Stalin and Lenin,
> or to assert that these conflicts simply show what a poor
> Leninist Stalin was. But this is to misread the nature of
> Bolshevik politics. Bolsheviks, believers in the virtues of
> intra-party ultracentralism, rarely practised what they
> preached before coming to power. It was normal to argue with
> and resist Lenin, even if not with success.[6]

Certainly Stalin's great advantages as a determined practical
fighter on the ground vastly outweighed his lack of sophistication or
track-record as a theoretician. And he was not alone in realising that
the revolution needed loyal activists in Russia rather than hair-
splitting intellectuals sitting around in European coffee-houses. By
1912 Lenin, in Isaac Deutscher's words,

> . . . was anxious to get for himself a maximum of elbow-room.
> He rid himself of the ham-stringing connexion with the
> Mensheviks. . . . Now he was out to knock his organization
> into shape. In the preceding splits he parted company with his
> ablest colleagues. His latest decision to burn all boats behind
> him left him with few outstanding associates . . . Lenin turned

his back on the emigré intelligentsia. He picked practical
workers of the underground for the new Central Committee.[7]

At the Prague Conference in 1912, Lenin had Stalin, in his
absence, co-opted on to the Central Committee and then made a
member of the Russian Bureau which directed revolutionary activities in Russia. Including Stalin, three of the four Bureau members
had been in charge of the Party's work in Baku. As Deutscher writes:
'The job ahead, Lenin thought, required men of grit, pertinacity,
and acumen, men like the leaders of Baku. In Krupskaya's files the
code name for the Baku group had been "The Horses". Lenin now
put his horses into harness.'[8]

Stalin's importance to Lenin was not based solely on his dedication
to the Bolshevik cause in the Caucasus. The very fact that Stalin was a
Georgian gave Lenin a chance to evolve with Stalin a policy towards
the nationalities inside Russia which would have both credibility and
authority. Following the Prague Conference, Lenin wrote to the
writer Maxim Gorky: 'About nationalism, I fully agree with you that
we have to bear down harder. We have here a wonderful Georgian
who has undertaken to write a long article. . . . We will take care
of this matter.'[9] Stalin's contribution, which Lenin described as
'very good', was to steer a careful course between national self-
determination and the Marxist position which predicted the ultimate
withering away of all nationalities and nationalism. The expedient
answer in the meantime was regional autonomy which, as Stalin
wrote, 'does not divide people according to nations, it does not
strengthen national barriers; on the contrary, it breaks down these
barriers and unites the population in such a manner as to open the
way for division of a different kind, division according to classes'.[10]

The nationalities question was just one of many problems facing
Lenin. His determination to ensure Bolshevism's place at the sharp
end of the revolutionary proletarian movement required policies and
platforms designed not just to win theoretical discussions among
intellectuals but the hearts and minds of people in factories and
fields. It was the peasants who would present the greatest challenge.

Within a month of writing the article on the nationality question,
Stalin was arrested and sent into unproductive exile. By the time he
was freed four years later in 1917, the need to find a viable basis for
alliance with the peasants had become a top priority. Up till then, the

working assumption had been that Russia would first have to undergo a bourgeois democratic revolution which would overthrow the Tsar and the aristocracy, leaving power in the hands of the middle classes.

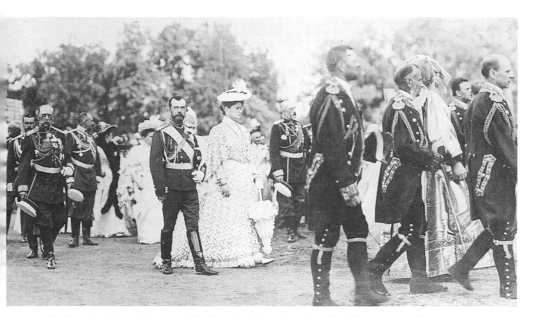

**13 Nicholas II and his court. The Tsar, ineffectual and easily influenced, could neither advance towards the reforms for which the 1905 revolutionaries had fought, nor re-establish the thorough autocracy of his father Alexander III. In 1914, fatally, he plunged into war with Germany, and utter defeat.**

As Lenin had said in 1905:

> The Russian revolution will begin to assume its real sweep, will really assume the widest revolutionary sweep possible in the epoch of bourgeois-democratic revolution, only when the bourgeoisie recoils from it and when the masses of the peasantry come out as active revolutionaries side by side with the proletariat. . . . The proletariat must carry to completion the democratic revolution, by allying to itself the mass of the peasantry.[11]

By 1917 Lenin realised that circumstances had changed, that the first revolutionary stage was giving way to the second stage 'which must', Lenin wrote in April 1917, 'place power in the hands of the proletariat and the poorest strata of the peasantry'. What were those

14  A suffering people. Women hauling rafts on the Volga, 1913. Nowhere in Europe were social divisions wider, and class hatred proportionally stronger, than in imperial Russia.

15  The February Revolution, 1917, overthrew the Tsar. Symbols of the old regime, like this statue of Alexander III, were overturned.

circumstances? First, there had been the 1905 revolution which, though a failure, in effect represented the bourgeois revolutionary stage. It forced Tsar Nicholas II to concede some power to a pseudo-parliament, the Duma; it provided the revolutionaries with what Lenin called a 'dress rehearsal', and it brought peasant grievances to the surface with a vengeance but no solution. Many peasants wanted to own the land they worked. Reforms designed to enable them to do so had insufficient time before war and revolution intervened to become properly operative.

The second factor in bringing the revolution closer was the progress of the First World War. Casualties were very high and morale correspondingly low. Food riots, strikes, demonstrations and clashes between workers and troops engulfed the capital Petrograd in early 1917. On 27 February whole regiments of the military garrison mutinied, Tsar Nicholas II abdicated and power passed to the Provisional Government watched over closely by the Soviet (Council) of Workers' and Soldiers' Deputies. This was the February Revolution, and Lenin, Trotsky, Zinoviev, Bukharin and Stalin all missed it. Lenin and Zinoviev were in Zurich, Trotsky and Bukharin were in New York, Stalin was in exile in Siberia.

Stalin got to Petrograd first, arriving by train on 12 March. The Bolsheviks in the capital had come out of hiding, had begun to publish *Pravda*, and were proceeding to reconstitute the Russian Bureau of the Central Committee. On the day of his arrival, Stalin's position was discussed, as the minutes record: 'Concerning Stalin, it was reported that he had been an agent of the Central Committee in 1912, and therefore it would be advisable to have him as a member of the Bureau of the Central Committee. However, in view of certain personal characteristics, the Bureau decided to give him only a consulting vote.'[12] It is commonly believed that Stalin's imperious, cold and rude treatment of fellow-exiles gave rise to the comment about 'certain personal characteristics'. Stalin did not let that or the diminution of his position in 1912 get in his way.

By the next day he was a full voting member. His next move was to take control of *Pravda* together with fellow exile Lev Kamenev. Under them, the paper's policy in the first eight issues changed. There was to be: conditional support for the Provisional Government; unification with the Mensheviks in a common front; and Russian soldiers were to hold the line in the war until peace could be definitely concluded. These were now the order of the day. *Pravda's* policy was at sharp odds with Lenin's recommendations, as the historian Roy Medvedev writes: 'There may have been indignation in the Petrograd organization, but the articles in *Pravda* served as a guide for all the party organizations in Russia. Until Lenin arrived in Petrograd, Stalin in effect stood at the head not only of *Pravda* but of the entire party.'[13]

This wasn't the only sign of Stalin's independence from Lenin at that time. Anxious to have his views about the nature and possibilities of revolution disseminated in his absence, Lenin sent *Pravda* a number of letters from abroad. Stalin and Kamenev shortened the first letter and did not publish the following three. When Lenin did return he submitted his plan for the impending struggle to *Pravda* for publication. The very next day Kamenev, with Stalin's approval, printed a critical reply to Lenin's proposals.

This shows Stalin's self-confidence in following his instincts, as well as Lenin's lack of dictatorial authority over his colleagues. Stalin failed to anticipate that Lenin's thinking would have taken him further than anyone else's, and that on his return to Russia Lenin would be at the stage where 'power in the hands of the proletariat and the poorest strata of the peasantry' seemed a realistic possibility.

Lenin reached Petrograd on 16 April 1917, his journey facilitated by the Germans, who knew that Lenin was advocating Russia's withdrawal from the war. There were crowds of people at the Finland Station to meet him, among them Ilya Shkapa.

> He was really a very ordinary man. Even his speech surprised
> me. It was guttural, his was an expansive way of speaking.
> However, despite the fact that his speech sounded guttural and
> he didn't pronounce words clearly, he inspired the people with
> his incredible thinking and deeply held convictions. He spoke
> passionately, loudly and even penetratingly. And I thought,
> what a revolutionary . . . Lenin for me became a standard,
> his appeal amazed me and I was not even nineteen years old.
> I took this on my part as a signal which I had to serve. And I
> decided this was the man who was leading the country forward
> to a successful conclusion to the war. My father at the time was
> at the front and I longed for him to survive and return, and
> Lenin claimed: 'Long live peace and long live the social
> revolution.' I decided only the Bolshevik party, and not the

Socialist Revolutionaries or the Mensheviks, could lead our
people forward to a successful and happy life.

Before the Bolsheviks could lead the people, they needed to win
them over. As always, the greatest challenge was the peasants. Again,
Lenin and Stalin did not see eye to eye – Lenin had advocated land
nationalisation, whereas Stalin's policy was for the peasants to act on
their own behalf: 'We call upon them to organize and form revolutionary peasant committees, . . . take over the landed estates
through these committees, and cultivate the land in an organized
manner without authorization.'[14]

Lenin, alone of the Bolsheviks, realised that power could and
should be taken, and that precise, detailed policies in each area,
particularly agriculture, were less important than rallying people to
his cause. The peasants were the largest group to be won over and
what happened is crucial to an understanding not simply of the
October Revolution but of the key problem which Stalin solved with
such brutality in the 1920s and '30s.

The problem was that the peasants constituted over 80 per cent of
the population, while the Bolsheviks had only a tiny following
amongst them. A party representing the interests of the proletariat
against the capitalists could command the support of the peasants
only by concessions to them, or by force, or by a combination of the
two. Concessions to the peasants were effectively concessions to
capitalism, to some degree of private ownership of, or control over,
the land and its products. That, of course, was ideologically unacceptable to the Bolsheviks. To gain power, therefore, compromise
was necessary. Leaving a number of things unsaid about Bolshevik
agrarian policy was not enough. The party of the peasants was the
Socialist Revolutionaries. They had compiled a list of 242 peasant
mandates expressing their demands for the even distribution of land
among the working peasants, transfer of high-standard scientific
farms to communes, etc. By the end of August, Lenin had adopted
these 242 mandates into his own party's policy, but in doing so
strived to conceal any notion of concession, or of a deviation from
plan:

> The peasants want to keep their small farms, to set equal
> standards for all, and to make readjustments on an equalitarian

basis from time to time. Fine. No sensible socialist will differ with the peasant poor over this. . . . The crux of the matter lies in political power passing into the hands of the proletariat. When this has taken place, everything that is essential, basic, fundamental in the programme set out in the 242 mandates *will become feasible*. Life will show what modifications it will undergo as it is carried out. This is an issue of secondary importance. We are not doctrinaires. Our theory is a guide to action, not a dogma. We do not claim that Marx knew or Marxists know the road to socialism down to the last detail. It would be nonsense to claim anything of the kind.[15]

It was apparent at the time that a large crack had merely been papered over, as Ilya Shkapa remembers:

I must tell you that from the very beginning there were arguments between the peasants, even your average person, and the Bolsheviks. Lenin had agreed to the programme of the Socialist Revolutionaries to socialise the land, but the programme of the Bolsheviks was in favour of nationalising the land. This was the difference here between them. Nationalisation of the land meant that the distribution of the land would go to the power of the government . . . but the socialisation of the land as the Socialist Revolutionaries had put forward, this was considered to be the property of those communes that happened to be on this land already. And these communes dictated the following: that the land belonged only to those people who actually tilled it, worked on it. And Lenin stood back from his nationalisation of the land . . . and put forward his thinking that he agreed with the SRs and with the socialisation of the land.

John Reed's eyewitness account of the Russian Revolution, *Ten Days That Shook The World*, documents the argumentative, difficult and critical attempts to reconcile Bolshevik and peasant interests in stormy public meetings as power was being seized:

But none of us knew that a series of secret conferences was already going on between the Left Socialist Revolutionaries

**16 Street demonstration, Petrograd. Although the Provisional Government continued the war with Germany, it unleashed powerful forces hoping for peace, social change and national liberation. These demonstrators came from the subject territories of Poland and Lithuania – soon to be independent.**

and the Bolsheviki at Smolny [Bolshevik Headquarters] . . .
Wednesday morning, 28 November, after a terrible all-night
struggle, an agreement was reached. . . . Old Nathanson,
the white-bearded dean of the left wing of the Socialist
Revolutionaries, his voice trembling and tears in his eyes, read
the report of the 'wedding' of the Peasants' Soviets with the
Workers' and Soldiers' Soviets. At every mention of the word
'union' there was ecstatic applause.[16]

The basis of the 'union' was that the radical faction of the peasants'
party, the Left Socialist Revolutionaries, would take part in government, and the first fruit of the union was a land decree which
essentially embodied the key parts of the peasants' demands. Lenin
explained the tactic thus:

We Bolsheviks were opposed to the law. . . . Yet we signed it,
because we did not want to oppose the will of the majority of
the peasants. . . . We did not want to impose on the peasants
the idea that the equal division of land was useless, an idea
which was alien to them. Far better, we thought, if, by their
own experience and suffering, the peasants themselves came to
realise that equal division is nonsense. . . . That is why we
helped to divide the land, although we realised it was no
solution.[17]

It was a manoeuvre which worked in that the Bolsheviks secured
peasant support and wound up in power. But as we shall see, this was
a problem simply postponed. The land did not pass to the peasant
who tilled it but went increasingly to the old backward communes
and then by the early 1930s into total collectivisation by force. These
alliances with other revolutionaries were enough to loosen the tenu-
ous hold on power of the Provisional Government led by Alexander
Kerensky. The Bolsheviks and their allies achieved their authority
by a *coup* at the centre; they knew what they wanted and had the will
to achieve it.

For the people who still remember the revolution, no cynicism
about political tactics can diminish the sense of excitement and pride
they still feel at taking part in what they see as the greatest single
event this century. Ilya Shkapa says:

I kept watch at the Smolny Institute in a military overcoat.
They gave me a military overcoat although I wasn't a soldier
yet. And I took part in all of those goings-on during those very
confused times. It was a time when there was a lot of fighting
. . . and we did everything so that the revolution would be
victorious, the socialist revolution. . . . I was eventually given
a personal pension and in the book are written the following
words: 'Participant in the Great October Revolution'.

Nadezhda Ioffe, the daughter of Trotsky's close colleague Adolf
Ioffe, was then eleven years old.

My father came home on the night of the revolution [25
October 1917] saying, 'Come quick, power is ours,' and he
took us to Smolny and I heard Lenin speak. I remember the
clapping and the excitement. Some people cried out, 'Power,
but only for an hour.' I kept asking my father, 'What can I do?'
He answered, 'Study!'

Stalin's own part in those months is often obscure and yet should
not be underestimated. In April he was elected to the Central
Committee with the third largest number of votes after Lenin and
Zinoviev. When Lenin had to seek temporary refuge outside Petrograd, it was Stalin who shaved off the famous beard and moustache to
assist Lenin's disguise. At the secretly held Sixth Party Congress in
August, it was Stalin who gave the Central Committee's report –
usually Lenin's task – and the main speech on the political situation.
Yet at this same Congress, Stalin was prepared to allow Lenin to
stand trial on conspiracy charges, a view overturned by the Party. As
for the events of the October Revolution itself, the seizure of power
in Petrograd and Moscow, Stalin's role appears to have dwindled as
events unfolded. John Reed's book, *Ten Days That Shook The World*,
was described by Lenin himself as 'a truthful and most vivid
exposition of the events'. Reed mentions Stalin twice in 351 pages.
Stalin for his part banned the book when he came to power, and mere
possession of it was enough to land people in the camps. By then he
was in charge of the country's history as well as its present. This is the
entry for 24–25 October in the *Biographical Chronicle* accompanying

Stalin's published works: 'V. I. Lenin and J. V. Stalin direct the October armed uprising.'

**17 Lenin underground. On his return to the cauldron of revolutionary Russia in April 1917 the Provisional Government ordered Lenin's arrest for conspiracy. This was the disguise he adopted, after being shaved by Stalin. This photograph was taken to make up a fake identity card.**

There is in fact no authentic record of Stalin directing anything, making any major decisions, being on any barricades, rallying any troops, workers or peasants, capturing any post offices or government buildings. The truth is that Stalin spent the revolution in editorial charge of *Pravda* and it is in that capacity that his role is of importance. On the eve of the revolution, leading Bolsheviks Kamenev and Zinoviev argued against the seizure of power by an armed uprising. Lenin called them 'strike-breakers' and 'traitors to the revolution'. Stalin published Kamenev's letter to *Pravda* defending his *own* position and then defended Kamenev when he offered his resignation. The resignation was accepted, Stalin offered his own, and it was refused. These events are important because they show that Stalin's position was itself moderate and conciliatory both within the Party and vis-à-vis political tactics outside, and because, years later, he was to use this incident as proof of Zinoviev's and Kamenev's treachery, without ever mentioning his own role.

Deutscher suggests a possible reason for the comparative slightness of Stalin's role: 'In part this was the result of ineffectiveness of the Central Committee, within which Stalin's own weight was much greater than outside it.'[18] This suggests that Stalin, the practical revolutionary, was already showing a predilection for committee work and organisation – a tendency which was to be instrumental in his rise to power. After all, he lived and worked among a group of men who excelled in fields in which he did not: theory, oratory and military action. He needed a sphere to dominate and perhaps had found it by October 1917.

**18 July 1917. Street fighting on Nevsky Prospekt, Petrograd, as the tsarist police broke up a Bolshevik demonstration.**

The Politburo had been formed in early October with Stalin one of its seven members, and by the end of the month the new cabinet – the Soviet of People's Commissars – was announced. The only new post was Commissar for Nationalities and the holder was Stalin. A month later, the Central Committee delegated the right to decide 'all emergency questions' to a four-man team of Lenin, Stalin, Trotsky and Sverdlov. Neither his deviation from Lenin's views nor his minor role during the seizure of power had hampered Stalin's steady progress towards a place at the top of the Bolshevik leadership.

# 3 THE STRUGGLE FOR POWER

'It is difficult to reconcile oneself with the fact that the failures of the movement with which all our lives were linked lie in the movement itself, its own miscalculations and failures.' This view comes from Alexander Tsipko of the Institute of the Economy of the World Socialist System, a Soviet academic who has studied the roots of Stalinism. It is easier, he says, to believe that enemies were to blame, or accidents, or Stalin himself for usurping power. This helps us *not* to think 'about the revolution itself, its own internal objective contradictions . . . the deep contradictions of the task begun by us in 1917 have still not become the subject of thoughtful and responsible analysis'.[1]

In trying to understand where Stalin's ideas and methods came from, the period between October 1917 and the death of Lenin in 1924 is crucial. These were critical years for the revolution and formative years for the Bolsheviks, including Stalin, who now carried the burden of creating a state out of an uprising. It was the clash between ideological goals and practical circumstances that created the contradictions Tsipko writes about. To understand Stalin, we have to understand the way Lenin tried to resolve the clash – a process Stalin witnessed at first hand and took part in.

'We shall now proceed to construct the Socialist order!' had been Lenin's ringing words on the night when the Bolsheviks seized power. The gap between revolutionary aspirations and socialist practice started to open immediately. Some of the plans now sound hopelessly Utopian: the abolition of the police, the army and all bureaucracy; the abolition of money; the state itself to wither away. Others were not so Utopian: freedom of the press; democracy; equalisation of all salaries to that of a competent worker. Some plans were feasible and happened: withdrawal from the First World War; nationalisation of banks and industry; confiscation of landed estates.

Others were feasible and did not happen: direct administration of industry by elected committees of workers; free self-determination for all the nationalities; the passing of power to the Soviets (workers', soldiers' and peasants' councils) – a policy closely associated with the aims of the revolution but in fact dropped by Lenin in mid-July 1917. A central tenet, whose status hovered between hope and belief, was that the workers of the world would unite and that revolution would spread, buttressing the Russian one and liberating all downtrodden masses oppressed by war and exploitation. The failure of the world revolution to be sparked alight from the Russian one curbed many aspirations and forced the Bolsheviks into an even more militant defence of their beleaguered position.

What the Bolsheviks faced was hostility aimed directly at them: from the old order they had displaced, from the mistrustful peasantry, from the other political parties, from sections of the military and from the outside world. In response, the Bolsheviks rejected the idea of a democratic alliance on as broad a front as possible, preferring to turn in on themselves. The factor that, more than anything else, came to determine what followed the revolution was the nature of Bolshevism itself. This, no less than the gaining of power, was Lenin's responsibility. This was the central part of Lenin's legacy. This was what his successors would fight for the right to defend. This was the basis of Stalin's second and infinitely more bloody and traumatic revolution. To put it another way, it was Lenin's triumph to secure power for the Bolshevik party and Stalin's task to hold on to it securely. But what was the nature and basis of that power?

The answer is that the nature of the power was rule by the Party as the 'vanguard of the proletariat' along Marxist lines, as adapted and codified by Lenin. The basis was the legitimacy conferred on the Party by the fact that, as Lenin said in November 1917: 'The second All-Russian Congress of Soviets gave the majority to the Bolshevik party. Only a Government formed by this party can therefore be a Soviet Government.'[2] As to *how* the power was to be used, Lenin said: 'The proletariat needs state power, a centralised organisation of force, an organisation of violence, both to crush the resistance of the exploiters and to *lead* the enormous mass of the population – the peasants, the petty bourgeoisie, and semi-proletarians – in the work of organising a socialist economy.'[3] We shall see later what latitude

Lenin, and even more Stalin, found in that word *'lead'* which Lenin himself italicised.

It had not begun as a one-party state. In order to bring the peasants on to their side, the Bolsheviks gave cabinet posts to seven Left Socialist Revolutionaries. But they resigned in March 1918 in protest over the Treaty of Brest–Litovsk – the pact which pulled Russia out of the First World War. As each difficulty arose in the period following the October Revolution, the effect was to strengthen the role and power of the Bolshevik party, even if that was not the prime intention. Soon it would be hard to distinguish between a problem for the country and a threat to Bolshevism.

A key landmark in the creation of a one-party state was the ending of the democratic process in Russia. This process had been started by the 1905 revolution and speeded on by the February Revolution in 1917. In November of that year, 41.6 million people had voted in elections to the Constituent Assembly, the new parliamentary body. The results have never been absolutely established but it is clear that the Bolsheviks only obtained about a quarter of the vote, and that the parties representing the peasants had gained the upper hand. When the Constituent Assembly met on 5 January 1918 it was also clear that the Bolsheviks were not going to tolerate any kind of parliament. Ilya Shkapa remembers the day and his part in what happened:

> I took a rifle which was simply given to me and lay down.
> And they shot through my overcoat in several places. There
> were battles, there was opposition . . . there was a massive
> amount of people who were in favour of an open Constituent
> Assembly. The Bolsheviks decided to dispense with this and a
> battle took place and we decided to disband the Constituent
> Assembly.

The next day, Lenin embodied in law what Shkapa and the others had done and dissolved the Constituent Assembly by decree: 'To relinquish the sovereign power of the Soviets, to relinquish the Soviet Republic won by the people, for the sake of the bourgeois parliamentary system and the Constituent Assembly, would now be a step backwards and would cause the collapse of the October workers' and peasants' revolution.'[4]

Stalin's daughter Svetlana is unequivocal in condemning the fate of democracy at the hands of the Bolsheviks. She believes that:

19 Lenin inspecting his troops, Red Square, Moscow (now the capital once more), 25 May 1919. The war against the counter-revolutionary Whites and the Allied intervention was raging across Russia.

20 Stalin and Kalinin flank Lenin at the Eighth Party Congress, March 1919. 'Koba Stalin', as he had called himself before the revolution, signed himself 'J. Stalin' from now on.

'. . . democracy had just been born in Russia and was murdered in the crib by the October Revolution. Because what proceeded later was never a democracy, as we understand it, and was never a prosperity, and never brought to Russia anything which was promised.'

This was certainly no time to be able to deliver promises. The new state's back was to the wall. First the Treaty of Brest–Litovsk was signed, which entailed ceding huge tracts of land to Germany and its allies. Lenin was supported only by Stalin in seeing the need to get out of the war no matter what, particularly as worldwide revolution was not about to come to their aid. Then Germany, Austria and Turkey invaded, a corps of 40,000 Czech troops which had gone over to the Tsar occupied a vast area east of the Volga, and there was a small intervention by allied forces at the periphery of Soviet territory. Their role was minor but no doubt contributed to the sense of encirclement. Foreign invasion was then accompanied by civil war itself as Cossacks and pro-tsarist forces attacked the Red Army, newly founded under Trotsky's command. The Soviet response was to fight on all fronts with full mobilisation and all resources nationalised under central control.

This was the era and system of government known as 'war communism', and Stalin took full advantage of it to become a ruthless and egotistical military leader. He went to Tsaritsyn on the Volga to expedite the supply and distribution of food; his treatment of friend and foe alike was peremptory and brutal, as Soviet historian Roy Medvedev explains:

> Truly Stalin spared no-one. He didn't hesitate to have dozens
> of real enemies of Soviet power shot; but he also destroyed
> anyone even suspected of ties with the counterrevolution . . .
> arrested on Stalin's orders were almost all the military
> specialists on the staff of the [Soviet] military district. They
> were placed on a barge on the Volga. This floating prison
> suddenly sank with most of its prisoners.[5]

Stalin's mistrust of military specialists brought him into sharp conflict with Trotsky, with whom Lenin sided. As the Civil War went on, the rivalry between Stalin and Trotsky grew. Trotsky was the outstanding military leader, while Stalin's blend of obstinacy, loyalty, attention to detail and capacity for hard work made him no friends but kept him at Lenin's right hand. He was put by Lenin on

**21** Trotsky (*centre*), as Commissar for War, in 1921 won the glory of successful command — and earned the undying enmity of Stalin.

to a succession of key military committees, and both he and Trotsky were awarded the prestigious Order of the Red Banner.

Stalin's last post in the field came in 1920 when he served as political commissar on the south-west front in the brief war with Poland. In that conflict, begun by a Polish invasion, the Red Army had initial successes but was routed before Warsaw by Pilsudski. The Red Army commander, Tukhachevsky, blamed Stalin for not coming to his aid. This reverse helped to persuade Lenin that the export of revolution did not find ready buyers internationally.

Under Lenin's express direction, the use of terror became routine in the Civil War. It had started within weeks of the October Revolution when the Bolsheviks intercepted a telegram calling for a general strike of all state employees. The response was to set up, as a short-term measure, an organisation to root out and destroy forces and people hostile to the revolution – the Cheka. Although the Cheka was intended to defend the revolution against enemies within, it was also seen by its founder, Felix Dzerzhinsky, as an agency to recruit and discipline forced labour. From the start, Lenin endorsed the need for the new state to have a machinery for repressing. 'The state is an instrument for coercion. Formerly it was the coercion of the whole people by a handful of moneybags; but we desire to transform the state into an institution for enforcing the will of the people. We want to organise violence in the name of the interests of the workers.'[6]

A string of factors served to widen the targets and scope of the Cheka: the Civil War with its enemies inside the country itself; an assassination attempt on Lenin by a Left Socialist Revolutionary which put that party in the firing-line; the critical food shortages which cast suspicion on rich peasants – or kulaks – for hoarding grain; and the new state's deep hostility to the Church. Lenin's instructions, some of them still not included in Soviet editions of his works, spelt out the importance of terror:

> Cannot a further 20 thousand or so Petrograd workers be mobilised, plus 10 thousand or so of the bourgeoisie, machine-guns be posted to the rear of them, a few hundred shot and a real mass assault . . . assured?[7]

and:

> Under the guise of 'greens' [partisan groups during the Civil War] we shall go forward for 10–20 versts [measurement of distance] and hang kulaks, priests and landowners. Bounty: 100,000 roubles for every man hanged.[8]

and:

> Famine is the only time when we can beat the enemy (the Church) over the head. . . . Right now . . . when people are being eaten in famine-stricken areas, we can carry out the expropriation of Church valuables with the most furious and ruthless energy. . . . We must crush their resistance with such cruelty that they will not forget it for decades.[9]

**22 A Cheka execution cell in Kiev. Both sides in the Civil War took ferocious reprisals against their opponents.**

Stalin had been in at the birth of the Cheka and thereafter was appointed to a string of commissions and committees to guide and define its work. In response to direction and encouragement from above and enjoying considerable latitude of movement, the Cheka under Lenin took hostages, executed without trial and started the prison-camp (or Gulag) system which became rapidly filled with 'enemies of the people'.

Still the problems mounted. The successful military engagements of the Civil War were increasingly overshadowed by the problem of peasant uprisings against the Bolsheviks, or communists as they were now renamed. Lenin dreamed of increasing the scale of agricultural units. He was already outwitting the peasants, according to H. G. Wells whom he met in 1920:

'We have in places large-scale agriculture. The government is already running big estates with workers instead of peasants where conditions are favourable. That can spread. It can be

**23 Victims of Red Terror in the Ukraine.**

extended first to one province, then another. The peasants of
the other provinces, selfish and illiterate, will not know what
is happening until their turn comes!' It may be difficult to
defeat the Russian peasant en masse; but in detail there is no
difficulty at all. At the mention of the peasant, Lenin's head
came nearer mine; his manner became confidential. As if after
all the peasant *might overhear*.[10]

But the peasants were in rampant opposition. Peasant armies in
the Volga region, in Tambov Province, in West Siberia, in the
Ukraine – all over the country, in fact – took on the Red Army in
protest against the forced requisitioning by the state of their grain.
The Civil War had totally disrupted farming; with the market
abolished by 'war communism', the only way to obtain food was by
force. Ilya Shkapa explains:

Look what was happening. They go and look for the bread
which the peasants hide, and search for and remove everything
which they find and punish them for this . . . village people
came up to me as a communist and asked me these questions:

'What do you have in common with these scoundrels? Look
and see how they behave towards the peasants, they're taking
away from us our very last grain, we are hungry and if you are
going to continue doing this . . . then we will rise up against you.'

According to the historian Robert Conquest, as many as 2 million
people may have died in the Peasant War, over twice as many as were
killed in the Civil War itself. The chaos in agriculture brought a new
and ever more terrible problem: famine. By 1921, over 5 million were
dead from starvation. The writer Nina Berberova, who lived in
Petrograd at the time, remembers: 'A city completely dead: dark at
night, dark in the evenings, in the winter evenings – can you
imagine? . . . No electricity, no heat. It was a terrible city, because
there was nothing. . . . It was a terrible sight: people just dying.'

Ludmilla Shapiro was in Moscow, by then the capital city of
Russia: 'You could often see people who walked from the famine-
stricken areas of the Soviet Union . . . in the hope of finding food
there. By that time they were usually so weak that they mostly died
on the street, so as a child I saw many deaths . . . whole families
dying on the sidewalks.'

**24 Peasants suspected of cannibalism
photographed with half-eaten bodies,
Orenburg in the Urals, 1921.**

Lenin's response was a dramatic U-turn in policy in order to appease the peasants. In March 1921, at the Tenth Party Congress, he spelt out the seriousness of the problem: 'We know that so long as there is no revolution in other countries, only agreement with the peasantry can save the socialist revolution in Russia.'[11] The plan to win over the peasants was called the New Economic Policy or NEP. It entailed a double concession: freedom for the peasants to trade their products, and access to commodities for purchase which would serve as an incentive to sell their goods freely in the market. The commodities would be obtained by relaxing both internal commerce and foreign trade restrictions. Lenin made it plain that, although this was a retreat towards capitalism, there was no other option. Harry Young was a member of the British Communist Party sent over to Moscow in the early 1920s:

> Lenin spoke to the Congress like a Dutch uncle, or like
> a grandad speaking to his wayward children . . . he was

**25 Lenin at the Tenth Party Congress, March 1921, where he announced the New Economic Policy (NEP) aimed at reconciling the peasants.**

administering a bitter pill. And they had to take it. And he just very quietly said, 'We can't go on like this any longer, comrades' . . . and there was a sort of subdued hush when people realised that a major transformation had got to take place.

One of the ironies of the NEP was that what seemed on the face of it to be a liberating move was in fact buttressed by a series of strict qualifying measures. Lenin made it plain that the 'retreat' was only temporary and that it would be highly disciplined. In a letter to Kamenev in March 1922, Lenin declared: 'It is a great mistake to think that the NEP put an end to terror; we shall again have recourse to terror and to economic terror.'[12] Furthermore, not only did the NEP *not* give rise to political pluralism, but there was to be a total ban on factions within the Communist Party itself. 'Comrades,' said Lenin, 'this is no time to have an opposition. Either you're on this side, or on the other, but then your weapon must be a gun, and not an opposition.'[13] This last point sharply reflected an incident earlier in the congress. There had been a rebellion at the Kronstadt naval base which, though staunchly loyal in the October Revolution and the Civil War, had become totally disillusioned with the communist monopoly of power, use of terror and failure to fulfil revolutionary aspirations. The revolt had been put down brutally by 50,000 troops led by 300 delegates sent out from the Party Congress.

Meanwhile, there were important changes going on in the Party itself. The majority of the membership had joined during the Civil War and, as historian Moshe Lewin writes, 'They did not have the culture, general or political, which most of the old guard shared, and what they brought into the ranks was of necessity a new and different political culture characterized by strong militaristic overtones and, quite naturally, by deep authoritarianism.'[14] Then, as the NEP began, the first big purge of the Party occurred. 180,000 were expelled and the new members were even more removed from the Bolshevik old guard – they were often illiterate workers, less questioning and more subservient.

In 1922 Stalin was appointed General Secretary of the Party and, by controlling the system of appointments within the Party, both harnessed the loyalty of the newer members and transformed what had been a senior but routine job into the most powerful in the country. People were given their jobs in the new bureaucracy on the basis of their loyalty, rather than their qualifications. A new class, known as the 'Nomenklatura', evolved, whose obedience was repaid by privilege but who could be as easily dismissed as promoted. The historian Michael Voslensky was a high-ranking Soviet official with first-hand experience of the system.

> Aspirants to social promotion were animated by a genuine desire to carry out the slightest whim of those who had appointed them. The key to Stalin's historic ascent lay in that trivial fact; he succeeded in concentrating all appointments to key positions in the country in his own hands and those of his apparatus, and it was by this use of political qualifications that he assured himself of the complete devotion of the whole of the new ruling class, the Nomenklatura.[15]

It was a process which took years and which no one guessed that Stalin would undertake. Nadezhda Ioffe, the daughter of an Old Bolshevik, remembers her father's generation's attitude to Stalin:

> Nobody felt he represented any danger. For example: Zinoviev and Kamenev would not have liked to see Bukharin having the role of General Secretary, and Bukharin would not have liked to see Zinoviev having that post, and all of them agreed that they were afraid of Trotsky . . . but nobody seemed particularly opposed to the idea of Stalin having the post and that's why it happened in the end – he got such a large amount of power in his hands.

Soviet academic Alexander Tsipko sees Stalinism as, above all, the tragedy of the Bolshevik old guard: 'It is this old guard that created that political mechanism, a weapon of absolute total power, which Stalin utilised for his egotistical purposes. . . . After all it was precisely the old guard which already during Lenin's lifetime voluntarily handed over to Stalin the vast power created by the revolution.'[16] Lenin himself did not at first foresee what would happen, though he did remark of Stalin, according to Trotsky, that: 'This cook can only serve peppery dishes.' Indeed, Lenin defended Stalin in front of the Party from attack for having too many senior posts.

The fact is that the Stalin of the early 1920s was not the Stalin who was to dominate the whole country a decade later. Furthermore, the particular propensity Stalin showed for arbitrary violence against the Party was completely alien to Lenin. Lenin believed in the use of terror against the Party's opponents, but not out of personal vindictiveness. *Within* the Party, the use of terror was taboo. Lenin derived his authority from his command of the argument rather than of the Cheka. Given that the indications of Stalin's true nature were sketchy at best in the early 1920s, and that Lenin was increasingly frail and sick by then, it was almost by chance that Lenin glimpsed something in Stalin which suddenly made him anxious about the man he had supported so long and promoted so high.

Lenin's realisation that Stalin might abuse the power he held came at the end of 1922 when he was too ill to do much about it. His misgiving about Stalin's ruthless approach had been triggered by his brutal suppression of the independence of his native Georgia in 1921. The Commissar for Nationalities had arranged an insurrection which called for fraternal Soviet assistance. Lenin did not baulk at that – he signed the necessary authorisations for the invasion. He, like Stalin, wanted Georgia firmly inside the fold, but he wanted it done tactfully. His advice to the Georgian communists was: 'not to apply the Russian stereotype but skilfully and flexibly to create tactics of their own based on great willingness to make concessions to all manner of petty-bourgeois elements'.[17]

It was the subsequent high-handed ferocity of the suppression of Georgian nationalism by Stalin and Sergo Ordzhonikidze (both Georgian themselves) which unnerved Lenin and Trotsky, whose aid Lenin sought to defend his views in the Central Committee. Lenin realised what a terrible impression Stalin's methods gave the other nationalities and other countries. He also hated 'Great Russian chauvinism' – the idea that Stalin, despite his Georgian origins, held Russia to be automatically superior.

Lenin was also struck by Stalin's capacity for excessive rudeness, which came out both in the Georgian affair and in Stalin's abusive treatment of Lenin's wife Krupskaya. It wasn't that, late in life, Lenin had grown squeamish about ruthlessness, indeed as recently as May 1922 he had advised the Commissar for Justice that: 'The courts must not ban terror – to promise that would be deception or self-deception – but must . . . legalise it as a principle.'[18] It was rather that he suddenly saw Stalin in a new light. The Central

Committee had put Stalin in charge of Lenin's medical supervision; neither his doctors, nor Stalin, nor his own health allowed him much time for work. Limited in his powers to change matters, Lenin committed his fears to paper in what became known as his Testament. He wrote of Stalin that, having become General Secretary, he '. . . has unlimited authority concentrated in his hands, and I am not sure whether he will always be capable of using that authority with sufficient caution'.[19] Lenin went on to discuss five other leaders – Trotsky, Zinoviev, Kamenev, Bukharin and Pyatakov – in a manner which suggests that none of them merited his blessing as his possible successor. Nine days later he added a postscript to his remarks about Stalin, describing him as 'too rude' – a defect 'intolerable in a general secretary'.[20] Lenin suggested that a way be found of transferring Stalin from the post. Yet Lenin did not call for Stalin's removal from the leadership, intending him to continue to share with the others in the running of the Party.

Soviet historian Roy Medvedev has analysed the Testament closely:

> . . . if there is a central thought in the Testament, it is that none of the men listed by Lenin should be allowed to occupy the place in the party that he himself had held. In Lenin's thinking, his appraisals would act as a bridle with which the party could restrain the political ambitions and vanity of its most outstanding leaders.[21]

The Testament contained much more besides Lenin's judgement about the leadership. The historian Moshe Lewin sums up its themes:

> No violent measures as a way of transforming the social structures of the country! The cultural revolution first, an undertaking with the peasants, and – an eminently necessary measure – slowness as the supreme virtue; in addition, an important discovery, a new vision on Lenin's part of socialism as a 'regime of civilized cooperators'.[22]

These ideas, such as the advice to remove Stalin, were left by Lenin to take their chances alone, without him to push and argue for them.

The Testament was not to be opened except on Lenin's instruc-

26 Lenin during his last illness. He suffered his first stroke in May 1922, and a second in December. It was after this that he dictated his Testament, with its postscript warning against Stalin. After that he lingered, helpless, for a full year. He died in January 1924.

tions or by Krupskaya after his death. In 1923, Lenin suffered paralysis and loss of speech after a stroke. He died on 21 January 1924. Nadezhda Ioffe heard the news at the Congress of Soviets:

> I have never seen so many people, especially men, who were in tears. I was sitting somewhere in a corner and sitting next to me was an elderly man – he looked like a worker. He turned around and said to me: 'Little one, what are we going to do? What's going to happen now?' He himself was crying.

The queues of people to pay their last respects were seemingly endless – soldiers, workers and peasants. Anna Larina remembers the effect on Party members:

> Party members were called out according to a list to take part in the guard of honour, and I went along with my father. And at the back of the Hall of Columns there was a little room where people sat in mournful silence suffering the effects of this death. Of course, it was difficult to foresee what was to come later, after Lenin's death. But now I have the feeling that they were sort of doomed.

Stalin's public part in Lenin's funeral was respectful and discreet. He was one of the coffin-bearers, he took turns in the guard of honour, and he was one of the speakers at the special session of the Congress of Soviets on 26 January 1924, when Petrograd was re-named Leningrad. His speech, as befitted the ex-seminarian, con-sisted of a series of vows couched in biblical language: 'Departing from us, Comrade Lenin enjoined us to hold high and guard the purity of the great title of member of the party. We vow to you, Comrade Lenin, that we shall fulfil your behest with honour!'[23]

Stalin's private role in Lenin's funeral is associated firstly with giving Trotsky the wrong date so that Trotsky missed it completely, and secondly with the decision to preserve Lenin's body by embalm-ing. The former is folklore and almost certainly not true. As to the latter, whether this was at Stalin's instigation or not, the cult of Lenin, of which this was the literal embodiment, became increas-ingly important to Stalin. Over the following months and years, Stalin built up the idea both of Lenin's infallibility and of himself as sole interpreter of Lenin's works. Thus to disagree with him was – heresy of heresies – to disagree with Lenin.

However, first he had to jump the hurdle of Lenin's Testament, which was circulated by Krupskaya amongst the top Party leadership at the Thirteenth Party Congress in 1924. Stalin's gambit was to offer his resignation and at the same time make himself politically indispensable to Zinoviev and Kamenev. It worked. Lenin's Testa-ment was, after all, flattering to none of the top leadership and was thereafter suppressed.

Iosif Itskov was in the Party apparatus in 1924 and saw how Stalin kept a low profile then, as a moderate and a conciliator:

> He tried to stay in the shadows. He was a man who – well, he
> was always wearing a mask, you would say. He tried to play the
> role of peace-maker. . . . He was a man whose wishes, whose
> aim was very clear, but you could never tell how he was going
> to accomplish it. He accomplished it in the most cunning way.
> And he allowed nothing to get in his way.

Stalin made sure that his ambition was well covered up: 'To lead the Party otherwise than collectively is impossible. Now that Ilyich [Lenin] is not with us it is silly to dream of such a thing, it is silly to talk about it.'[24] Stalin worked his way towards power by a series of alliances designed to isolate his enemies and particularly his arch-rival Trotsky. John McDonald in *Strategy in Poker, Business and War* wrote of these groupings: 'Nothing was needed more by these men than a little game theory, and only one had it.'[25]

Stalin also attacked Trotsky on the theoretical front, arguing that socialism *could* be built in Russia alone. By polarising the argument he managed to isolate Trotsky as a defeatist and rally Party workers demoralised by the failure of Trotsky's 'world revolution'. Gradually Stalin got the upper hand, helped by Trotsky's own ill-suitedness to close political in-fighting. By 1927, Stalin's grip upon the Party was sufficient to deliver him a majority when it mattered, whatever Trotsky's argument. Harry Young was present at the 1927 meeting when Trotsky was expelled from the Communist International or Comintern, the organisation which united foreign communist parties around the world. 'The meeting got very acrimonious. He defended the world revolution line and permanent revolution in the way that only Trotsky could. But of course, it was all to no avail. The thing had been thrashed out and decided in the Russian Communist Party Politburo and Central Committee.'

To a certain extent Stalin derived support from his control of the Party appointments system, but we should not underestimate the popular approval his views commanded, as historian Robert Service argues: 'Stalin won his battles in the 1920s to a large extent because political judgements were made in his favour among Bolshevik party officials and not only because he controlled the levers of bureaucratic authority. Many of Stalin's inclinations were shared by many Bolsheviks.'[26]

By 1927, in alliance with Nikolai Bukharin, Stalin had seen off Trotsky, Zinoviev and Kamenev. Bukharin had been closely ident-ified with the New Economic Policy from its inception and Stalin aligned himself resolutely behind Bukharin's views. But the NEP was coming under increasing strain. The causes were various: a feeling at the top that the NEP would run itself, that there was no need to *make* it work strategically; too much time spent on power struggles rather than on the economy; a lack of trained and skilled people who could think through the economic problems and find solutions; excessive interference from bureaucracy at local level designed to maintain the authority of the state within a market system. The signs that the NEP was failing became obvious by 1928.

27  Another funeral oration – by Voroshilov for the dead Dzerzhinsky, 1926. The brooding Stalin, to his left, was already winning the power struggle, isolating Trotsky and Zinoviev (*on the steps of the rostrum*).

28  Stalin at a football match in 1927. To his right, Kirov; behind them, Voroshilov and Kalinin.

Grain output was still below its pre-1914 levels, and industrial products were expensive, of poor quality and scarce. There was not much incentive for the peasants to sell their grain and spend the proceeds.

The NEP's worst enemy lay in the Party itself. A sizeable body of opinion regarded the NEP as an unacceptable concession to capitalism, and its lack of success did not help. The NEP was the runt of the ideological litter; as the 1920s proceeded, Stalin picked it up and stroked it from time to time, but he wasn't prepared to stop it from dying. In the end he killed it off himself, as he had warned he might: '. . . if we adhere to NEP it is because it serves the cause of socialism. When it ceases to serve the cause of socialism we shall get rid of it.'[27]

The trigger for a shift in policy away from the NEP came in early 1928, with the start of severe food shortages brought on by a huge shortfall in grain deliveries, as a result of the peasants' dissatisfaction with pricing. Stalin's response was to send out food requisition squads; Bukharin agreed, but not with the extreme levels of aggression employed by the squads. Panic and rumours of the NEP's abolition swept the countryside. At first Stalin denied the rumours. Then in May 1928 he reaffirmed the desirability of moving towards a collectivised form of agriculture. It was the start of a process of destruction intended to solve the peasant problem once and for all, in what the philosopher Leszek Kolakowski has called 'probably the most massive warlike operation ever conducted by a state against its own citizens'.[28]

# 4 'DROP BY DROP'

On 21 December 1929 Stalin celebrated his fiftieth birthday. Gone were Lenin's colleagues: Bukharin, Kamenev, Zinoviev, Trotsky, Rykov, Tomsky. By now Stalin's own men, or men he had made his own, were in place around him. They were photographed together on his birthday under the benign gaze of a Lenin statue: Sergo Ordzhonikidze, with whom Stalin had quelled Georgia; the dull-minded War Commissar Kliment Voroshilov, who, in honour of the occasion, rewrote the history of the Civil War around Stalin the mighty warrior; the economist Valerian Kuibyshev, who had successfully proposed changing the name of the city Tsaritsyn to Stalingrad; the weak-willed puppet President Mikhail Kalinin;

**29 Stalin on his fiftieth birthday in December 1929 with the circle now close to him: Ordzhonikidze, Voroshilov, Kuibyshev, Kalinin, Kaganovich and Kirov.**

Lazar Kaganovich – blindly loyal and mercilessly cruel; and Sergei Kirov, Stalin's trusted friend who ran the Leningrad Party Organisation. Three of the six were to meet with violent, untimely deaths – their loyalty to Stalin and importance in the Party were no guarantee of longevity. For the moment, though, they held privileged positions around the great leader on his birthday. Praise and greetings showered in on him from around the country. In reply he said that he was prepared to 'devote to the cause of the working class, to the cause of the proletarian revolution and world communism, all my strength, all my ability and, if need be, all my blood, drop by drop'.[1]

There were those who thought, but didn't say, that it would benefit everyone if he gave it all in one go. In the event it became clear within a week whose blood would in fact be shed. In a speech delivered at a Conference of Marxist students, Stalin spelt it out: '. . . we have passed from the policy of *restricting* the exploiting tendencies of the kulaks [wealthy peasants] to the policy of *eliminating* the kulaks as a class. It means that we have carried out, and are continuing to carry out, one of the decisive turns in our whole policy.'[2] A fundamental part of this 'turn' was that the whole of agriculture was to be collectivised, by force if necessary.

Collectivisation entailed the peasants moving lock, stock and barrel to farms owned equally by all its members, run co-operatively, and obliged to hand over a certain amount of produce to the state each year. No more individual farms. No more individual farmers selling their goods independently. No more NEP. It was a move which had considerable support within the Party from people who believed that the NEP was an aberration and that Lenin had compromised with capitalism. Abdurakhman Avtorkhanov was a graduate student at the Institute of Red Professors. It was there in 1928 that Stalin made his speech presenting the policy of collectivisation: 'I of course was on Stalin's side, because I thought . . . well, Lenin himself said that NEP was a pause. And so Stalin said: 'The pause has finished, and we are returning to socialism and communism.''

Many, particularly on the left of the Communist Party, saw the peasants as the obstacle to progress because the peasant would always work for himself rather than for the state. According to the Soviet academic Alexander Tsipko, this class approach, shared by most Bolsheviks, caused 'monstrous strain in a country in which 80 per cent of the population were seen as an obstacle on the path to an ideal

**30 The ideal of collectivisation. A posed photograph in the Ukraine, 1929.**

society. Because of this in the twenties the leaders of the party had come to find themselves in a besieged fortress . . . surrounded by a commodity-and-peasant world.'[3] Lenin had created that world through the NEP in response to the post-revolution crisis in agriculture. A key question under Stalin was the same as it had been under Lenin: how to get the grain out of the countryside? Stalin decided that the answer was to abandon appeasement for force. He justified the move on the ground that the kulaks were the class enemy, that they hoarded grain and wouldn't hand it over, that they would do all they could to sabotage agriculture. He even devised a theory which explained how, as socialism advanced, the enemies which remained would fight even harder – even more vigilance and ruthlessness would be needed.

Yet the experiences of those who took part in, or were the victims of forced collectivisation and anti-kulak campaigns, do not tally with Stalin's public analysis of the problem. In the first place, mass grain-hoarding was a myth. Sarra Babyonyshev's husband was a communist activist, sent by the Regional Party Committee into the north Caucasus to requisition grain by force:

> It was considered that for some reason the peasants were
> hiding it . . . were storing the grain somewhere underground.
> He saw that this wasn't true – children were dying of
> starvation, the peasants really were dying of starvation because
> they had no grain. He sent the Regional Party Committee a
> telegram: 'There is no wheat, people are dying of starvation,
> help them.'

A friend had advised him not to send the telegram because everyone in the Regional Committee knew the villagers had no grain. He did send it however, was expelled from the Party, fired from his job, and two years later he was arrested and died in a labour camp. As for the kulaks, described by Lenin as 'blood-suckers grown rich on the want suffered by the people', politicians and agricultural experts failed throughout the 1920s and '30s to agree either on a definition of what constituted a kulak, or how many there might be. It is a moot point whether any kulaks had even survived with their land and hired labour much beyond the October Revolution. The historian Moshe Lewin answers the question 'who was the kulak?' in this way: 'It is, in the first place, he who is declared to be such by the authorities.'[4]

Again, experience on the ground confirms the shakiness of Stalin's analysis. Mykola Pishy lived in the Ukraine throughout the forced collectivisation and the destruction of the kulaks.

> The kulaks – I mean the real kulaks – had a lot of land before
> the October Revolution. But the majority of them didn't have
> much land and couldn't keep farm labourers. They were
> dispossessed only because they refused to join the collective
> farm scheme. Then they were driven out of their houses. Their
> farms were taken and the authorities just considered them as
> 'kulaks'. There were masses of them.

Because the definition of kulak was arbitrary, the so-called middle and even poor peasants were often caught up in the net. Soviet historian Roy Medvedev believes that: 'It would hardly be sinning against the truth to put the total number of "dispossessed kulaks" at close to one million families, of which not fewer than half were exiled to the northern and eastern regions of the country.'[5]

According to the 1928 *Statistical Handbook USSR* calculation of

**31** The peasants were tenacious opponents of collectivisation. Millions met death by famine or liquidation as a result.

the average size of a kulak family, this would mean that around 6.5 million people were dispossessed. Western historians put the figures even higher. Moshe Lewin estimates that 'several million households, to a total of 10 million persons, or more, must have been deported, of whom a great many must have perished'.[6] Robert Conquest, agreeing broadly with this figure, puts the death-toll in the anti-kulak campaign at 3 million people. An operation on that scale could not go unnoticed. Abdurakhman Avtorkhanov stopped at a small town on the journey by train from Grozny to Moscow in 1930. He saw

> endless fields of people – women, children, old people – and universal wailing. They were being loaded on to cattle trucks to be sent off to Siberia. I was there for fifteen minutes and I asked the station master there, 'What's this? What's happening here?' and he said, 'What's up with you? Have you just landed from the moon or maybe you've just arrived from Persia? This is collectivisation and the elimination of the kulaks as a class.'

And it turned out that there were so many people, and not enough trains that, with the cold weather, people were literally just dying there.

It is clear that the Party must have known that there weren't any real kulaks left, that there was precious little grain to hoard, and that the state, *en route* to socialism, was hardly going to be much troubled by resistance from those it repressed. So what was Stalin's real aim? The Soviet writer, Lyudmila Saraskina:

> If you imagine that Stalin wanted to improve the harvest or to improve the lot of the peasant, then you're just fooling yourself. . . . Collectivisation was a bloody, terrible and monstrous means of the seizure of absolute power because the free peasant and the master of the land, the farmer, constituted one of the main obstacles on the path to the absolute feudal power that Stalin really wanted.

The tactics of grain seizures, forced collectivisation and elimination of the kulaks brought an even worse disaster down on the peasants – famine. The harvests had been poor. By throwing the better-off peasants from their land, the state destroyed its best farmers; those peasants that remained slaughtered their livestock *en masse*, both for food and in order to withhold them from the new collectives. Then the requisition squads from the Party and the OGPU (the state security agency, formerly the Cheka) arrived. The result was catastrophic, particularly in the rich farming land of the Ukraine. It seems clear that what happened there was intentional. Mykola Pishy remembers the squads arriving at his home to take away their food: 'My mother spoke up. "Please leave us something. We've got five children in the family. They'll die." Vasil – the leader – answered, "I don't care about your children. I care about my party-ticket."'

Alisa Maslo has lived all her life in the small village of Targan, where 362 people died from the famine:

> They went from house to house and they took away everything to the last grain . . . and this included ours. And they really left the family to certain famine death. And so my grandma died and then one of my brothers. . . . My mother was lying in

**32 Starved corpses lie abandoned in the street during the Ukraine famine, Kharkov, 1933.**

bed swollen with hunger . . . my other brother died. And I told my mother that 'we're the only two left', that my brother was also dead. Up came the cart and the man took my brother and dragged him to the cart, and then my own *live* mother. I started crying and the man said, 'Go to the orphanage where at least you'll get some soup. She will die anyway, why should I come here a second time?' And so I became an orphan.

Alexandra Ovdiuk was at school then: 'In 1933 it really was frightening. Every day somebody did not show up for school. The children were very scared and all swollen up. I'll never forget this. There were a lot of them who died in our class.'

During the famine, the Soviet Union exported grain, it guarded it in granaries with soldiers, it let it rot in piles, but it would not allow it to be used to feed the hungry. Merely snipping a few ears of corn in a field was an offence which landed people in Siberian prison camps. People ate leaves and weeds and whatever they could get hold of. Some, like a neighbour of Mykola Pishy, resorted to cannibalism.

Ivan was a good specialist – a joiner, a tailor, a shoe-maker – a good fellow who could turn his hand to anything. But the

famine was awful and he got to the end of his tether. He was so
hungry that he killed his child, and ate the meat – of his own
child. His wife was dead scared. She went to the village council
to report on him. She told how her husband had gone mad and
had killed his own child. So he was taken away. No one knows
where.

In all, about 7 million people died in the 1932–3 man-made
famine. What did the Party make of it? 'No-one was keeping count,'
said Khrushchev, then a rising star. 'All we knew was that people
were dying in enormous numbers.'[7] And what of the Party activists
who went out with the men of the OGPU to seize the grain from the
hungry? Lev Kopelev was one of them:

**33  Bodies collected for mass burial, Ukraine, 1933.**

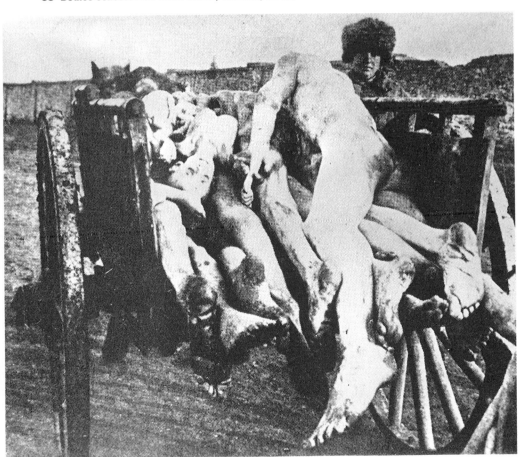

> We did not discuss it, we did not object, because we were
> convinced that the disaster was not so much the fault of
> the Party and State, as the result of inexorable 'objective'
> circumstances. We were convinced that the famine was caused
> by the opposition of suicidally unconscientious peasants,
> enemy intrigues and the inexperience and weakness of the
> lower ranks of workers.[8]

It wasn't just the Party which didn't discuss the famine. The record of western newspaper reporters and visitors to the country is shameful. Walter Duranty of the *New York Times* categorically denied the existence of the famine in his authoritative columns, while telling British Consular officials in Moscow in *private* that 'as many as 10 million people may have died directly or indirectly from lack of food.'[9] George Bernard Shaw visited with wilful myopia, not seeing a single undernourished person in Russia, young or old: 'Were they padded? Were their hollow cheeks distended by pieces of india rubber inside?'[10] The left-wing social scientists Sidney and Beatrice Webb concluded about the treatment of the kulaks that 'the Soviet Government could hardly have acted otherwise than it did'.[11]

Naomi Mitchison went to Russia in 1932, as a member of the Society for Socialist Inquiry and Propaganda, which had grown out of the Fabian Society: 'I think we were all taken into the mood of thinking that something wonderful had happened and perhaps we were in a way part of it.' Even so, as soon as she took a train journey south, she started to see things that didn't quite fit. 'Outside there were these people begging, and that seemed – it seemed odd . . . people, one realised, were hungry, and if one had a sandwich over, it disappeared.'

Malcolm Muggeridge was almost alone in having the wit to go to the Ukraine to see the full horror of what was happening, and in having the courage to report the horrors absolutely faithfully: 'The fields are neglected and full of weeds, no cattle are to be seen anywhere and few horses, only the military and the OGPU are well fed, the rest of the population obviously starving, obviously terrorised.'[12] Muggeridge filed his story and left Moscow before he could be thrown out. Most other newspapermen valued their continued accreditation in the Soviet Union more than the truth.

In tandem with the transformation of agriculture went the total reconstruction and modernisation of industry. The two were inextricably linked. The fields would feed the factories, the factories would build tractors and harvesters. Goods made in the cities would be paid for by the workers in the collective farms. The policy had a clear ideological purpose. The bond between town and country was intended to bring the two classes together, as Stalin said: '. . . to strengthen the alliance of the peasantry with the working class, the leading force in the alliance, gradually to *remould* the peasantry, its mentality and its production, *along collectivist lines*, and thus to bring about the conditions for the abolition of classes.'[13]

But industrialisation was also born out of economic necessity, as Stalin recognised: 'We are fifty or a hundred years behind the

**34 The city of Magnitogorsk under construction, a major enterprise of the Soviet industrialisation programme.**

advanced countries. We must make good this distance in ten years. Either we do it, or we shall go under.'[14] Moreover, agriculture was not intended to be in equal harness alongside industry; the idea was that industrialisation would be in part *funded* by agriculture. The exact method to be used had been hotly debated throughout the NEP period. Bukharin believed that the key was for industrial goods to be cheap and plentiful, as he argued prophetically:

> If we, who in essence . . . have a state monopoly, do not push, press and whip our cadres [nuclei of key party members at every level] spurring them to cheaper production, to produce better, then . . . we have before us all the prerequisites of monopolistic decay. The role played by competition in capitalist society . . . must with us be played by the constant pressure arising from the needs of the masses.[15]

But Bukharin's views, underpinned by his belief in moving ahead slowly with the peasants, were sharply challenged by the economist Preobrazhensky, who believed that the state should buy low and sell high, both to accumulate wealth to fund industry and to squeeze private capital in the countryside. By the late twenties, Bukharin had lost the argument and his position. Industrialisation was now the order of the day. The finance had to come from somewhere, as Stalin explained in April 1929:

> In addition to the usual taxes, direct and indirect, which the peasantry pays to the state, the peasantry also pays a certain supertax in the form of an over-payment for manufactured goods, and in the form of an under-payment received for agricultural produce. . . . We need this supertax to stimulate the development of our industry and to do away with backwardness.[16]

The basic device for propelling the country forward was the Five Year Plan of 1928 which would lay out targets for industrial growth and achievements. Fulfilment of the plan became more than a way of life, it became the reason for it. Lev Kopelev worked as an activist in factories as he did in agriculture:

**35 An image which changed lives, urging young Bolsheviks to reshape the world.**

We were raised as the fanatical adepts of a new creed, the only true *religion* of scientific socialism. The Party became our church . . . the works of Marx, Engels and Lenin were accepted as holy writ, and Stalin was the infallible high priest. Factories, mines, blast furnaces, locomotives, tractors, work-benches, turbines were transformed into objects of a cult, the sacramental objects blessed from on high: 'Technology solves everything!' Men genuflected to these objects in poetry, prose, painting, film, music.[17]

The men and women who exceeded their production targets became national heroes. Alexei Stakhanov broke all records for cutting coal in the Donbass mine where he worked and the enthusiastic workers who tried to emulate him were known as Stakhanovites. Alexander Avdeyenko, also a Donbass steelworker in the 1920s, had seen a Soviet poster on a railway station which changed his life: 'It was of the world, shackled in chains which encircled it. Smashing the chains was a blacksmith – a Soviet blacksmith. I wanted to be that blacksmith.'

Avdeyenko went to Magnitogorsk where a gigantic city of blast furnaces, factories and smelting works was under construction:

> I drove a railway tank engine. It was small and powerful and very beautiful. I was very proud of it. It was very useful to Magnitogorsk, carrying the molten iron in eight-ton hoppers, six or eight at a time. I blew the whistle as much as possible. I didn't have to, but I wanted to. I was building the heartland of the working class.

But this popular and widespread enthusiasm for industrialisation was being harnessed and directed by a growing bureaucracy driven ever harder and harder from the top. In the summer of 1929, a new watchword was handed down: 'The Five Year Plan must be fulfilled in four years.' The result was that planning became 'bacchanalian', as historian Hiroaki Kuromiya describes:

> In August 1929 the Council of Labor and Defense worked on an upward revision of the plan for the nonferrous metallurgy industry: the annual output of smelted copper was to increase in five years to 150,000 tons instead of 85,450 as in the original plan; the annual production of aluminum was projected to skyrocket by forty times to 200,000 tons![18]

In fact only 860 tons of aluminium were produced. Planning itself became nigh on impossible. There were too few planning specialists, too few coherent targets, too much upward revision of goals, too much jockeying for resources, too many construction projects started without accurate budgeting or even definite approval (in order to present a *fait accompli* to the distributors of investment).

The tractor factory in Stalingrad exemplified the problems. On 17 June 1930 Stalin sent this message to the plant on its opening day when the first tractor was rolled out: 'Greetings and congratulations on their victory to the workers and executive personnel of the giant Red Banner Tractor Works, the first in the USSR.'[19] But the first tractor was in fact a wooden dummy. To fulfil already unrealistic plans, huge numbers of new, illiterate workers had been taken on, many of them peasants. The factory had lacked skilled men, sufficient equipment and enough time from the start.

Attempts to slow the pace were treated as sabotage and punished ruthlessly, in line with Stalin's view that: 'People who talk about the necessity of *reducing* the rate of development of our industry are enemies of socialism, agents of our class enemies.'[20] Factory managers who couldn't make deliveries because of shortages of raw materials were branded as saboteurs. Workers who didn't understand their machines, which then broke down, were wreckers. Railwaymen who refused to drive excessively laden trains over bridges were traitors. In 1928, fifty-five people were arrested for sabotage and treason at the Shakhty mine in the Donbass. It led to the first of a number of 'show trials' which rammed home to the Soviet people the message that there were saboteurs throughout society, working for foreign capitalist interests.

Alexander Avdeyenko never saw or heard of a single genuine case of 'wrecking' in his whole time in industry. He is adamant about the Shakhty trial:

> This was a trumped-up trial, thought up by Stalin to justify the
> failure of his projects, so that he could say to the people – look,
> there are saboteurs and if they hadn't messed up the whole
> thing then everything would have been all right. He couldn't
> say the obvious, which was that we were building very fine
> factories, but we just didn't know how to manage them. That
> we had built wonderful machines, but had put peasants in
> charge of their operation and they didn't know how to use
> them.

Only four of the accused in the Shakhty case got off. Five were executed and the rest imprisoned. Throughout industry from top to bottom, people were arrested and tried, exiled or shot. The sheer turnover in personnel created its own chaos. Evidence of guilt was of minor importance, especially as Stalin announced that some of the wreckers in society were clever enough to conceal themselves by never actually sabotaging anything. And yet in spite of the setbacks, and even given the contemporary exaggerations of Soviet industrial achievements, factories and dams were built, railway lines laid, heavy industry built up and the country electrified. Had this not occurred, it is unlikely that the Soviet Union could have even begun to resist the Nazi attack on them in the Second World War. The price in human lives and misery was, as in agriculture, enormous.

In both agriculture and industry Stalin's purpose was to a great

extent ideological and his methods highly divisive, as Hiroaki
Kuromiya writes:

> Stalin, far from rallying the entire nation, even split it. . . .
> Stalin deliberately sought the support of particular political
> constituencies, the Communists, Komsomols, and industrial
> workers, by pitting them against the alleged class enemies.
> It was from among these constituencies that the main
> beneficiaries of Stalin's revolution, 'a new class' or a 'new
> Soviet élite' sprang. . . . The class-war ideology of the
> industrialization drive created a basis for the survival of the
> regime.[21]

In the process, had the peasants indeed been bled dry to supply the
crucial transfusion of resources into industry? Therein lay, after all,
both hallowed Party theory and the justification for the sacrifices the
country had made. The historian Robert Conquest has assessed fresh
studies of this question and believes the traditional view may be
mistaken:

> Recent research by a Soviet scholar (A. A. Barsov)
> magisterially analysed by a Western one (James Millar) seems
> to indicate that, wholly against expectation, there was a
> definite – though probably slight – input from the industrial
> into the agricultural sector over the years 1928–32, rather than
> the other way round; and that the intense and desperate
> squeeze on the kolkhoz [collective farm] peasants was not quite
> enough to balance the inefficiencies and disruption due to the
> collectivisation itself.[22]

Peasants collectivised by force and industrial workers were not the
only people building the new socialist state with their bare hands.
There was a third group: prisoners sentenced to forced labour. This
was an old idea which, like show trials, the use of terror and the
prison camp system, went back to Lenin. On the eve of the October
Revolution, Lenin wrote a pamphlet entitled 'Can the Bolsheviks
Retain State Power?' In this Lenin argued: 'We must not only break
resistance of every kind. We must also *compel the capitalists to work*
within the framework of the new state organisation . . . we must . . .
employ them *in the service of the state.* "He who does not work,

neither shall he eat" – this is the fundamental, the first and most important rule.'[23]

The plan came into effect during Lenin's lifetime. The first permanent camp was officially established in 1923 on the Solovetsky Islands, 250 miles north of Archangel, and cut off from the mainland by ice floes from October until June. The first prisoners, apart from some criminals, were the sailors from the Kronstadt mutiny and pro-tsarist counter-revolutionaries. It soon filled up with priests (victims of the anti-religious campaigns), political prisoners, and more common criminals. Oleg Volkov was sent there in 1928, arrested on trumped-up charges. His crime had been to refuse to spy on the Greek embassy in Moscow, where he was a translator. The work at Solovki was in forests, quarries and brickyards:

36 The writer Maxim Gorky was often wheeled out to 'inspect' the camps, and endorse their regime. Here he is (*centre*) with the Chekists at one of the first and worst, on the Solovetsky Islands, in 1929.

> However hard you worked, you still never really could get
> warm. We'd try and warm ourselves up by camp fires, but of
> course camp fires were really prohibited because it was against
> regulations, and you wouldn't fulfil the norm if you spent the
> time making them. . . . The regime was really quite ruthless
> on the sites where they were responsible for felling timber and
> if you failed to fulfil the norm then you could well be shot for
> it. I saw that myself.

By the time of Stalin's fiftieth birthday in 1929, there were around
half a million people in the camp system. It is worth bearing in mind
that the total had grown to this figure during the years when power in
the Soviet Union had been shared by Stalin with others, such as
Zinoviev, Kamenev and, particularly, Bukharin. This was the
period of the NEP, associated in the minds of many with a relaxation
of authoritarianism and an increase in social, cultural and artistic
diversity. Throughout that time, the state security organisation,
under the top political leadership, had increased both its vigilance
and its arbitrary and ever more widespread use of repression. In
1929, a conference of higher prison officials declared that:

> The Five-Year Plan . . . requires tasks involving a great
> demand for unskilled labor. Local conditions sometimes
> present serious obstacles to the recruitment of labor. It is here
> that the places of confinement, having at their disposal excess
> labor in great quantities . . . can come to the assistance of those
> economic enterprises which experience a labor shortage.[24]

Countless industrial schemes thereafter made use of forced labour,
particularly in the early stages of site clearance, preparation and basic
construction. Prisoners found themselves building factories, cities,
railways, dams and harbours. They also mined, fished, farmed and
cut timber. This was the means whereby the OGPU consolidated its
dominant position, alongside that of the Party, in Soviet life. By
1931, there were around 2 million people in the forced-labour camp
system.

Camps sprang up across whole regions of the country; these areas
became known as being under OGPU, rather than Soviet control.
The OGPU administered the system from start to finish, from the
arrest of a man on the street to the completion of contracts using his

labour, but otherwise it was like any other economic enterprise. As the economic role of the OGPU grew their demand for forced labour increased, which in turn led to the setting of arrest quotas.

**37 Stalin with Bukharin (*in cap*) and Ordzhonikidze, 1930. With the abandonment of NEP in 1929, Bukharin's star was waning.**

Lenin's prescription 'He who does not work, neither shall he eat' was the basis of the food-rationing system in the labour camps. The hard worker was given extra rations, and there was a careful system of allocation for each level of work output. The historians David Dallin and Boris Nicolaevsky made a special study of forced labour:

> The lowest scale of food rations for prisoners is the minimum allotment to the least efficient workers – the 'shirkers' and 'slackers'. It is intentionally set so low as to make subsistence impossible. . . . The intention is obviously to compel the 'shirker' to revert to efficient work. On the other hand, it also means a gradual weakening of the prisoner and eventual death.[25]

The exact economics are hard to work out, given the paucity of data. Nevertheless, it is clear that the OGPU increasingly exploited

38 Forced labour on the building of the Belomor Canal which began in 1931. It cost around 100,000 lives.

39 At any one time, up to 125,000 men and women worked and lived in camps along the canal.

the financial advantage of using forced labour, and expanded its operations accordingly.

Economic viability, however, cannot begin to justify the forced-labour camp system, while some of the projects were not merely unprofitable but downright ridiculous. The most tragic example is the Belomor Canal, planned to give the Soviet navy access to the White Sea through a string of waterways. For the first time ever, the OGPU had been assigned the whole contract. Construction began in November 1931, involving a total of about 250,000 workers. The turnover was fast because the regime was extremely cruel: the work had to be done by hand with picks and wheelbarrows. No heavy machinery was used on the canal because such machinery had to be purchased abroad, and the OGPU were told: 'Not one kopek of foreign exchange.'[26] They had no need of machinery though, because they had so much slave labour.

In 1933, the distinguished author Maxim Gorky was asked by Stalin to visit the canal and put together a book explaining how socially useful forced labour was for rehabilitating offenders. Gorky had already performed the same service in 1929 at Solovki, where he studiously turned a blind eye to anything and everything untoward. Gorky took a party of 120 writers, artists and musicians to Belomor.

Alexander Avdeyenko had become a writer by then, and was invited along. They were entertained lavishly by the OGPU on the way, and then shown a prepared cluster of neat log cabins where beds had sheets and pillows and where the cafeteria had a long menu of delicious food. The prisoners they were allowed to meet were well-drilled, as Avdeyenko remembers: 'They would answer us by saying that they'd committed some crime or other . . . or somebody else would say that they had concealed grain from the state and refused to hand it over – that they had damaged the country by doing so.'

The visitors asked their OGPU hosts if anyone had died during construction and were told that they had, of course, but declined to answer the question 'Do you have a lot of cemeteries?' The OGPU did not volunteer any information about how many people had died and, for their part, the writers and artists and musicians did not ask. The visitors from the world of creative arts returned to Moscow and produced a lavishly illustrated volume extolling the virtues of both the canal and the use of forced labour. Avdeyenko again:

> We arrived at the canal with the already formed opinion that
> everything was well, that this was one of the great Socialist
> experiments in construction work, and that it was one of the
> strokes of genius of the great Stalin himself. By that time we,
> together with the rest of the Soviet people had committed a
> gross error, had been completely misled as to how much we
> actually knew about the methods being applied to achieve
> these results.

The prisoners had been promised amnesty on completion of the canal. That day came on 2 August 1933, when Stalin came to open it, accompanied by the head of the OGPU, Genrikh Yagoda, and Sergei Kirov, the Leningrad Party boss in whose area of control the canal fell. Only 72,000 were freed, thousands were kept on to maintain the canal and the rest were transferred either to the Baikal–Amur railway in the Far East or to the Moscow–Volga Canal. The Belomor Canal proved to be of questionable strategic value, being bombed by the Luftwaffe early in the war. About 100,000 people are believed to have died building it.

By 1933, Stalin's policies in agriculture and industry had drastically changed Soviet life – and death. Around 11 million people were killed by famine, forced dispossessions, resettlements and the anti-kulak campaign. The death-toll and totals of arrest in industry have not yet become known. The camp population was swelling all the time, reaching some 5 million people by 1935. A great many, maybe 80 per cent, were peasants, most of whom were to die in the camps. Robert Conquest has calculated peasant deaths from all these causes to total around 14.5 million. These are, he stresses, 'conservative estimates, and quite certainly do not overstate the truth'.[27] The mass arrests, purges and shootings of the late 1930s – what Conquest has called the 'Great Terror' – are not included in this figure and were all to come. However, the most modest of recent Soviet estimates puts population losses in the 1930s at about 10 million.

We can perhaps gauge Stalin's feelings about the losses from what he told the Conference of Marxist Students in 1929: '. . . it is now ridiculous and foolish to discourse at length on dekulakisation. When the head is off, one does not mourn for the hair.'[28]

# 5 **TERROR**

> They came at night and there was a knock on the door.
> 'Open the door,' they shouted. . . . I got up and the children
> followed me in a panic. Husbands had been taken away before
> . . . we knew very well what was going on. . . . I managed to
> give him a loaf of bread and some underwear; it was Saturday,
> the day when he had to have a wash and a change. The work in
> the field had been sweaty, hard and dusty. 'Well,' he said,
> 'don't cry, don't worry, I've done nothing wrong. I haven't
> harmed a soul, I'll be back soon.'

Tatyana Matusevich's husband was not a recalcitrant kulak, nor a spy, nor a supporter of the vilified Trotsky. He was a Byelorussian peasant who worked hard as the foreman on a state farm just outside Minsk. He supported collectivisation and still he was arrested.

By 1932, a number of senior figures in the party and leadership were growing extremely anxious about Stalin's policies and methods. Since collectivisation, and amidst the excesses of industrialisation, a number of informal groups had met to discuss how to restrain or remove General Secretary Stalin. The most important was led by Martemyan Ryutin, who circulated clandestinely a two-hundred page attack, fifty pages of which were devoted to Stalin's own personality. Stalin was described as 'the evil genius of the Russian Revolution who, actuated by vindictiveness and lust for power, has brought the revolution to the edge of the abyss'.[1] Ryutin and his supporters wanted Stalin removed, democracy within the Party, slower industrialisation and an end to formal collectivisation. Ryutin did not mince matters: 'It is shameful for proletarian revolutionaries to tolerate any longer Stalin's yoke, his arbitrariness, his scorn for the Party and the labouring masses. Whoever fails to see this yoke, to feel its arbitrariness, this oppression, whoever fails to be indignant at it, is a slave, no Leninist and no proletarian revolutionary.'[2]

**40** There were times in Stalin's family life when he was happy. This picnic at Sochi with his wife (*centre*) and the Voroshilovs was in 1929.

**41** Nadezhda died by her own hand on the night of 8 November 1932 – shot with a pistol given to her by her brother. Life with the man Stalin had become was intolerable for her.

**42** The three motherless children of Stalin on a rare visit to Stalin's mother in Georgia. Yakov (*centre*) and Nadezhda's children Vasili and Svetlana.

Ryutin, it is said, even considered the possibility of having to assassinate Stalin to rid the country of him, but his group never made any plans for this. Stalin was quick to respond. The group was arrested on the charge of attempting '. . . to form an underground bourgeois kulak organisation under a fake "Marxist–Leninist" banner for the purpose of restoring capitalism'.[3]

Stalin called for the death penalty, although its use against Party members had been expressly forbidden under Lenin. The issue went before the Politburo and Stalin was defeated by an opposition led, it is believed, by the Leningrad Party boss, Sergei Kirov. Ryutin and his followers were expelled from the Party and banished from Moscow. It was a crucial moment, as historian Stephen Cohen explains:

> The 'Ryutin Affair', as it became known, was a turning point
> in the politics of the thirties. On one level, Stalin's defeat
> merely reaffirmed the sacrosanct prohibition against shooting
> party members. On another, however, it demonstrated that
> Politburo moderates were now determined to resist his
> grasp for greater, more arbitrary power within and over the
> party. . . . At the same time, as later became clear, the Ryutin
> Affair dates Stalin's determination to rid himself of all such
> restraints represented by the existing Bolshevik Party, its élite
> and its political traditions.[4]

There were criticisms of Stalin closer to home, though, from his own wife. Nadezhda Alliluyeva was the daughter of staunch Old Bolsheviks; it was at her family home that Lenin had sought temporary refuge in 1917. Stalin had known the family since the old underground days before the revolution and had married Nadezhda in February 1919. There was an age gap of twenty-one years between them. Nadezhda was spirited and independent; she worked in Lenin's secretariat during the Civil War and in the late 1920s went to the Industrial Academy to study synthetic-fibre production. She worked, brought up the children and ran a friendly family home. She was not afraid to argue with Stalin, and told him on several occasions that she did not want his henchman, Lavrenti Beria, then rising ruthlessly up the ranks of the secret police, to come to her house. She and Stalin quarrelled frequently and seriously. On 8 November, at a Kremlin banquet to celebrate the fifteenth anniversary of the revolution, Stalin rudely urged her to have a drink. Some say he threw a lighted cigarette at her. She was highly strung and it was evidently the last straw. She shot herself dead that night. Stalin's daughter, Svetlana, is in no doubt that her mother's suicide was not motivated by purely personal considerations.

> She was in disagreement with our father on many things. It was the time when collectivisation was going. It was the time when the party was dealing cruelly with people . . . and she had a mind of her own, you see. My aunt, who stayed in our house immediately after she died, told me later that she had left a letter that she obviously wrote that night. It was a very accusatory letter to father . . . accusatory in the way that could make him think that she was very much against his policies at the time and that she would be sympathising with the opposition, with people who were against collectivisation.

Stalin's response was one of bitter resentment rather than grief, as Soviet historian Roy Medvedev describes:

> Stalin came to view the coffin before the memorial service. After approaching the coffin, he suddenly made a gesture as though to push the coffin away and said distinctly, 'She left me as an enemy!' Then he turned away and departed. He did not attend his wife's memorial service or burial . . .[5]

Whatever suspicions Stalin had that his authority was in question were confirmed at the Seventeenth Party Congress of 1934. Party congresses had become a lot less frequent under Stalin than they had been under Lenin; they became venues for policy endorsement rather than real debate. The Seventeenth Party Congress, or 'Congress of Victors' as it was known, was also an opportunity to rejoice at the so-called achievements in agriculture and industry. As Stalin told the gathered delegates, '. . . there is nothing to prove and, it seems, no-one to fight. Everyone sees that the line of the Party has triumphed.'[6]

In fact, Stalin still had to prove he was really in charge, and the people he had to fight were, he believed, all around him. An official Soviet history published in 1962, confirms that there were anti-Stalin discussions held in private at the Congress:

A number of delegates of the Congress, and above all those who remembered Lenin's testament, considered that the time had come to remove Stalin from the post of secretary general to transfer him to another function, because, certain of his infallibility, he was beginning to ignore the principle of collective work and was again becoming rude.[7]

**43 Stalin at the Seventeenth Party Congress, February 1934. Despite the fawning support of his cronies, he got a glimpse of his unpopularity in the secret ballot of delegates.**

At one of these conversations, attended by senior leaders of the Party, including members of the Politburo, Sergei Kirov, the man who had argued for Ryutin's life to be spared, was offered the post of General Secretary. He refused. Kirov was a moderate, but a moderate within the general hard line; it was Kirov who proposed that a report by Stalin on behalf of the Central Committee be regarded as a resolution of the whole Congress. The motion was carried unanimously. That report contained a line aimed at the Party's policy on industrialisation, but had a wider application in the context of challenges within the Party itself.

> . . . we must not lull the Party, but sharpen its vigilance; we must not lull it to sleep, but keep it ready for action; not disarm it, but arm it . . .[8]

It was at the voting in the Congress for membership to the Central Committee that Stalin obtained the clearest picture of his real popularity in the Party. When the ballot boxes were opened, it was discovered that only three votes had been cast against Kirov, while, according to Roy Medvedev, '. . . 270 delegates voted against Stalin, who was elected only because there were exactly as many candidates as there were members to be elected.'[9]

The pro-Stalin elections commission chairman Vladimir Zatonsky went straight to the loyal henchman Lazar Kaganovich. Soviet historian Anton Antonov-Ovseyenko takes up the story:

> Kaganovich asked him to wait a few minutes and left the room. When he returned, he asked how many votes Kirov had lost. 'Three,' answered Zatonsky. 'Leave the same number against Comrade Stalin,' Central Committee Secretary Kaganovich ordered. 'Destroy the rest. This misunderstanding must be eliminated immediately.' And so they did.[10]

Kirov was both a close family friend of Stalin and politically loyal to him. According to another Stalin henchman, Anastas Mikoyan, Kirov went to see Stalin and told him he had refused the offer to replace him as General Secretary. Kirov was '. . . met with hostility and a will to revenge against the whole Congress and of course Kirov personally'.[11]

On 1 December 1934 Kirov was shot dead in the Leningrad Party headquarters. His bodyguard had been mysteriously detained downstairs by men of the NKVD (the state security agency, previously OGPU). Stalin was informed immediately. Vladimir Alliluyev, Stalin's nephew, is adamant:

> Stalin had nothing to do with that murder. I could say more to
> you than that. My mother was with Stalin when they phoned
> him and informed him that Kirov had been murdered. And my
> mother said to me, neither before nor after it had she ever seen
> Stalin in the state he was after receiving that phone call. And
> moreover Stalin knew full well that this murder would be
> linked with his name, after the Seventeenth Congress – that
> was clear and understandable to him.

That evening a decree was issued calling for the immediate application of the death penalty for acts of terror with no possibility of pardon. Stalin arrived in Leningrad at dawn the next day, accompanied by his closest colleagues and Genrikh Yagoda, the head of the NKVD. Kirov's killer, a thirty-year-old misfit named Nikolayev, was brought before Stalin. He fell on his knees, saying that he 'did the deed on orders and in the Party's name'.[12] The day after, Kirov's bodyguard was battered to death by the NKVD men bringing him in for questioning. These three men were then sent to the camps, where they too died. Disconcerting evidence leaked out that Nikolaev had been given target practice by the NKVD and that he had been arrested twice previously in Kirov's vicinity with a pistol. On both occasions he was quickly released. Most members of the Leningrad NKVD were arrested, the top leadership receiving strangely lenient sentences and being taken to the camps in comfort where they received gifts of radios and records. They survived until 1937, when they were shot. The NKVD defector Alexander Orlov recalled being told that: 'The whole affair is so dangerous that it is healthier not to know too much about it.'[13]

Nikita Khrushchev established a commission of inquiry into Kirov's murder when he came to power. However, when he read the commission's conclusions he stated: 'As long as imperialism exists in the world, we will not be able to publish this document.'[14] Khrushchev is said to have dropped a number of hints that Stalin was behind the murder, but confirmation that this was his judgement only came in July 1989 when the Soviet magazine *Ogonyok* published an extract of Khrushchev's recollections in which he said: 'This murder was organised from above. I consider that it was organised by Yagoda, who could act only on the secret instructions of Stalin, received as they say, eye to eye.'[15]

The evidence upon which Khrushchev's verdict was based is believed to have been subsequently falsified and destroyed. It consisted amongst other things of documents and the testimony of eye-witnesses. However, a last link to that evidence survives. Olga Shatunovskaya was appointed by Khrushchev to the commission of inquiry into the murder of Kirov. She is a veteran Party member, dedicated and, as Khrushchev described her, 'incorruptible'. She recalls clearly that Nikolayev had been expelled from the Party and then upon reinstatement begged to be assigned not to a factory, but to Party work: 'The NKVD latched on to this, that he was dissatisfied, and he wrote them a letter saying: "I am ready for anything now. I hate Kirov." And they organised it. At the inquiry before Stalin he said: "For four months the NKVD prepared me and convinced me that it was necessary for the Party and the country."'

Shatunovskaya is definite that the motive for the murder lay in the offer of the General Secretaryship to Kirov: 'Of course, after this when Stalin found out he decided to remove him and Kirov realised this. When he came back from the Seventeenth Congress he told his friends and family: "My head is now on the block." I had all these testimonies from his friends and family and now they have been destroyed.'

Shatunovskaya had also spoken to the surviving NKVD guards and confirms that Nikolayev had been caught previously with a loaded revolver and a map of Smolny in his briefcase and was then released. She is adamant about the ultimate responsibility for the assassination, based strictly on the evidence collected by the commission: 'It had been irrefutably proved that the murder of Kirov was organised by Stalin, through Yagoda and the NKVD.'

Kirov's murder then gave Stalin the justification for removing any last taboos about not killing members of the Party. He would never again be outvoted as he had been over Ryutin.

The reverberations of Kirov's murder started to be felt immediately. Ludmilla Shapiro was among the crowds watching Kirov's body being carried in state through Moscow:

At the head of the procession was, of course, the coffin carried
by eight people. The main pall-bearer was Stalin . . . he was on
the right-hand side and he passed very near us. His face looked
tragic; whether it was good play-acting or whatever, we didn't
know then . . . the whole procession – it was a grey winter
afternoon – somehow had a very sombre quality, much
worse than many others that we witnessed, and the sense of
foreboding gripped us, as it did very many of the people I
talked to afterwards . . . and I feel that this wasn't hindsight,
but a genuine feeling that something bad had begun with this
mysterious assassination.

**44 A murder which caused many more.** *Left to right*: Zhdanov, Kaganovich, Molotov,
Voroshilov and Stalin carry the bier of the assassinated Kirov, December 1934. At the
Seventeenth Party Congress, the Leningrad party boss had seemed to Stalin to be a
popular and therefore dangerous rival. It was Kirov's death sentence.

The waves of arrests which followed were so overwhelming that they became known as the 'Kirov flood'. Robert Conquest explains:

> Everyone who was remotely connected with the case was seized. One woman had worked as a librarian at the 'Young Communist Club' in Leningrad which had been disbanded in the mid-twenties but with which Nikolayev had in some way been associated. Not only was she arrested, but also her sister with whom she lived, her sister's husband, the secretary of her Party cell, and all those who had recommended her for jobs.[16]

According to Conquest, within a few months 30–40,000 Leningraders had been arrested. The camps filled up, trials were followed by executions, the sense that enemies of the people were everywhere and that *no one* could be trusted enveloped the entire country. What, though, was Stalin's motive? To help understand this, we have to stand back far enough to trace the patterns of respite and repression in the thirties which match the phases in the evolution of both Stalin the despot and the Stalinist system: of authoritarian rule by means of terror.

First, of course, came forced collectivisation and the famine, accompanied by the fierce and often frantic pace of industrialisation. Then the years 1933–4, between the Ryutin affair and the murder of Kirov, were an interlude of relaxed rates of growth – a greater emphasis on light industry, a series of concessions to the peasants, the first discussions about a new 'democratic' Soviet constitution, the recall to public positions of oppositionists like Bukharin, even a feeling that the creative intelligentsia would be given more freedom. Some attempt was made to exert authority over the Party through the purge of 1933 – purge in its strict sense of sweeping the party clean of hostile and corrupt elements within, not by the bullet but by removing the Party card. But the Party closed ranks and hindered the purge process as officials within the local bureaucracy sought to protect their positions. This phase of respite, which Kirov endorsed, was seen by Stalin as a threat to his authority. He sensed a mood at every level in the country to put a halt to excesses and institute a more coherent, regular mode of government. In the wake of such moods, the historian Moshe Lewin explains:

Stalin, and some around him, were turning violently antibureaucratic. This was the direction from which he sensed a growing opposition against his way of ruling. Soon, after 1934 and Kirov's assassination, would come the 'enemies of the people' orgy and the bloody purges that epitomised the blossoming of Stalinist autocracy, the period of 'high Stalinism'. But there were no enemies around, no agents of foreign intelligence agencies. It was the administrative party and its leaders, the Stalinists, who were caught up in the industrialisation crisis and were now losing their power and lives. There also was a new and growing social structure and bureaucracy, products of the same revolution and of a reality that was here to stay, whatever the havoc wreaked on them by the purges. Thus, the same period that saw the making of 'Stalinism' also saw the emergence, timid at first, of a second authoritarian model in the Soviet state: bureaucratic in its attitudes, but not based intrinsically on coercion; oligarchic but opposed to capricious autocracy. This 'version' was Stalin's real enemy; there was no other.[17]

For the moment, though, there was to be another period of comparative respite. The lull in 1935–6 which followed the sweeping ferocity of the 'Kirov flood' appeared to offer the hope of a brighter and safer future. A commission was established in February 1935 to prepare a new Soviet constitution. Chaired by Stalin, it included Bukharin, who was back in limited favour.

The Stalin Constitution, as it was called, was drafted to a great extent by Bukharin himself. As his biographer Stephen Cohen writes:

> . . . , though few people, including Bukharin, took seriously the official claim that the constitution guaranteed real 'democratization', it provided for many inside and outside the party further evidence that an era of civil peace and legality had begun, that 'people will have more room. They can no longer be pushed aside'.[18]

At the same time, a huge propaganda machine was pushing the cult of Stalin into every corner of the work-place, street and home. Huge parades in Red Square, films in the cinema, statues and paintings all proclaimed the good fortune of the Soviet people in having Stalin to guide and care for them. Many, like Alexander Avdeyenko, swallowed it hook, line and sinker:

> Looking back on my life, I now see that period as one of sincere enthusiasm. as genuine human happiness, and yet, at the same time, as self-hypnosis in the first place from the personality cult of Stalin. It would have been impossible for a common mortal to withstand the onslaught of Stalin, of the apparatus which was Stalin's, or the pressure which was put on people's reason, heart and soul. Day and night radio told us that Stalin was the greatest man on earth – the greatest statesman, the father of the nation, the genius of all time. . . . Man wants to believe in something great.

Stephen Cohen assesses this period of time:

> 'Historically Stalinism was, to use a Soviet metaphor, two towering and inseparable mountains, a mountain of national accomplishment alongside a mountain of crimes. The accomplishments cannot be lightly dismissed. During the first decade of Stalin's leadership, memorialized officially as the first and second five year plans for collectivization and industrialization, a mostly backward, agrarian, illiterate society was transformed into a predominantly industrial, urban, and literate one. For millions of people, the 1930s were a time of willingly heroic sacrifice, educational opportunity, and upward mobility.[19]

By 1936, Stalin had secured the legal power he needed. The highly restrictive system of internal passports was in place. Article 58 of the Criminal Code, and particularly its catch-all Section 10, made virtually anything imaginable an offence against the Soviet state. New, repressive laws had been passed, such as the one which extended punishment, including execution, to twelve-year-olds.

The NKVD, its teeth sharpened by forced collectivisation and industrialisation, was ready. The prison-camp system, operated by the NKVD under the acronym Gulag, was spreading across the country. It was ever-hungry for forced labour. The terror which was unleashed went beyond the bureaucracy Stalin distrusted, and the Party, now placed literally at his disposal, after the murder of Kirov.

Ordinary people up and down the country had their lives changed irrevocably. What happened to them is a key part of Stalin's legacy today – the sorrow and the guilt and the loss.

The Soviet Union became split like a country wracked by civil war. A continuous, shifting invisible line ran through factory, office, farm, street and home, cutting off the 'enemies of the people' from the rest. Fear spread, as no one knew which side of the line they were on. As historian Moshe Lewin writes:

> . . . not just some action – however innocent – but even a shadow of doubt about the party line and the leader's wisdom was already the beginning of treason – because doubt was bound to end up serving foreign intelligence services and was thus worthy of being cut down prophylactically , even if it was still buried somewhere in the subconscious.[20]

Lives came to be dominated by a permanent state of social crisis. Trivia, like an innocent mistake at work, or the jealousy of a neighbour, or an accidental muddle in the confusion of paper work in the growing state bureaucracy could turn lethal. 'Every Communist must be a Chekist,' Lenin had said; under Stalin the whole nation was urged to become an informer. It was a way of showing your loyalty. It became a means of settling old scores, or of taking your boss's job, or the flat of a friend; even, it was said, someone else's wife or husband. A key part of the chaos in Soviet society became the moral despair forced on so many by having to lie or keep silent out of fear.

There is a huge block of flats near the Kremlin in Moscow known as the 'House on the Embankment'. This gaunt edifice has been home to many of the political, military, academic and creative leaders in Soviet society. When it was built in 1931 the atmosphere was very congenial, but then the turnover in occupancy of the flats became rapid. Tamara Ter-Yegiazarova has lived there from the beginning.

> It became vastly more difficult to socialise because nobody knew who was informing on them . . . in the morning when you left your flat, you saw that a flat had been sealed and that those people were no longer there. Of course, your state of mind was utter terror, because nobody knew whether they would be arrested. . . . People turned in on themselves.

The reasons for arrest were arbitrary and often fatuous: telling a joke, laughing at a joke or failing to laugh at one, having a relative or friend who had been arrested, or just being in the wrong place at the wrong time. Olga Sliozberg was denounced with ninety-nine others, including her husband, for conspiracy to kill Lazar Kaganovich. As with so many others, they came for her at night:

> My son had woken up, and I said, 'Little son, get up and go to your granny – I'm going away for a while.' . . . Then I went to the little girl – she was four years old, he was six. She was sleeping with her nose into the pillow. I turned her round and she started smiling. What could I do? I kissed her and left. This was terrible and the worst thing was that during the years that I sat in prison, I thought constantly about my children all the time.

The arrests increased dramatically during 1936 as Stalin consolidated his total grip on the machinery of repression. In a surprise move which showed the shape of things to come, Zinoviev and Kamenev were put on trial for conspiring with Trotsky and murdering Kirov. They were made to confess in exchange for their lives and were promptly shot. Then Yagoda was suddenly replaced as head of the NKVD by Nikolai Yezhov, the 'bloodthirsty dwarf'. Yezhov set out his stall with brisk candour in a speech to NKVD executives: 'Of course there will be innocent victims in this fight against fascist agents. We are launching a major attack on the enemy; let there be no resentment if we bump someone with an elbow. Better that ten innocent people should suffer than one spy get away. When you cut down the forest, woodchips fly.'[21] Now the full terror was unleashed. Now there were no holds barred, no remaining taboos. Anyone could be guilty, anything could happen.

Wilhelmina Slavutskaya was a totally loyal Comintern agent who had already carried out highly risky undercover operations in Germany. When she received the knock on the door at night and subsequent tough NKVD interrogations, she thought it was training practice for her next mission. Nine months in the Lubyanka convinced her otherwise. When she was sent to the equally dreaded Butyrka Prison in Moscow, she realised the scale of the mass-arrests from the unbearably cramped conditions. 'We lay just the way

45 In the dwarfish Yezhov, Stalin found an NKVD killer who would carry out his orders without question. Here they are celebrating the twentieth anniversary of the Cheka — now the NKVD — on 20 December 1937.

sardines do in a tin . . . every row had a woman who was in charge and she would give the order, "Let's turn over on to the other side", and the only way you could turn from one side to the other was if everybody did it together.'

The conditions were part of the punishment. The basic device for breaking the resistance of those from whom confessions were required was known as the 'Conveyor'. This involved a continuous process of interrogation which could go on for days. It would break all but a handful who were subjected to it. Beatings, being confined in a tiny space and urinated on by guards, blood-chilling threats to one's loved ones, mental as well as physical abuse – all played their part in the NKVD repertoire. Actual torture also went on, retroactively legitimised by Stalin in 1939:

> The Central Committee . . . explains that the application of
> methods of physical pressure in NKVD practice is permissible
> from 1937 on. . . . The Central Committee . . . considers
> that physical pressure should still be used obligatorily, as an
> exception applicable to known and obstinate enemies of the
> people, as a method both justifiable and appropriate.[22]

The aim was to obtain confession, which, as Robert Conquest says,
'. . . is the logical thing to go for when the accused are not guilty and
there is no genuine evidence'.[23]

The State Prosecutor, Andrei Vyshinsky, held that if the confession was actually written by the accused it would look more
'voluntary'. 'I personally prefer a half confession in the defendant's
own handwriting to a full confession in the investigator's writing.'[24]

The anguish of the relatives and friends who waited for news of
those arrested can only be guessed at. They queued with food and
clothing parcels to hand in at prison gates. They waited at the
information hatch at No. 24 Kuznetsky Bridge in Moscow for the
slightest clue. Some, like Maya Klyashtornaya, know no more today
than they did then:

> I waited for my father; I waited for my father a very long time.
> I would scrutinise faces and think to myself, 'well perhaps he
> just doesn't know that I am still alive.' But then afterwards I
> thought that he must have died much earlier, that he'd given in
> and that it had been even more tragic for him than I had
> imagined, but where, when and how?

Many people did not survive their time in prison. They were shot
in cellars whose walls needed regular whitewashing. The bodies
were disposed of in various ways, but never with proper burial. The
Moscow NKVD sent some for incineration at the Donskoi Cemetery; the ashes were then scattered in an unmarked section only
recently accorded a memorial stone in remembrance of the unknown
victims who died between 1930 and 1942.

Other bodies received even less consideration, as Valentina
Yushina chanced to see. As a child she used to play with friends on a
piece of waste-ground near another Moscow cemetery:

Once we came here to play and we saw that there was a van.
And from the van they were unloading absolutely naked
bodies. We wanted to get closer but they wouldn't let us.
We stood there waiting until they unloaded the very last
body. There were three people, wearing rubber gloves, dark
overalls and rubber aprons. They were taking them from the
car with hooks. They were removing them with hooks. We saw
this twice on that day. I also saw this the next day.

For those who survived prison, the next hurdle was the journey to
any one of the hundreds of camps which pockmarked the map of the
Soviet Union. The usual method was a painfully slow railway journey
in an overloaded cattle-truck, as Wilhelmina Slavutskaya recalls:
'What they gave us to eat – and I don't know whether they were just
tormenting us, making fun of us or why it was – but what they gave us
to eat was salted fish. And they gave us nothing to drink.'

Some were sent to camp for execution there – those it is thought
whose sentences included the phrase 'without right of correspon-
dence'. Others were immediately incarcerated in isolation cells
within the camp itself, for weeks or even months, if they lived that
long. For the rest, camp meant work: hard labour in often ferocious
conditions with inadequate food and clothing. The memories of the
camp survivors interlock in a telling way. They simultaneously bear
witness to a host of individual experiences, and yet speak of the single
experience of a whole country.

*Ilya Shkapa*: They didn't need gas chambers because the
frost finished you off. . . . When I collected firewood for the
heating, the following phenomenon surprised me: it sounded
like something blowing, but it turned out that it was my
breathing. In the frost it sounded like a pipe. That's how it
was down there.

*Olga Sliozberg*: It was an awful lot, sixteen – eighteen trees to
cut down. The Brigadier would come and check. And then we
went back home again: a five-, six-kilometre walk. There was
practically no day there anyway, this was in the Arctic Circle.
So of course, we left at night and we arrived at night. The
middle of the day was sort of grey.

**46 – 52 Four victims remember.**
*Clockwise from bottom left*: Oleg
Volkov, Ilya Shkapa, Olga Sliozberg,
and (*below*) Wilhelmina Slavutskaya.
The NKVD confiscated all the latter's
early personal photos.

*Wilhelmina Slavutskaya*: We were going along in file. The dogs were part of the convoy and had been trained. It was very hot, and even though they had warned us that if we took one step to the side, they would shoot, this chap saw a little stream. . . . He jumped out of the line and bent over to drink. A dog jumped on him and they immediately shot him. He was a young man . . . even now I dream about that scene.

*Oleg Volkov*: I remember the mosquitoes punishment, where they would stand a man in the middle of those ghastly northern bogs, which are so full of mosquitoes, with his hands tied behind his back. You can imagine what torture that must be, and the people ended up absolutely covered in blood from mosquito bites.

The Soviet writer, Lev Razgon, himself a camp survivor, points out the closeness of the relationship between the system of repression and the country itself:

Tolstoy said that nothing tells us so much about the character of the state as its prisons. With all their cruelty, the camps were a reflection of the country as a whole. It was a splinter of society; the country became one big camp. Forced labour, suppression of personal qualities, great violence and cruelty – these were exaggerations of Soviet life. It was organic rather than ordained.

A common cry was that, if only Stalin knew what was happening, he'd soon put a stop to it. But Stalin knew all about it. When his daughter Svetlana interceded on behalf of a schoolfriend's father, he had the man freed but made it clear that she should never come to him again with a similar request. Khrushchev described Stalin at that time as 'a very distrustful man, sickly suspicious. . . . Everywhere and in everything he saw "enemies", "two-facers" and "spies".'[25]

The more power he had, the more threatened he felt. It was a characteristic he enshrined in his own ideology, as he explained it to the Plenum of the Central Committee: '. . . the more we move forward, the more success we have, then the more wrathful become the remnants of the beaten exploiter classes, the more quickly they turn to sharper forms of struggle, the more mischief they do the Soviet state . . . as the last resort of the doomed.'[26]

On 2 March 1938 Stalin launched the Great Show Trial. There had been many other show trials before, but this was to be the crowning glory. Three members of Lenin's Politburo were in the dock: Bukharin, Rykov and Krestinsky. They, with eighteen others including Yagoda, were accused of a host of crimes which involved wrecking, espionage and conspiring with Trotsky. Sir Fitzroy Maclean, then Second Secretary at the British embassy in Moscow, attended the trial:

> Fifty odd years later it's still one of the most horrifying experiences of my life. It was unbelievable that human beings could have been manipulated in the way they were. . . . They had worked out together as it were a play, a scheme of things, in which they were all taking part, and they obviously to some extent had come to believe in its truth.

Despite the confessions that had been obtained from the accused beforehand and the careful rehearsal of their testimony, the trial did not go completely smoothly. First, Krestinsky pleaded 'not guilty' and had to be taken away and forcibly reminded of his script. Then the prosecutor Vyshinsky was rash enough to question Yagoda about the murder of Kirov. Yagoda, of course, knew the truth of the matter and his answers started to suggest he might begin to tell it. Vyshinsky dropped the subject abruptly. Lastly, Bukharin turned the tables on the whole trial by admitting everything in general and absolutely nothing in particular. It was a brave performance, but to no avail. All but three minor figures were executed.

From Stalin's point of view, the obtaining of Bukharin's and the others' confessions and deaths must have greatly outweighed any of the hiccups at the trial itself. But how are we to understand the confessions? One need look no further than fear for oneself or for one's family. Most confessions were extracted under torture or the threat of it, or under intense psychological pressure about what would be done to loved ones. Indeed often what was threatened had in fact already happened to wife, husband, child or friend. The promises of safe passage were almost invariably hollow. Bukharin was, perhaps, a special case in that he had not been tortured, although he did fear for the safety of his wife and baby son. His widow, Anna Larina, underplays this motive in favour of the idea of confession as a last service to the Party: 'He was a child of his time, a

**53 & 54 Nikolai Bukharin and his wife Anna Larina before his arrest. Bukharin confessed to grotesque crimes in general, but made a mockery of the indictment in its particulars. Anna Larina was sent to the camps, and did not see her young son for nineteen years.**

child of the Party, he was devoted to it, and a great deal can be explained in this way. It explains his capitulation; he thought that it was in the interests of the unity of the Party.'

The 'last service to the Party' argument does not, of course, explain the confessions of non-Party members. The atmosphere of the witchhunt and inquisition may have induced a desperate 'group' willingness to admit that one's soul had been sold to the devil. Moshe Lewin believes that this was totally intentional:

> The effort here on the part of the regime – or was it mainly caused by the pathological mind of the top leader? – was geared to tapping the psychological and cultural predispositions of a disoriented population in the midst of a crisis of values and a cultural no man's land by making them accept a 'demonology' offered by the regime.[27]

In the shadows, between victim and interrogator, lurked the informer, often combining the characteristics of both persecuted and persecutor. Valentin Astrov, a young turk of the Institute of Red

Professors, was arrested, deprived of his Party card, and then released in 1937. The explanation is simple. During interrogation he, like many others, had been 'turned'.

He made a grotesque confession of his own imaginary guilt and implored Bukharin to do likewise. How many others Astrov implicated is not known, but to this day he sees this form of work for the NKVD as the only way he could cling on to the lifeline offered by the Party to those turning informer:

> Some of my friends were Chekists . . . we were all
> communists . . . I have never thought collaboration with the
> Soviet Socialist Security organs to be dishonourable, not now,
> not before – when I hadn't given my pledge – and not when I
> had agreed to work with them. They offered me the one thread
> that tied me to *my* Party, and the conditions were such that
> there was nothing else I could do.

Purges ravaged the ranks of the Party, the academic establishment, the sciences, medicine, economics, the judiciary and the NKVD itself. Despite the imminent war in Europe, Marshal Tukhachevsky was arrested and shot, followed by at least 40,000 of the top military commanders in the country. The arts were not spared. Amongst the many arrested and killed were the writer Isaac Babel, the theatre director Vsevolod Meyerhold and the poet Osip Mandelstam. Poems like this one, written in 1933, came to the attention of Stalin, himself a poet in his youth, and resulted in Mandelstam's exile and subsequent death in a labour camp.

> We exist, without sensing our country beneath us.
> Ten steps away our words can't be heard.
>
> But where there are enough of us for half a conversation
> They always commemorate the Kremlin mountaineer.
>
> His fat fingers slimy as worms,
> His words dependable as weights of measure.
>
> The cockroach moustaches chuckle,
> His top-boots gleam.
>
> And round him a riff-raff of scraggy-necked chiefs,
> He plays with these half men, lackeys,
>
> Who warble, or miaow, or whimper.
> He alone prods and probes.[28]

Others, like Boris Pasternak and the poet Anna Akhmatova, were ostracised and could not get their works published. Anna Akhmatova wrote in the Foreword to 'Requiem':

> During the terrible years of Yezhovshchina [the Yezhov era] I spent seventeen months in the prison queues in Leningrad. One day someone recognised me. Then a woman with lips blue with cold, who was standing behind me and of course had never heard of my name, came out of the numbness which affected us all and whispered in my ear (we all spoke in whispers there), 'Can you describe this?'
> I said, 'I can!'
> Then something resembling a smile slipped over what had once been her face.[29]

Some leading figures like the trade unionist Mikhail Tomsky and Stalin's old comrade Sergo Ordzhonikidze escaped by suicide. Others, such as Valerian Kuibyshev and Maxim Gorky, died under suspicious circumstances. Being closely related to those at the top did not ensure safety. The wife of Kalinin, the President of the Soviet Union, was herself arrested and spent seven years in prison. Members of the Old Bolshevik families of both Stalin's late wives were arrested and shot. As the old Georgian revolutionary Budu Mdivani is said to have told his interrogator: 'I have known Stalin for thirty years. Stalin won't rest until he has butchered us all, beginning with the unweaned baby and ending with the blind great-grandmother.'[30]

There is no doubt of Stalin's *personal* responsibility for a great many of the executions. Soviet historian General Volkogonov was given unprecedented access to the Soviet archives in the course of writing his recent biography of Stalin.

> With my own eyes, I saw tens, hundreds of documents bearing Stalin's signature confirming the death sentence on enormous numbers of lists of people. The most devastating group of documents that I found was dated 12 December 1938 – Stalin and Molotov signed about thirty lists whose overall content was 3,182 people condemned to death in one day. Then he went off with Molotov to watch a film in the evening.

**55  A Leningrad café, 1937. Not all Russians were in the Gulag. For many, life was getting better.**

**56  The killing abated, the cult of personality did not. This 1939 sports parade in Moscow was dominated by the image of the wise leader.**

Yet there were only so many hours in Stalin's day, and the system of terror he headed needed hundreds of thousands, perhaps millions of people to go along with him. From Molotov, Kaganovich and the other 'Stalinists' at the top, through the ranks of the NKVD and the judiciary, to the guards in the camps and the secretaries who typed order forms for bullets and barbed wire – all these people shouldered a part of the responsibility for making the system work. The writer and camp survivor Lev Razgon despises these faceless people more than the camp guards he saw all the time: 'They signed the papers, they agreed to it, they affirmed what was written on the paper and did nothing else. But . . . they are much worse than those stupid people with keys on their belts who actually shut us in.'

By late 1938 Stalin and the bureaucracy were in an increasing state of tension. The more Stalin applied the pressure, the more society was in flux and the less he felt in control. The terror itself was taking on a life of its own and that too had to be kept under his thumb. The paradoxes built up, as historian Moshe Lewin explains:

> The rank and file had lost power; reality became what a few people decided it was. The Stalinists gave the power to Stalin and lost it in the process. But as power was concentrated on Stalin, the more he amassed, the more fragmented and multi-centred the administration became. Because Stalin couldn't direct it all.[31]

The way out of the spiral was to wind down the terror. The first Party Congress since the Seventeenth was held in March 1939. Of the 1,966 delegates to the Congress of Victors in 1934, 1,108 had since been arrested. Only thirty-five of the old rank-and-file members attended as delegates in 1939. This was a fitting tribute to Stalin's talent for revenge, at the way the voting had gone against him five years before. Yezhov was now replaced as NKVD boss and the excesses blamed on him. Lavrenti Beria, now in charge, ironically presided over the reining-in of the NKVD. The pace of arrests and shootings started to slow.

In trying to calculate the scale of the repressions, new evidence forces re-evaluation of old judgements. It is clear that it was not only the Party, the bureaucracy and the intelligentsia which fell victim to the terror of the late thirties. The Byelorussian writer Ales Adamovich, now an elected People's Deputy, argues that: 'We suffer from a very false premise that people killed the kulaks between 1929 and 1933 and that from 1937 to 1940 it was the intelligentsia, the Party workers who were killed. . . . What we have to realise is that throughout that time ordinary people were being killed.'

It was perhaps Stalin's brutal policy against the nationalities which lay behind scenes such as those Sir Fitzroy Maclean witnessed in Azerbaijan in 1937: 'I remember seeing people being herded into trucks and put on board ship and sent across the Caspian . . . when you looked out of the window of the train you'd see trains quite often going the other way with cattle-trucks, with hopeless faces looking out.' But there seems little doubt that peasants were being rounded up long after forced collectivisation.

Tatyana Matusevich's husband, the state farm-worker whose arrest opened this chapter, was typical of the people Lev Razgon met when he was sent to the camps in 1938:

> The largest mass of people in the camps were peasants . . . and they perished first, from cold and hunger because they worked with all their strength . . . these people preserved a specific feeling of dignity. Sometimes they refused certain types of work . . . when this happened they were accused of counter-revolutionary sabotage and there was only one way out and that was death. And therefore, amongst all this mass of people that were killed, the majority weren't Party workers or the intelligentsia. They were simple people and the mass of these graves are scattered all around our country.

The indications are that peasants were going to these graves not from camps alone, but also direct from NKVD headquarters. It seems that this process persisted after the deceleration of the terror and up to 1941.

In 1943, graves holding over 9,000 bodies of people killed around 1938 were found in Vinnitsa in the Ukraine. Since then a succession of mass graves has been found, including some outside major cities such as Minsk, Kiev and Novosibirsk, and one with possibly 40,000 bodies in the Kirov region of Donetsk. At Chelyabinsk in the Urals, a burial site was exhumed in 1989, containing some of the more than 80,000 people thought to have been killed there in the 1930s. The indications are that these are in the main the graves of ordinary people. Zenon Pozniak is the archaeologist who, together with an archaeological group from the Academy of Sciences of Byelorussia, led the excavation and analysis of the many burial plots which cover the floor of Kuropaty Forest close to Minsk. He found such persistent examples of home-made footwear and primitive rural artefacts that he is certain the graves contain 'very simple people'. He has also researched the circumstances of their deaths:

> They were shot by NKVD soldiers in NKVD uniform. They shot them from behind, in the back and pushed them into the pit. When that group was finished, they covered the corpses with sand like a layer cake. They got the contents of the next lorry and shot them, and in that way they filled the pit right up to the top . . . people who lived in the villages nearby told us that . . . the earth would breathe. Some people weren't actually dead when they were buried, and the earth breathed and heaved and the blood came through.

Tatyana Matusevich, following her husband's arrest, got a job doing nightguard duty at the state farm opposite Kuropaty Forest:

> I saw and heard everything on earth. How the people were crying, screaming, when they were brought there to be killed off . . . there were women screaming: 'Oh my God, my children!' There were different kinds of shots – sometimes single, sometimes altogether. They were barbarians . . . innocent human beings were executed – quite innocent.

Zenon Pozniak has counted 510 burial pits in Kuropaty and calculates that each one contains upwards of 150 bodies. This could mean there are around 75,000 people buried there. However, there were apparently as many as 1,000 pits originally, before roads and new construction encroached on the Forest. The number of victims could be very much higher. We do not yet know the full scale of these atrocities, but Kuropaty has, as Ales Adamovich says, turned abstract statistics into terrible evidence:

**57 Recently exhumed victims of the NKVD killing fields at Kuropaty, near Minsk, where execution squads maintained a deadly body count in the forest between 1937 and 1941.**

We can now point to a specific place and say it was in these pits that tens of thousands of people lie buried–simple people, simple and perhaps not so simple, who were killed between 1937 and 1940. This gives the whole story a reality without which it was simply a series of numbers and statistics, counted in millions . . . and this reality has shaken people. And after Kuropaty now they're opening up Bykovnya outside Kiev, another site outside Alma-Ata, Gorky, outside Irkutsk, they're discovering Kuropatys all over the place.

As more of these sites are uncovered and analysed, overall death figures might well have to be revised. Furthermore, we may get a clearer sense of whether there was indeed a continuing assault upon the peasants, and if so, why.

It is difficult to assess how many people suffered and died under Stalin during the purge years of the 1930s; estimates in and out of the Soviet Union vary widely. Much basic information is not yet available. Some will never be. For example, the 1937 census revealed such an embarrassing drop in the expected Soviet population, that

Stalin had the data confiscated and the demographers and statisticians shot.

A clue to the scale of the tragedy came in 1956 when, under Khrushchev, the Politburo asked the KGB for statistics. There are two sources for the answer: Anastas Mikoyan quoted by his son Sergo, and the veteran party worker, Olga Shatunovskaya. Their versions broadly tally. Around 19 million people were arrested by the KGB's predecessors between 1935 and 1940. Of these, at least 7 million were executed or died and the balance passed into the Gulag or exile. We do not know how the KGB arrived at these totals, nor how diligent and uncompromising they were in reaching them. Needless to say, many of the millions who went into the camps subsequently died there. The KGB figures can be put together with Robert Conquest's calculation of 7 million peasant dead from the 1932 – 3 famine and perhaps a further 3 million dead from forced collectivisation and dekulakisation before 1935. This means a death toll of at least 17 million people between 1929 and 1940. By 1941 around 9 million people were in the Gulag.

All this, and then war.

# 6 INTO THE WAR

> Our government made not a few blunders; there were
> moments of desperation in 1941 and 1942 when our army
> retreated, abandoned our native villages and cities . . . because
> it had no choice. Another nation might have said to the
> government, 'You have not justified our expectations, get out;
> we will set up a new government which will sign a peace with
> Germany and give us repose.' But the Russian people did not
> take that road because it had faith in the policy of its
> government. Thank you, great Russian people, for your trust.[1]
>
> J. V. Stalin, 24 May 1945

In Stalin's personality a capacity for excess, sometimes overwhelmed by paranoia, always struggled with a calculating, cautious pragmatism. This was as true in foreign as in domestic affairs. The difference was one of balance; in foreign affairs it was the cautious realist who usually prevailed. In the diplomatic game of the 1930s, in which Soviet Russia was an incongruous but not unskilful player, Stalin never changed his broad view that he must preserve the workers' state from international capitalist encirclement, until such time as the contradictions of capitalism brought forth that international union of socialist republics of which the USSR was the exemplar.

The Comintern, based in Moscow, was intended in the 1920s to be the forcing house of this new upheaval of the international proletariat, without which, Lenin had believed, the Soviet state might not survive. Its activities were no help to the public image of the Soviet Union when, later, the time came to dissemble about its revolutionary aims. Since it was always asked to put the interests of the Soviet state first, the Comintern was not in fact the incubator of indigenous revolution which the bourgeois states feared. Communist parties abroad, and the intelligence which their sympathisers gathered for Moscow, provided Stalin with far better information and support than any other state enjoyed beyond its own ethnic boundaries.

Their reward was subordination and incessant purging. Many a Comintern idealist was to wake in a Soviet prison cell, unable to believe in his coming liquidation. ('Anything which is a necessity from the standpoint of Soviet Russia is also a necessity from the standpoint of the world revolution,' was Stalin's convenient dictum.)[2] Stalin's murderous fury fell with particular intent on the 'heretics' of his own movement. 'National' communists like the Hungarian Bela Kun, the Germans Willi Munzenberg and Fritz Platten, and disillusioned agents like Ignace Reiss, were murdered as surely outside the USSR, as they were liquidated within it. Trotsky and all his children were hunted down like animals. European socialists and social democrats were anathematised as 'social-fascists' with whom no co-operation was possible in the capitalist crisis which followed the Great Depression. The argument was that, as capitalism inevitably collapsed, the real enemy was any competitor for the allegiance of the proletariat. On the very eve of the breakthrough of real fascism in Germany the Executive Committee of the Comintern roundly declared: 'We shall not be able to strike and destroy the class-enemy of the workers, the bourgeoisie, unless our main attack is directed against Social Democracy, the chief prop of the bourgeoisie.'[3]

Ironically, relations were better with the country where real fascism was a growing force. There had been much to draw Germany and the Soviet Union together. Both regarded the new nation states created after the Treaty of Versailles around their borders with loathing. Stalin never forgot that Imperial Russia had ruled half of Poland, Finland and the three Baltic states of Lithuania, Latvia and Estonia. The Soviet Union stood aloof from the 'robbers' league', declining to join the League of Nations. Germany, the principal victim of Versailles, made a natural partner for the Soviet Union in the 1920s. At Rapallo in 1922 the two states had signed an agreement to strengthen their economic links. The infant army of the Weimar Republic trained on Russian soil, developing ties which would later damn many of their military hosts when the Soviet Army was purged in 1937. Stalin admired the Germans, and had some knowledge of the language. 'Ech, together with the Germans we would have been invincible,' he murmured to his daughter long after.[4]

When the Nazis seized power in 1933 Stalin did nothing. The German communists had made common cause with the Nazis in destroying Weimar democracy: 'After Hitler, our turn!' It was their turn to be rounded up and liquidated. Stalin watched this with the same apparent equanimity he had shown more than six years before, when Chiang Kai-shek massacred the Chinese communists. The Soviet Union was the first country in the world to conclude a treaty with the new Nazi regime, on 6 May 1933. Stalin showed a grudging admiration for Hitler's short way with dissenters in his own party in the 1934 Roehm purge. But by this time the Soviet line was changing, and that of the Comintern with it. Much of the powerful French party had been in open revolt, calling for a popular front. Stalin's agents in Germany reported to him the new truculence of the Nazis towards the Soviets.

The Soviet Union reversed its position and joined the League of Nations. There, its Commissar for Foreign Affairs, Maxim Litvinov, cut a figure as a firm advocate of collective security. Litvinov was the much-travelled Bolshevik adventurer who had once been caught passing bank-notes from Stalin's robberies. Now he had to pass himself off as a respectable diplomat. A Jew married to an Englishwoman, his sympathies lay with a putative western alliance. No voice called more loudly for sanctions against Mussolini, or a United Front in Europe between the communists and those quondam agents of the bourgeoisie, the socialists.

The returns were meagre. A defence pact was signed with France, but its unenthusiastic ratification by the French showed the suspicion in which the Soviet Union was still held. Even a Popular Front government in France failed to quieten mutual suspicions, whilst in Spain the Popular Front was actually overthrown by Franco's insurrection. The Russians came to the assistance of the Spanish Republic, while the western democracies kept their distance, but they brought it in their own special way, with NKVD men in attendance well trained to sniff out Trotskyite deviationists and liquidate them. From Stalin's point of view the inertia of the democracies, following hard on their failure to act against Hitler's treaty-breaking entry into the Rhineland, was proof enough that they would be happy to see the wave of fascist aggression turned against an isolated Soviet Union. Stalin had accommodated the Comintern to moderate, even rightwing, allies abroad. He had paraded a new democratic constitution for the USSR (while millions of Soviet citizens vanished into the Gulag), incorporating all the classic liberties. He had stood up to fascism in Spain. He concluded a treaty with the Czechs, who plainly stood in Hitler's path, to be activated when France met its own treaty obligations. The lack of response heightened his sense of isolation.

The years 1936–9 mark, therefore, a period when the growing threat of the Axis powers (Germany, Italy and Japan, who signed their own Anti-Comintern Pact in 1937) failed to bring the Soviet Union closer to the western democracies. Stalin's purges consumed almost everyone who had had foreign contacts, be they Marshal Tukhachevsky and his officers who had once trained with the Germans and whose creatures they were now declared to be, or the advisers, soldiers and international supporters who had become dangerously exposed to the infectious idealism of Spain. The blow to Soviet military efficiency was enormous, emphasised by senior historians like Alexander Samsonov. 'This loss cannot simply be measured by the loss of people like Tukhachevsky and Blyukher . . . more than 43,000 senior army officers and party workers were liquidated by Stalinist repression . . . who were the best prepared, the best qualified, and the best dedicated to their country.'

Samsonov's estimate has been challenged recently by Soviet scholars like Georgi Kumanev as not representing the real scale of the Stalin crimes:

> According to archive files, in the short period from 27
> February 1937 to 12 November 1938, the NKVD was
> sanctioned by Stalin, Molotov and Kaganovich to shoot 38,679
> military personnel. Add to this 3,000 men shot in the fleet, and
> those liquidated before and after these dates . . . the overall
> figure of those purged is far higher. In 1941 there was a
> shortfall of 66,000 officers.[5]

The morale of the army collapsed. Enough of the horror was reported to increase the repugnance which much western opinion felt for Stalin. He reciprocated. As Austria was absorbed by the Nazis and Chamberlain, and Daladier manoeuvred to hand the Sudeten-land to Hitler without war, Stalin's justifiable suspicion that they meant to turn Hitler eastward increased. In fact, everyone except Hitler was playing the same game: to make sure that the risks of war, especially on two fronts, were avoided. Even those who did not think that appeasement would bring avoidance, but merely postponement, wanted to see others exhausted or satiated first. Hitler played

**58 May Day 1937. Five marshals of the Red Army take the salute in Red Square below Stalin and Yezhov (*centre*). Eleven days later Tukhachevsky (*extreme left*) was arrested and subsequently shot. Two marshals, many generals and around 50,000 senior military personnel went to their deaths after him.**

according to different rules, but the war he craved still involved the freest hand he could get to take on his victims one at a time.

The British and French had a poor opinion of Russian military capacity after the purge of the Red Army. They doubted its ability to come to the aid of the Czechs in 1938. But at the height of the Sudeten crisis the Soviet ambassador in Prague delivered to President Benes an assurance of Soviet help provided France also acted, and more generally if it were requested by the League of Nations. Since such help would have had to come through Poland or Rumania, two countries with good reason to fear the Soviet Union, its provision on a large scale was impossible. But the effort was made, and Stalin could say that no commensurate conditional assurance had been made by the French about their treaty obligations. They, as much as the

British, were desperate to buy Hitler off, to use the threat of war to control his appetites, not the reality to destroy him. The Russians had been snubbed by the Munich agreement, and by Chamberlain's frigid distaste of Bolshevism. It is difficult to disagree with Isaac Deutscher's verdict: 'The unwritten maxim of Munich was to keep Russia out of Europe. Not only the great and seemingly great powers of the west wished to exclude Russia. The governments of the small eastern European nations as well squealed at the great bear: 'Stay where you are, stay in your lair.'''[6]

What was Stalin to do? He despised the western bourgeois democrats. He feared and half-admired Hitler. And he had another fear. Since the Japanese had moved into Manchuria in 1931 they had an extensive land frontier with the Soviet Union. They were eager members of the Anti-Comintern pact. They had mauled Russia before. And those who attributed fiendish powers to British intelligence, as Stalin did (and to some who did not), it seemed obvious that a priority of the western imperialists must be to turn Japan away from its vulnerable colonial possessions towards the eastern USSR. The border was alive with tensions and incidents. At Lake Khasan in 1938 and at Khalkhin-Gol the following year there was heavy fighting, in which the Russians under General Zhukov gave a good account of themselves. The Japanese had richer pickings elsewhere, but for Stalin this was the old nightmare of encirclement in a new form: a war on two fronts against the Axis powers, while the rest of the world looked on.

Accordingly, Stalin signalled his availability to both sides. On 10 March 1939, he spoke at the Eighteenth Congress of the Soviet Communist Party of the intention 'to be cautious and not allow our country to be pulled into conflicts by warmongers who are accustomed to have others pull chestnuts out of the fire for them'.[7] The speech was ambiguous. It could be read as encouragement to the Germans to buy Russian neutrality, or as a reminder to the British and French that they would pay a price for ignoring the Soviet potential. (Only afterwards would Molotov shamelessly claim it as the precursor of the pact with Germany he had just signed, when 'the historical foresight of Comrade Stalin was brilliantly confirmed'.[8])

This was premature pro-fascism. Comrade Stalin's historical foresight was given a sharper nudge while the Congress was still sitting. Hitler occupied the rump of Czechoslovakia. It was obvious that

Poland would be next. And then? Litvinov was allowed one last try to bring Britain and France into a pact which guaranteed not just Poland but all of the Baltic states. Any guarantee to any of them was useless without Soviet participation. The British and French procrastinated. Elaborate guarantees were unilaterally bestowed by Litvinov on the Baltic states. Ironically, in view of later events, Latvia was told that any intrusion on its sovereignty would be intolerable to the Soviet Union. The Latvians should feel 'confident of the readiness of the Soviet Union to prove in deeds, if necessary, its interest in the full preservation by the Latvian Republic of its independent statehood and its political and economic independence'.[9] To the Soviet Union it looked as though the reluctance to aid the Baltic states was a western hint to Hitler that that was the route he might take into the Soviet Union. In May 1939 Litvinov was dismissed and replaced by the drab and taciturn Molotov. It was a hint which the Germans could understand. Stalin had given up what hope he might have had of collective security.

In fact, relations with the Germans had never been broken off completely. Molotov made his approaches in late May. The Germans responded cautiously. Both sides knew that a partition of Poland, and Soviet hegemony to the east, would be the price for Stalin. The Germans had dined at this table before, in the time of the tsars. An Anglo-French mission, slow to travel, unhappy in arrival, toiled in Moscow at the old problem of which Soviet guarantees the suspicious Poles and Rumanians might accept. One day the mission was told by the Soviet negotiator, Voroshilov, that the talks were adjourned. Under the noses of the unwitting British and French, Hitler and Stalin constructed a non-aggression treaty which shook the world. It offered German credits for machine tools and armaments in exchange for Russian neutrality. A secret protocol, whose accompanying maps carry the bold signature of Stalin and the crudely crayoned lines where he sought at the last moment to enclose more territory, accompanied the pact. It gave him that part of Poland wrung from Bolshevik Russia after 1917, and a sphere of influence that included all his Baltic neighbours, Finland, Latvia, Lithuania and Estonia. The Anglo-French mission was flabbergasted, older hands less so. Sir Fitzroy Maclean was in the British Embassy in Moscow at the time:

Stalin was being offered on the one hand by Hitler what he
hoped meant peace, which he needed very badly to pull the
Soviet Union together, plus very considerable territorial gains,
the Baltic states, half of Poland, Finland, odd bits of the
Balkans, all for keeping out of war, which he wanted to do
anyway. We were offering him a front-line position in the nastiest
war there'd ever been. And that didn't appeal to him at all.

The pact bought time. Time to recover from the purges and the
blood-letting. Time to rebuild the armed forces. In crude terms, it
also gave Stalin what must have seemed a painless route to re-acquire
the lost Baltic empire of the tsars. In retrospect Stalin's *legerdemain*
has always been justified in the Soviet Union, despite the slump in his
reputation elsewhere. But around the fiftieth anniversary of the
August 23rd Pact it has been Soviet historians like Mikhail Semi-
ryaga who have argued that Stalin's short-term gains were more than
cancelled out by the greater gain to Germany: its ability to fight on
one front at a time, to perfect the blitzkrieg techniques which later
took millions of Russian lives, and to demoralise anti-fascists everywhere.

For the moment Stalin was well pleased. He was photographed
affably playing cards with von Ribbentrop, his hand carefully concealed. After the successful German onslaught on Poland the Red
Army moved into position in what now became Western Ukraine and
Western Byelorussia. The NKVD followed, to prepare the inhabitants for their voluntary sovietisation. As became known later, some
15,000 Polish officers were murdered in cold blood by the NKVD at
Katyn and elsewhere. (On this subject Stalin displayed his gallows
humour. When asked later by the Free Poles, then his allies, what
had happened to the officers, he replied, 'They fled to Manchuria.')
On 28 September a new Treaty of Friendship was signed, binding
these two grave-robbers still closer together. Around 800 German
and Austrian communists were handed over to the tender mercies of
the Gestapo. Molotov proudly told the Supreme Soviet that: 'It
proved enough for Poland to be dealt one swift blow, first by the
German Army and then by the Red Army, to wipe out all remains of
this misshapen offspring of the Versailles Treaty.'[10]

Stalin never had quite this gall. At the celebrations for the

**60 High stakes. Ribbentrop playing cards with Stalin, 1939.**

anniversary of the revolution on a freezing November day, Voroshi-lov was filmed on the Mausoleum droning on in endless, nervous justification for this embrace of the Nazis, and the return of the Red Army to the 'old frontiers'. Occasionally Stalin paced in and out of frame, the flaps of his fur hat down, glowering balefully at Voroshi-lov. The *Vozhd* (Leader) knew what history would make of his arrangements. The second treaty, which spoke of friendship as well as frontiers, is too much for senior Soviet historians today. Alexander Samsonov draws a distinction between the August and September treaties: 'The [first] was a treaty of non-aggression, so it would have been possible to continue talks with Britain and France. . . . The second pact . . . both politically and ideologically reinterpreted the whole of our traditional position in relation to fascism and fascist Germany as such . . . a terrible mistake.'

Stalin on his sixtieth birthday cabled Hitler in response to his congratulations that the friendship of their peoples 'cemented by blood has every reason to be lasting and firm'.[11]

The Finns were the first to receive his demands for territory, to move the Soviet frontier further from Leningrad. They refused and

**60** Ribbentrop signs the Nazi–Soviet Pact, 23 August 1939. Much relieved, Stalin and Molotov (*centre*) look on.

**61** New allies. Nazi and Soviet troops offer mutual congratulations on the partition of Poland, 1939.

**62** The Polish officers shot in the Katyn Forest by the NKVD in 1939 — exhumed by the Germans in 1943.

went to war, for some months inflicting defeats and heavy casualties on an unprepared Red Army, which suffered 100,000 casualties before the Finns sued for peace. For this aggression the Soviet Union was expelled from the League of Nations. The three Baltic republics were easier prey. Soviet troops were stationed there in large numbers in 1939. In 1940, after Hitler had occupied Norway and Denmark and moved against France, the Red Army presided over the 'voluntary' absorption of the Baltic states into the Soviet Union, and the first of the NKVD purges began. The pretence that this was joyfully welcomed by the native Balts fooled no one. Stalin was imposing a Soviet regime at the point of the bayonet. Bessarabia was taken from the Rumanians and annexed.

There was a double price to pay for these territorial gains. The economic agreements signed with Germany committed the Soviet Union to regular and increasing supplies of raw materials for the German war effort.[12] They were made punctiliously, right up to June 1941. In exchange for naval assistance Soviet ports were available for use by the German fleet. Then there was the humiliation of an appeasement as thorough, and more cynical, than that of Chamberlain had been. Every triumph of German arms brought its congratulatory cable from Molotov. Foreign communist parties competed in their denunciations of the 'imperialist war' and their exhortations to sabotage the anti-fascist war effort. Molotov went to Berlin in 1940, where Hitler dangled before him the prospect of booty from the break-up of the British empire. Throughout the latter part of 1940, Stalin found Russian influence squeezed out of the Balkans and stealthy German pressure around his perimeter. Instead of a four-power carve-up as proposed by the Germans, he concluded a non-aggression treaty with the Japanese, telling their envoy that they were fellow-Asiatics, and accelerated Soviet war production, especially in less vulnerable areas to the east. The Soviet Union was spending over 30 per cent of its national budget on armaments in 1940. It had 4 million men under arms and was by some margin the largest producer of aircraft in the world.

In this sense, then, Stalin was readier for war in 1941 than at the time of the pact. He had extended his frontiers and expanded his armaments, and he would not have to fight on two fronts. But in 1939, or 1940, he could have had the second front against Germany for which he was soon noisily clamouring. In 1941 he faced the German blitzkreig alone, and it was fuelled by the spoils of conquered Europe, usefully supplemented by Soviet oil. He also faced it with a profound misunderstanding of Hitler's psychology. Discomforted when Hitler fell upon the Yugoslavs, he could still persuade himself that this put paid to another campaigning year from the Wehrmacht.

German planes were now overflying the Soviet Union with insolent regularity – the air force was told not to force them down. Sources as diverse as the Soviet spy Richard Sorge in Tokyo and the British, fresh from interrogating Rudolf Hess, warned that a German attack was imminent. It was dismissed as provocation and intrigue. Stalin was contemptuous of Sorge's warnings. According to Marshal Timoshenko, 'The boss said: "This (unprintable word) of ours has turned up, running businesses on the side and whore-houses in Japan, and has deigned to tell us the date of the German attack – 22nd June. Would you suggest that I believe him too?" '[13]

Stalin preferred to address a letter to Hitler, and to believe the Führer's reply, which blandly stated that troops had been moved east so that they would not be monitored by the RAF! Even when the German ambassador Schulenberg, at great risk to himself, conveyed the same warning as Stalin's overseas agents, this too was seen as disinformation. Stalin chose to believe Hitler.

On 14 June 1941 all Soviet media carried a statement about 'the obvious absurdity of rumours about a forthcoming war' which should be discounted.[14] No private warnings to the military counterbalanced this military disclaimer. Admiral Kuznetsov, who saw Stalin at this time, found him still obsessed with an Anglo-US conspiracy to force him into war with Germany. Meanwhile, 3 million men crouched on the frontier, waiting for the deadline: 4 a.m., 22 June 1941. One of them, a German conscript with a communist background, courageously crossed the lines to confirm the precise moment of the attack. Stalin had him shot for 'disinformation'. Private Alfred Liskow was to be the last casualty of the 'imperialist war'. The Great Patriotic War was about to begin.

The Germans fell upon the Soviet armies like a whirlwind. Soviet generals demanded a response. The most Stalin had agreed with Marshal Timoshenko was that they should be told that a German attack might be launched and, if so, that it should be treated as a provocation. By the time this tortuous message, sent during the night, had reached the troops in the field, a thousand Soviet aircraft had been destroyed and the Germans were a hundred miles inside the new frontiers that Stalin had acquired with the 1939 pact. Molotov was handed the formal declaration of war and it was he, not Stalin, who broadcast the news to the Russian people. Stalin himself was prostrate. For a week he rarely emerged from his villa at Kuntsevo. His name disappeared from the newspapers. For ten days the Soviet Union was leaderless. His daughter remembers how shattered he was:

> He never went missing. . . . He was, however, shocked and depressed because he didn't believe that the Germans would do that. He was visited by one of my aunts during these very early days, and she found him quite depressed too, saying, 'Things are very bad. You have to leave Moscow, you have to take your children, your family, and go to the Urals.'

On 1 July Stalin pulled himself together. It was announced that he was head of a State Defence Committee, with Molotov, Voroshilov, Malenkov and Beria. He nerved himself to broadcast, and the low, depressed voice struck a new note of fraternity: 'Comrades, citizens, brothers and sisters, fighting men of our Army and Navy, I am speaking to you, my friends. . . .'[15] He defended the pact whilst admitting that most of its territorial gains had already vanished, and he called for a scorched-earth policy against the invaders on Russian soil. To the troops at the front this meant standing firm, even if encircled. In the initial speed of the German advance whole armies were surrounded, cut off and forced to surrender.

The new defence fortifications had proved useless. Units were ordered to attack when only tactical retreat might save them. Despite individual acts of heroism the front was in chaos. Within a week the Germans were in Minsk. Within a month they had advanced 450 miles on a wide front, striking north towards Leningrad, in the centre through Smolensk towards Moscow, and southwards towards the Black Sea. Two of the three senior marshals in command were sacked for their failures. General Pavlov, who lost Minsk, was shot after court martial, and General Kirponos, who lost Kiev, was killed in action. At the centre Stalin was reasserting himself. He became Defence Commissar, then Commander-in-Chief. He took charge of

**63 Anxious crowds in Moscow listen in bewilderment to the news of the German invasion.**

negotiations with Beaverbrook and Harriman, when they arrived to represent the British and US governments. Valentin Berezhkov became his interpreter at that time. 'He looked quite different from what I had been imagining for myself, from all these newsreels and

64 Russian prisoners caught up in the German advance eastwards. Of the 3 million captured only a handful would see their homeland again.

65 Yakov Stalin captured by the Germans, 1941. His father could not be seen to acknowledge that he had a son who had surrendered. Overtures to exchange him for the highest-ranking Germans were rebuffed, and Yakov killed himself (or was murdered) in a prison camp in 1943.

sculptures and so on. He looked very frail, very ill, with a grey face and small pocks all over his nose and cheeks. And my first thought was that maybe it was not Stalin, maybe it was someone else.'

It *was* Stalin, now embarked on four years in which he ran the Soviet war effort, and its foreign relations, from a simple office in the Kremlin. He learned how to be a commander-in-chief as he went along, and many paid with their lives for his mistakes. But he did learn. And he pushed through, with Malenkov, the relocation of Soviet industry behind the Urals, away from the aggressor, so that within a year Soviet production could pick up again, although the Germans had overrun so much of Russia's industrial and agricultural capacity.

Like the soldiers who died in the path of the panzer armies, the workers who rebuilt their factories almost by hand, and the men and women who toiled long hours in them, were the true heroes of the war. And Stalin eventually found a voice to address them. It was not the ideology of Marxism–Leninism but the ancient Russian wrath against the invader which spilled out of him when he spoke at the celebrations for the October Revolution, first at Mayakovsky metro station, then atop the Mausoleum. He evoked the struggle against foreign intervention after the revolution, and went further back, to the legendary heroes who had beaten off invasions before, from Alexander Nevsky to Suvorov. The resolution of the public man was hard earned. Privately he had doubts. As the Germans gathered themselves after the fall of Smolensk for their attack on Moscow, all departments of the Soviet government were evacuated to Kuibyshev on the Volga. Three million Russians were captured, including Stalin's elder son. Countless others had fallen – some shot by the NKVD for alleged desertion. Half the land under grain crops and 40 per cent of the railroads were in German hands.

Stalin himself seems to have had two moments where his pessimism again overwhelmed him. There was a day when he appeared at the railway station, pacing the platform before he was due to board a train that would take him, too, out of Moscow. According to his daughter, it was only then, at the last moment, that he changed his mind: 'All the household goods were packed, and the train was on the rails all ready to move. And within half an hour he called his chief bodyguards and said, "We're not going, we're staying." And so they decided to stay, and to have a big parade on Red Square.'

It was the most crucial decision of his life. Another was taken for him – by Hitler. Alexander Samsonov describes it:

> Stalin's thoughts about something like a Treaty of
> Brest–Litovsk appeared in October 1941 when the German
> fascist army group of von Bock was already on the outskirts of
> Moscow. . . . Precisely on 15 October Stalin entrusted Beria,
> who was a member of the State Committee for Defence, to use
> the state security channels to explore the possibility . . . of
> surrendering the Ukraine and a whole collection of other
> territories belonging to us, and start negotiating for peace.
> Feelers were put out, but Hitler was convinced that the
> problem of taking Moscow and the victorious conclusion of the
> war with the Soviet Union was only a matter of days and he
> refused to negotiate. . . . The image of Stalin as an adamant
> commander-in-chief fades when we discover facts of that kind.

Hitler's belief that he could crush the Russians within days was wildly wrong. Leningrad was surrounded and starving, Moscow almost encircled. Survivors of the Leningrad siege like Gennadi Beglov hold Stalin responsible for the error which left most of the city's supplies concentrated in the Badayevsky warehouses, where they were destroyed by the Germans in full view of the city:

> I lost my parents and sixteen of my closest relatives,
> grandmother, grandfather, everybody. . . . Why couldn't they
> have distributed these provisions a month before the Germans
> assaulted Leningrad? Several hundred thousand people would
> still be alive as a result of such a measure, so the responsibility
> for this crime must be borne by Stalin himself, and those who
> commanded on the Leningrad front.

Stalin's priority was Moscow. He moved his far eastern reserves and every available gun back into the capital. The Red Army fought the Germans to a standstill on the perimeter of Moscow. Russian pride and patriotism were touched. They could fight back. They had the assistance now of the trucks and supplies coming in from the Anglo-Americans, but it was not yet a world war. At this crucial juncture the Japanese had not turned on the democracies. Stalin fought in Moscow as alone in his conflict as Churchill had been in the Battle of Britain. He learned that he had to work with an able new

# Soviet annexations 1939-1940

Miles
0       100

**FINLAND**

Petrozavodsk

Vyborg

Helsinki

Leningrad

**ESTONIA**
*Russian before 1917*
*Independent 1918-1939*

Tallin (Reval)

**PART OF FINLAND**
*Russian before 1917*
*Finnish 1918-1939*

Pskov

**LATVIA**
*Russian before 1914*
*Independent 1920-1939*

Riga

**S O V I E T**

**U N I O N**

*Baltic Sea*

**LITHUANIA**
*Russian before 1914*
*Independent 1919-1939*

Memel

Kaunas (Kovno)

Vilna

Königsberg

East Prussia

Grodno

Minsk

**EASTERN POLAND**
*Russian before 1914*
*Polish 1919-1939*

Warsaw

**P O L A N D**

Pinsk

Lublin

Kiev

Zhitomir

Turnov

Lvov

Przemysl

Kamenets-Podolsk

**BESSARABIA**
*Russian before 1917*
*Rumanian 1918-1940*

**EASTERN GALICIA**
*Austrian before 1918*
*Polish 1918-1939*

SLOVAKIA

Uzhgorod

Balta

**H U N G A R Y**

**BUKOVINA**
*Austrian before 1918*
*Rumanian 1918-1940*

Jassy

Kishinev

Odessa

**R U M A N I A**

*Black Sea*

Occupied by Russia between
October 1939 and December 1940

The German Reich in December 1939

Under German political control or
influence by December 1940

**66** Lessons in German order. Zoya Kosmodemyanskaya on her way to be hanged in November 1941. The placard 'Arsonist' is hung around her neck. The story of her fortitude under torture made her a national heroine.

**67** Hanging of partisans, Minsk, Byelorussia, 1941.

generation of military commanders, to hoard reserves, to fight a flexible war of movement. Khrushchev noticed the change in him: 'He had pulled himself together, straightened up, and was acting like a real soldier. He had also started to think of himself as a great military strategist, which made it harder to argue with him.'[16]

He was still to make terrible errors when the Germans regrouped and tried again in the spring of 1942. At Kharkov an army of 200,000 men was destroyed pressing on into a German trap on Stalin's orders. Khrushchev, the political commissar with the defeated Timoshenko, was summoned back to Moscow. Stalin took no responsibility and talked darkly of how encircled commanders had been executed in the First World War. Every commander feared him.

Together with the heroism of the Russian troops and factory workers, and the help of his allies, Stalin now had critical help from his rival dictator. Whereas he had tempered his ideology and learned from his mistakes, Hitler did neither. The failure of the initial blitzkrieg meant that the Germans could only tilt the long-run odds on the eastern front by detaching the non-Russian peoples permanently from Stalin's heartland. But the Nazi ideology had no place in it for these Slav *Untermenschen*. In the granaries of Byelorussia and the Ukraine land was not returned to the peasants, though in the Baltic, Caucasian and Muslim regions there was conciliation, redistribution and some local autonomy. The east European plain was to be held for incoming German colonists. Meanwhile, its inhabitants could be brutalised. The Russian liberation army which the captured General Vlasov tried to form with German help was never given the credibility it needed to attract support. That support went instead to the partisans, and to the steadfast defenders of a dozen cities and salients which, in 1942–3, held out against the invader. And Stalin's government struck a note of Russian patriotism. Marxist dogma bowed to the recognition of religion, and of ethnic identity. The Comintern was dissolved, lest there be misunderstandings in the international anti-fascist alliance.

In the summer of 1942 the Germans broke loose and drove hard for the Caucasus and the Volga. The city of Stalingrad joined beleaguered Leningrad in the annals of the Patriotic War. A raw Soviet army was driven into Stalingrad and surrounded. One of the young recruits was the artist Boris Birger:

**68 The long siege of Leningrad. This couple are dragging their dead child to burial.**

**69 Stalingrad — decisive battle of the war, where the German army of von Paulus was cut off and surrounded until the last remnants surrendered in February 1943.**

> Just imagine boys of eighteen who when they came to the war
> believed that we had everything . . . and found themselves
> under the German bombers, absolutely helpless without any
> anti-aircraft artillery, without any good weapons. The only
> thing that worked properly were 1895 model rifles, the ones
> used in the First World War. And we were starving.

The defenders held on and defied the encircling Germans. Fresh troops (and winter weather) now trapped the Germans in their turn. Field Marshal von Paulus surrendered with the frozen survivors of his army. It was the greatest German military reverse of the war, achieved in the city that bore Stalin's name. The blockade of Leningrad had been breached for the first time, too. There were terrible battles ahead, but all, including the ferocious tank battles at Kursk, simply confirmed that the tide had turned. The Soviet armies were now better led and equipped with superior weapons like the T34 tank. This flood of new equipment, from the relocated Russian factories and abroad, would reach its peak in 1944. Sooner or later the Germans would be pushed out. Stalin, working long hours, using his prodigious memory to good effect, pored over his battle plans. As the war went better, so he was closely identified with the winning of it. He promoted himself to Marshal as the cult took a new form. Fresh generations of young people went to war 'For the Motherland! For Stalin!' with a renewal of the enthusiasm of the Old Bolsheviks.

Even in the darkest days, Stalin had kept his nerve in the long poker game with his new allies. Early visitors found him clamouring for that second front he could have created in 1939. With Moscow under siege he did not forget to push before Anthony Eden an agreement which would leave him with all the territory he had gained from his deal with Hitler. The Free Poles, now his allies, were treated with an initial sinister jocularity, which hardened into suspicion. Stalin awaited his many visitors well-briefed and tireless. He argued that they should come to him, because he could not leave his duties at the front (in fact he only visited the combat areas once in the whole war). He was skilful at exploiting weaknesses and divisions, and assuming the moral ground. He did this over the failure of the western allies to establish a second front in Northern Europe in 1942, in addition to the heavy fighting in North Africa, and returned to the theme with more justice when they opted to fight their way up

**70 Exhausted survivors of the Polish Home Army surrender after the failure of the Warsaw Uprising.**

through Italy rather than invade France in 1943. When the London Poles dared to raise the issue of the Katyn massacre – the mass graves having been discovered by the Germans in April 1943 and heavily exploited in their propaganda – Stalin denounced them as Fascists and set about constructing a more pliant Polish 'Committee of National Liberation' of his own. With the other governments-in-exile based in London, like the Czechs, he maintained cordial relations. An identity of interest remained.

In November 1943 Stalin climbed aboard an aeroplane for the first time. He was going to Teheran, which he had persuaded Roosevelt and Churchill should be the site of the first allied summit. There he played on the differences between them, and won the prize he most wanted: agreement on the 1941 border with Poland, whatever the London Poles might say. They were to be compensated with richer German lands to the west, and here, even Churchill thought, would have a stable state. The Poles saw no reason why they should not have the frontiers from which, as the first victims of 1939, they had been dispossessed. Confirmation of his hold on eastern Poland and the Baltic states was not Stalin's only strategic prize at Teheran. He also saw Churchill's plans for an allied move through the Balkans and into Yugoslavia overruled in favour of a frontal assault on France, striking directly at the Ruhr. He had seen, correctly, that his allies were beginning to worry about just how far the victorious Red Army would go.

In 1944 it went very far. Russian soil was cleansed of the invader. Slowly the predominance of men and materials swung inexorably to the Soviet side. While the allies invaded Normandy in June, Soviet troops were massing on the old Polish frontier. By September they were on the Vistula, looking across at Warsaw. There they stopped. The London Polish government ordered a general uprising of the Home Army in Warsaw, not co-ordinated with Moscow. The Poles meant to liberate their own capital. The insurrection was suppressed, Warsaw destroyed. Stalin kept the Red Army immobile. The last chestnuts he would ever have chosen to pull from this fire would be those of the London Poles. With the Home Army wiped out by the Germans he could recognise the National Liberation Committee as a provisional government. The London Poles had been hasty, but the sacrifice of the Home Army was never forgotten. Czeslaw Milosz expressed the bitterness seven years later:

> There was no logical reason for Russia to have helped Warsaw.
> The Russians were bringing the West not only liberation from
> Hitler, but liberation from the existing order, which they
> wanted to replace with a good order, namely their own. . . .
> The people dying in the streets were precisely those who could
> create most trouble for the new rulers.[17]

By the end of the year Soviet troops were moving into Rumania,
Bulgaria and Hungary. Tito's partisans were the dominant force in
Yugoslavia, allied with, but not subservient to, the Red Army. The
pattern of post-war influence was becoming clear. Stalin was willing
to play a game of percentages of influence with Churchill: a right-
wing monarchy preserved in Greece and the communists, who had
much natural support, suppressed; communism entrenched in
Rumania, and the right-wing monarchy and its own substantial
support neutralised. But his rules were of ideology and class, com-
bined with Russian national interest, as he made clear to the visiting
Yugoslav partisan leader Milovan Djilas: 'Stalin said that post-war
Europe wouldn't look the same as it had after the First World War.
Whoever occupied a territory would impose his own system on it.
There would no longer be the idea of a people independent nationally
but rather subordinate to a certain system.'

On their way back the Yugoslavs stopped in Kiev, noting the
thorough russification which was under way. Stalin was now the
master of Eastern Europe. He was also the genuinely popular leader
of a military power which had pressed all national and religious
sentiments, as well as the aid and goodwill of its allies, into the
struggle. As Stalin played host to those allies at Yalta the question
remained open. Would his temperament and aims be affected by
what he and the Soviet people had undergone, or would the Stalin of
the thirties re-emerge?

# 7 THE SOVIET SUPERPOWER

An ungainly dwarf of a man passed through gilded and
marbled imperial halls, and a path opened before him; radiant,
admiring glances followed him, while the ears of courtiers
strained to catch his every word. And he, sure of himself and
his works, obviously paid no attention to all this. His country
was in ruins, hungry, exhausted. But his armies and marshals,
heavy with fat and medals and drunk with vodka and victory,
had already trampled half of Europe under foot, and he was
convinced they would trample over the other half in the next
round. He knew that he was one of the cruellest, most despotic
figures in human history. But this did not worry him a bit, for
he was convinced that he was carrying out the will of history.[1]

Milovan Djilas: *Conversations with Stalin*

At Yalta in 1945 Stalin, the host, bestrode his world. Roosevelt was
visibly dying. Churchill brooded on his loss of real power. Stalin
could afford a certain bonhomie, though the sentiment never replaced hard bargaining. The allied armies stood at the Rhine, as well
as the Oder, but it was obvious to all that the immense Soviet effort
over three and a half years of war had played the predominant part in
bringing down Germany, whose unconditional surrender was now
awaited. Stalin acquiesced in the decision to build a United Nations
organisation in which the big powers would play a leading role,
secure from overruling by the smaller nations. (He secured for
himself extra votes for the Ukraine and Byelorussia.) He promised to
enter the war against Japan within three months of the end of the
European conflict.

In return he secured the recognition of his territorial gains at the
expense of Poland and Germany, and of what was now known as the
Lublin government. Of course there would be elections and self-
determination. Germany was to be put under four-power adminis-

**71  1945. Victory in Berlin. Soviet troops triumphant on the ruins of the Reichstag.**

tration, its industries broken up, reparations paid, and its eastern provinces torn away to compensate Poland. When asked what would happen to the people of East Prussia, Stalin expressed the view that 'when our soldiers arrive all the Germans will flee'.[2] The land would be left empty.

The Germans were indeed to suffer the full weight of Russian revenge for the barbarities they had inflicted since 1941. The Red Army had fought its way across Europe and seen those horrors. Its reprisals were terrible, the more so because this orgy of rape and killing seemed to be condoned from above. Milovan Djilas found himself in Stalin's bad books for his complaints about the behaviour of Soviet troops in Yugoslavia. Stalin had growled that if they wanted some fun with a woman why should he object? 'He took as an example a certain Soviet major who had attacked a woman while on leave in the USSR and had killed a man who tried to defend her, and Stalin said: "The man was sentenced to death, and I pardoned him and sent him back to the army because he was brave, and he became a hero of the Soviet Union."'

Thus chivalry was suspect. The young Lev Kopelev, a major in army intelligence, fluent in German, tried to prevent atrocities within his own unit. He was denounced by his fellow officers, who '. . . realised that this was clear evidence of ideological corruption, a link with alien, hostile petit bourgeois. . . . In East Prussia I had occupied myself with "saving Germans and their property and preaching pity for the Germans, in spite of the indignation of our officers and men".'[3]

Kopelev was first acquitted, then rearrested and sent to a labour camp. There he joined the tidal wave of prisoners who were flowing into the Gulag. They included all collaborators who were not killed out of hand. The western allies handed back under the Yalta agreement all Russian nationals who had served the German cause, including those who had not lived in Russia since the revolution and were not, technically, Soviet citizens. It was called 'Operation Keel Haul'. Some of these 'victims of Yalta' deserved retribution. Cossack and other units had committed atrocities on both western and eastern fronts. Those who had joined the renegade Russian General Vlasov, even if starvation had been their motive, were guilty of treason. But the net was flung much wider than over the million souls thus trawled.

**72 Cossack troops, awaiting deportation to the Soviet Union, hand in their weapons at Klagenfurt, Austria.**

Prisoners-of-war were suspect. Why had they surrendered, and not fought to the death? Stalin had hardened his heart over the fate of his own son, disowned because he had fallen prisoner to the Germans; he had died (either by suicide or murdered by British fellow-prisoners) in 1943. Stalin never signed the Geneva Convention to secure proper treatment for Soviet captives, who died in their millions, or survived, numb with fear. Alexander Solzhenitsyn had seen 'the downcast columns of returning war prisoners' in East Prussia – 'the only people around who were grieving and not celebrating'.[4] And it was not only prisoners. Those who had fought their way across Europe had also been exposed to the contamination of bourgeois life. The demobilised soldier might be a subversive time-bomb.

Modern Soviet historians like Mark Gefter echo Solzhenitsyn's view that Stalin saw parallels with the young men who had come home from an earlier war: 'Did he see in the young men in military coats without rank badges a species of future Decembrists, or was he again fearful of becoming unnecessary?'[5] The prestige of the Red Army was very high. It had sustained immense losses, and would do so to the very end of the war. (Stalin had thought nothing of 100,000 casualties in the final assault on Berlin.) What ideas would these troops bring home? 'Tsar Alexander got to Paris,' Stalin said ruefully to Harriman. He would have remembered that the Decembrists who rose against the Tsar were the officers who had also got to Paris, and picked up strange ideas of liberty. So why take chances? Solzhenitsyn, Kopelev, and thousands of other soldiers who invoked momentary suspicion were transformed from heroes to criminals almost overnight.

Whole nationalities were deported and their national republics expunged from the map. The Volga Germans were deported to Siberia. Ingush, Chechens and other Caucasian minorities, some of whom had aspired to independence sponsored by the Germans, followed them in 1943. So did the Crimean Tatars. In all, a million people from seven nationalities were wrenched from their homelands. The population of the labour camps soared. The Baltic states yielded up the victims of the third purge in as many years when they were seized back from the retreating Germans in 1944. The same happened on a grand scale in the Ukraine, where guerrilla warfare against the Soviet state persisted for four years after the war. Ukrainian separatists had fought with, and against, the Germans. In their suppression after 1944 many thousands of innocents were also rounded up. Stalin remarked that he would have deported every Ukrainian if he could, but a country the size of France made this impossible.

He had always been a hard man on the nationalities question. Now, at the climax of the Great Patriotic War, it was the contribution of Russia which he chose to mark in his victory speech, not that of the Soviet peoples as a whole. He who had been a commissar would now be a tsar. German banners were cast down at his feet as he reviewed the June victory parade in Red Square. He awarded himself the title of Generalissimo. A brief, thrifty entry into the war against Japan brought fresh territorial gains, and a shared occupation of Korea. Everything the tsars had aspired to and lost, he had restored.

The cost had been terrible. No full list of war casualties, military and civilian, has ever been produced in the Soviet Union. The commonest general estimate is 25 million dead, if we include those who starved or were killed both on the home front and secretly in the labour camps by the NKVD. Some of the casualties raise too many awkward questions. The latest estimate at the time of writing of military casualties is that 8.5 million men were killed in action, and 2.5 million died of wounds of the 30 million who bore arms. A further 5.8 million were taken prisoner, of whom 3.3 million died in captivity.[6]

**73 The reconstruction of a ravaged country. The Soviet Union in 1945 had lost 20 million dead, together with the majority of its livestock.**

Shattered cities had to be rebuilt, and industry revived. In the areas which had been occupied, production levels were only 30 per cent of pre-war achievements. The level of real wages was no more than half what it had been before Stalin had plunged into collectivisation and industrialisation in the late 1920s. Agriculture had been devastated by the loss of livestock, machinery and manpower. Consumer goods were non-existent. Stalin was right to worry as his armies came home. They had seen that not only the capitalist states, but also the feudal Balkans which they had liberated lived better than they did.

Boris Birger marched with the Red Army into Rumania:

> We knew that Rumania was not the richest country in Europe,
> but the standard of living was incomparable with the standard
> of living in Russia. Besides that, the shops had a great many
> things we'd long forgotten about. And the same in Bulgaria. A
> small country on the edge of Europe and the shops just
> stunned us.

Stalin had the popular acclaim of a war leader, not merely the bought plaudits of toadies. True, he shared it with his victorious generals, like Zhukov. But in the pause of victory, when what existed of public opinion was buoyed up by the returning troops, he could have put himself at its head, identified with its aims. To do this he would have needed substantial dividends from the policy of economic reparations which he advanced against western misgivings at the Potsdam Conference in 1945, and the retention for a long period of western aid. That aid carried strings with which Stalin had no intention of being tied, in a capitalist-dominated world order. Lend-Lease (to the Soviet Union and to Britain) was cut off immediately after the defeat of Japan. The Americans had found the Potsdam agreement on a four-power occupation of Germany a gloomy affair, and were dubious about Stalin's intentions in the Soviet zone. Potsdam itself drove the point home. 'The misery of the place and the conflict between the East and the West hangs over you the whole time,' the American diplomat John McCloy wrote home.[7]

Even if he had had time to weigh up the new western leaders, Truman and Attlee, whom he met at Potsdam, Stalin could not afford to trust them. Since they told him little and late about the atomic bomb and the Manhattan Project it was a fair inference that they did not trust him, and he had another priority which must inevitably clash with close western ties – the restoration of communist ideology within the Soviet Union itself.

Stalin's insistence on the renewal of the leadership of the Party had a double edge. In the war it had had to share primacy with the army, and to make a whole range of compromises with local needs and traditions, just as the Soviet state had made compromises and shared influence with its western allies. Now the army leadership and the wartime alliance could be downgraded. Zhukov and his colleagues were eased out from positions of influence, relegated to obscurity, and to some extent written out of the history books. From the

The Soviet Union
and Eastern Europe
1945–1948

Territory annexed by Russia 1939–1940, and re-incorporated in Russia in 1945

Former German and Czechoslovak territory annexed by Russia in 1945

States liberated by the Soviet army, and in which Communist regimes came to power between 1945 and 1948

Russian occupation zones in Austria (evacuated 1950) and Germany

British, French and American occupation zones

The 'Iron Curtain' in 1948

Frontier of pre-war Germany

Miles
0  100  200

White S.
Solovetski Islands

FINLAND

Vyborg

Belo
Ca

Leningrad

Tallin (Reval)

ESTONIA

Riga
LATVIA

LITHUANIA
Vilna

Königsberg

East
Prussia

Minsk

SOVIET

UNION

Stettin

Berlin

Warsaw
POLAND

GERMANY

Bonn

Dresden

Silesia

Cracow

Galicia

Lvov

Prague

CZECHOSLOVAKIA

FRANCE

Munich

Vienna

AUSTRIA

Budapest

HUNGARY

Bessarabia

Kishinev

SWITZ.

Trieste

YUGOSLAVIA

Belgrade

RUMANIA

Bucharest

Blac
Sea

ITALY

Adriatic Sea

Sofia

BULGARIA

Tirana

ALBANIA

GREECE

Aegean Sea

TURKEY

November 1945 celebrations of the revolution onwards there were few references to the wartime allies. A whole new generation had come forward in genuine idealism to join the Communist Party during the war. By the end of 1945 there were 5.5 million members, including the great mass of that administrative class of functionaries who were known as the Nomenklatura. They were exhorted to use the *'partiinost'* (party spirit) of Leninism, as redefined by Stalin, to restore 'Bolshevik consciousness' and to rebuild Leninism. They were to be the shock troops in the drive against that insidious western influence which Stalin feared had been brought back from the wars. As Deutscher neatly put it: 'His foreign policy was to keep Russia in Europe. His domestic policy was to keep her mind out of Europe.'[8]

**74 Stalin at the Potsdam Conference, 23 July 1945. The resplendent Generalissimo still carries his withered left arm awkwardly.**

Western diplomats in Moscow picked up early warning signals. Frank Roberts was in the British embassy:

> It wasn't high diplomacy, but for me it counted for a lot.
> George Kennan, who was my opposite number at the
> American embassy, and I had a monthly lunch with the then

*Times* correspondent in Moscow, Ray Parker. He afterwards became a communist. So he had rather good connections. One day he told us, I think it must have been April, shortly before the end of the war, that he thought we ought to know that the agitators, the lecturers who went round the factories and places like that to give a lead to the Russian people – which they couldn't quite put in *Pravda* – were stating that it was a pure chance that this war, which was now nearly at an end, had been fought with the English and American allies, against the Germans and Italians. This was pure chance . . . in the peacetime period we were just as much capitalist enemies as the Germans and the Italians and Japanese. But that gave one a feeling of how the Russians were meant to go into the peace and how Stalin himself was going into the peace.

In late 1945, according to his daughter Svetlana, Stalin fell ill. He was well enough to see Truman's informal envoy Averell Harriman at his Black Sea dacha and to talk about the conditions in which Soviet troops might be moved out of their forward occupation bases in Northern Iran and Manchuria. He hinted that there might be more western involvement in his European sphere of influence if he was permitted some say in Japan, where there was no Soviet presence except in the annexed territories. Later Harriman met Maxim Litvinov during an interval at the Bolshoi ballet. Litvinov, the apostle of co-operation with the West, had been lucky to escape with his life when he fell from office in 1939. He had been restored to favour as wartime ambassador to Washington. Now his star was plummeting again. Nothing could be done to prevent a decline in US–USSR relations, he said. 'I know what to do but I am powerless.'[9]

At the last conference of the wartime allies (of foreign ministers) at which he appeared, Stalin was still mixing geniality and demands for fresh bases. If he was anxious about the atomic bomb he hid this well, and appeared to go along with an empty American proposal for a UN commission on the uses of atomic energy. In Europe pro-Soviet communists were in coalition governments in Italy and France, and strong elsewhere. The British Labour government might have been expected to be sympathetic, despite its right-wing leadership. Even in the United States pro-Soviet sentiment was still strong. Stalin, however, was now about to help his ideological opponents in the west

1  Bolshevik poster urging a 'harvest' of the Poles and the White Russian army of General Wrangel.

2  1930s poster spurs collective workers to greater efforts. The 'MTS' (Machine Tractor Stations) allocated resources and policed agricultural collectivisation.

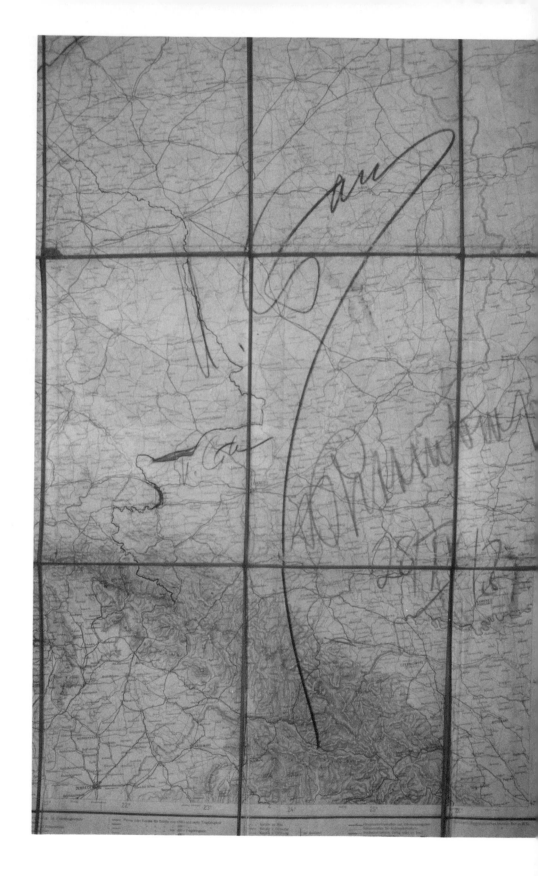

**8 (above)** Churchill, the dying Roosevelt and Stalin meet for the last time at Yalta. Stalin provided the lavish setting and called the tune.

**7 (left)** The map which accompanied the September 1939 Nazi–Soviet Friendship Treaty. Stalin has crudely crayoned in an attempted extension of the Russian zone of occupation in Poland, and autographed his endeavours.

9 Stalin and his heirs in the full glory of Socialist Realism, 1950. To his right: Malenkov, Kaganovich, Beria. To his left: Voroshilov, Molotov, Mikoyan and Khrushchev.

(who needed little enough excuse) to fashion what soon became known as the 'Cold War'.

On 9 February 1946 Stalin appeared at the Bolshoi Theatre to read out his election speech as a candidate for the Supreme Soviet. The war, he now said, had been a triumph of the superior Soviet system. Capitalism led inevitably to war and periodic crisis. It was for the Soviet Union to be vigilant, well-prepared and self-reliant. There was no talk of further disarmament.

A new Five Year Plan would be massively directed towards heavy industry. Huge targets were set for the production of coal, steel, oil and cement – all met during this and subsequent plans. This restored Soviet economy was to be buttressed by a dependent satellite system in Eastern Europe. In all the countries wholly or largely liberated by the Red Army, Soviet troops had stayed behind as the agents of change. The old social order had been thrown into disarray. Those who had by coalition or collaboration helped the Axis cause had been purged or had fled. The right-wing resistance movements, such as they were, were sidetracked and purged in their turn.

**75 Stalin was portrayed as presiding over vast plans to change the landscape and improve the harvest, mainly influenced by the quack biologist Lysenko. The slogan reads 'And We Will Conquer Drought'**

In Bulgaria, Hungary, Poland, Rumania, Yugoslavia and Albania the communists installed themselves in charge of the army and the police. Smaller parties were drawn into 'fronts', larger ones purged or banned. In the Soviet zone of Germany, stripped for reparations, the Social Democrats were banned. Only in Czechoslovakia, with its strong democratic traditions, and a government which had both stayed in London and been recognised by Stalin, was there a genuine, freely elected government in which the communists played the largest part.

In Hungary, by contrast, where the communists had polled only 16 per cent of the votes in a free election, there was never any question that they would not dominate the government, just as the Red Army dominated the country. Elections were not held in Poland and Rumania. As the west saw it, these events constituted a series of violations of the Yalta agreement. Stalin came from a different school. The revolution from above, which his armies and security police were imposing, caused no qualms to the former Commissar for Nationalities. Spheres of influence were to be used. He had been magnanimous with Finland. He was to pull his armies out of Iran and North Korea. Why should he, who believed in the revolution of the workers which would overthrow late capitalism, not help it along in countries so vital to the security of the Soviet Union?

There now followed a downward spiral of cause and effect, corkscrewing its way through the post-war settlement. The American diplomat George Kennan, musing in Moscow on Soviet intentions after Stalin's speech, sent his 'Long Telegram' to the State Department in February 1946 – 'the most influential cable in the history of the American Foreign Service'.[10]

He warned that Russian intentions were a mixture of ancient Russian insecurity fused with the ideology of Marxism. The Russians would see what they wanted to see abroad: states which both threatened them and were ripe to be undermined on class lines, as the clashes within capitalism developed. They were 'impervious to the logic of reason' but 'highly sensitive to the logic of force'. This telegram was widely circulated, and seized upon by those who saw recent defections and unmasked spy rings as pointing in the same global direction. Just weeks later, a public man underlined these private warnings in crude but vivid language.

Winston Churchill at Fulton, Missouri made his 'Iron Curtain' speech, with President Truman in the audience. He portrayed a new darkness fallen upon Eastern Europe, Soviet ambitions which must be resisted from a position of strength, and warned against any UN role in the management of atomic weaponry. There were many who thought that he wanted to suck the USA into a new Anglo-American policing role, in the interests of the British Empire, but contemporary events seemed to reinforce his words. On the day of the speech the press was full of a Canadian spy ring and Russian troop movements in Iran. Stalin responded with a polemic of his own. It was Churchill who sought world dominion, not he. The Eastern European states were peoples' democracies, not to be slandered. To signal his lack of expansionist intent Soviet troops were withdrawn from Iran, and Stalin had to watch the local communists there slaughtered by the Iranian government afterwards, as he had already allowed the British to eliminate the Greek Left in 1944.

76 Winston Churchill at Fulton, Missouri, March 1946, where he spoke of the new 'Iron Curtain' across Europe, before an attentive Harry Truman (*right*).

The age of blocs was dawning, and both sides carry responsibility for it. Open attacks on the Soviet Union increased Stalin's sense of isolation and his innate paranoia. He was playing from a weak hand until he had acquired and tested the atomic bomb. Thanks to his agents in Britain, Canada and the USA, and the captured German scientists who worked for him, he was closer to success than anyone knew. Despite a massive demobilisation, he had retained the largest land army in the world, although there was a desperate need for manpower on the home front. This was not enough. The instinct to close off his society from the west was overwhelming. Planes could not fly in. Those unfortunate Russians who had married foreigners could not move out. Tom Whitney was in the US embassy and later became a journalist in Moscow:

> Every dispatch that we sent by telegraph, or by telephone, or by mail out of the Soviet Union had first to be submitted to a Soviet censorship office . . . it had to have a censor's stamp of approval. Naturally, censors being people themselves, human beings who did not wish to have retribution visited on them for something that had their stamp on it – because there was a number and an initial or something like that that identified every individual censor – they were naturally over-cautious. . . . We ourselves were afraid to have contacts with ordinary Soviet people, by and large, because this could immediately lead to them being arrested. And we were surrounded by situations in which people were actually arrested and removed – they disappeared, and they were gone. Soviet employees in the American embassy – people with whom we were acquainted often-times.

Within the Soviet Union a new attack on nonconformists was launched, striking at the intelligentsia. Stalin was close to Andrei Zhdanov, the Leningrad Party chief – so close that he repeatedly urged his daughter to marry Zhdanov's son, which she did with her usual independence only after Zhdanov was dead. In the summer of 1946, Zhdanov launched a ferocious attack on two Leningrad writers: Anna Akhmatova and Mikhail Zoshchenko. Anna Akhmatova's first husband, the poet Nikolai Gumilev, had been shot in 1921. Her second husband and son had been sent to the camps, and her son, after release for war service, had been rearrested. She had not been published for twenty years before the war. After it, briefly tolerated, her poetry readings had been hugely popular in Moscow and Leningrad. So had the satirical work of Mikhail Zoshchenko.

**77** Zhdanov, scourge of the artists and intelligentsia, in full cry. On the left, Trofim Lysenko.

Zhdanov denounced him as an evil-intentioned hooligan, and Akhmatova as 'half-nun, half-whore'. The leaders of the Leningrad literary establishment were hauled off to Moscow to see Stalin who told them that the culprits had 'fallen under the influence of the petty-bourgeois ideology of literature hostile to us'.[11] The journals which published them 'do not have the right to adapt themselves to the taste of people who do not wish to recognise our regime'. Zhdanov, arbiter of all things cultural, launched his polemic against writers and musicians, and presumed to instruct Shostakovich and Prokofiev on correct socialist music. Behind him, though, was always the hand of Stalin. The old dictator had been a poet in his youth. He found time to read poets and novelists, as he had in the 1930s, and took them seriously. On occasion a favourable clearance from Zhdanov had to be overruled when the *Vozhd* took a different line. Hand in heavy hand with this discipline was a crude insensitivity for western artists and intellectuals. Svetlana reports her father's crony Kaganovich listening to Menuhin and Oistrakh playing Bach's 'Concerto for Two Violins': 'Suddenly Kaganovich turned to me and winked: 'See how our boy is beating the American!'''[12]

**78 & 79** Two victims
of Stalinist repression
— Anna Akhmatova and
Alexander Solzhenitsyn.

It is unlikely that Stalin ever realised how much the good opinion of Soviet Russia held by western intellectuals was dissipated by his intolerance. The prominence given to ludicrous boasts about Soviet inventions and the persecution of those who criticised Stalin's favourite quack biologist, Trofim Lysenko (including Zhdanov's own son), also left him isolated. The distance he sought from the west lent no enchantment to his image there. Western journalists like Tom Whitney found Lysenko's dominance both sinister and laughable: 'The assertion was even made that chromosomes and genes do not exist. They are fabrications of bourgeois science. Anybody could look into a microscope and see them, but they did not exist in the Soviet Union.'

Thus was the scene set for the cold year of 1947. In Russia there was once more the spectre of famine. The peasants had been pushed back into collectives. Currency reform wiped out their savings. (The old currency was exchanged for new at the ratio of 10 to 1.) When Khrushchev complained to Stalin that his Ukrainian fief faced starvation, Stalin's response was to send Kaganovich from Moscow to step up the repressions. Soviet destitution was far worse than anything endured in Western Europe, but there too governments appeared shaken by severe strains on war-weakened economies. The British were obliged to abandon their independent administration of their zone of Germany, and to hand over to the United States what were seen as their obligations to the Greek Right in the civil war in that country.

Germany was prostrate, much of its production in effect legally looted as reparations by the Soviet Union, Poland, France and Belgium. The closer British and American interests became in Germany, the more Stalin feared that their 'Bizone' would rebuild a new, capitalist state. With that he would make no deals. The hope that there might be a genuine four-power agreement on the future of Germany under joint administration diminished to zero. And when President Truman not merely picked up Britain's obligations to Greece and Turkey, but cast it in ideological terms in the Truman Doctrine, the screw of Cold War was turned still further. Anti-communism was boosted in the United States, production of atomic bombs was increased, and the National Security Council and CIA were set up. (In its first monthly 'situation report' the CIA claimed that the Soviet Union was 'presently incapable of military aggression outside Europe and Asia' but was 'deliberately conducting political, economic and psychological warfare against the United States'.[13])

True to his deal with Churchill, Stalin had done nothing to aid the Greek communists; he had left that to the Bulgarians and the Yugoslavs. But he was unlikely to ignore this new note in the voice of America.

That voice now spoke to Europe, West and East, of a European Recovery Plan which would boost European markets and export trade through American cash investment. As European production grew, so it would earn back what it had first received in subsidy. The plan was open to Soviet and Eastern European participation, but at the cost of ending their self-imposed economic isolation. As such it was unacceptable to Stalin, and the fact was well-known before the offer was made.

Stalin had believed that there would be another crisis of western capitalism after the war, as the capitalist countries struggled for markets. Here was the largest capitalist country offering to invest in the creation of a more integrated market for all. There was never any chance that he would accept Marshall Aid, as it came to be called. The obedient satellites fell into line. Only in Czechoslovakia, where the communists ruled in coalition, was there a prolonged and genuine debate. The Czech communist leader, Klement Gottwald, was summoned to Moscow to be given his orders – no deal. Marshall Aid passed the US Congress and achieved another purpose too. Europe became more divided; communists ceased to participate in any western coalition. The last shreds of democracy fell away in Eastern Europe.

Strictly speaking, what happened in Czechoslovakia in February 1948 was not a *coup*. The non-communist ministers resigned from the government, hoping to bring about its fall on the issue of communist interference with the police. Instead, the communist ministers stayed put, calling out street demonstrations and the workers' militia in their support. President Benes, a dying man, gave way. A communist government was installed with Jan Masaryk, son of the founder of Czechoslovakia, as non-party foreign minister. Within weeks he was found dead on the pavement beneath his window. No one knew if he had jumped or been pushed: whether it was suicide, murder by the Czech security police, or by their Soviet counterparts. Instead of open elections in May, there was the familiar pattern of a new constitution and voting for a single 'coalition' list under extreme coercion. The model was Stalinist; the slogan: 'With the Soviet Union for all time!'[14] Stalin undoubtedly approved but he did not instigate the February *coup*. He may not have known or cared how the backwash of this event spread out over Europe. Unless Britain and the US acted together, Ernest Bevin mused, 'Italy would go next.'[15]

**80 Marshall and Molotov drink a toast, London 1947. Despite the exploratory meeting, the Soviets turned down Marshall Aid – to private US relief.**

There was now another twist of the downward spiral. Those countries where Stalin had still felt he should tread carefully because of western sensitivity (Czechoslovakia, Poland and Hungary) began to lose their remaining pluralism. All the peoples' democracies, as they were often ironically called, began to take on the same characteristics. The Cominform set up in 1946 to facilitate co-operation between these countries and western parties, began to look dangerously like the old Comintern. This alarmed the west, and its hysteria fed Stalin's own neuroses about who was reliable and who was not.

He had his own cavalier way with national identity. When a Yugoslav delegation, including Milovan Djilas, came to visit him in 1948, he told them that it was time Yugoslavia absorbed Albania. This was the reverse of his real intention, but he was testing the Yugoslavs: 'He said, "We have agreed that you should swallow Albania." And I said, "It's not a matter of swallowing, it's a matter of unification." Molotov said, "But that is swallowing." '

Two months later, Stalin was firing off angry letters to Tito about Yugoslav insubordination. The Yugoslavs in their turn stayed away from the Cominform, and began an open show of defiance, buttressed by their greater degree of popular support. The pro-Russian faction of the Yugoslav party was eliminated over the next year, driving Stalin to a greater frenzy in his search for heretics, Titoists and Trotskyite wreckers allied to western imperialism. Devotion to the 'great Stalin' was to become as much a feature of the satellites as it was of the Motherland. A Pole who was then a communist cadre sums up the result:

> One thing is certain: if Stalin did not believe in the prospect
> of winning genuine political support of the population in
> the foreseeable future, and wanted to rely on the complete
> dependence of the East European leadership on him, he could
> not have chosen a better, more diabolically cunning method
> than that actually chosen: by imposing Stalinism on Eastern
> Europe he obtained not only a system of direct command over
> the entire institutional structure, but also a double grip on the
> local leadership – faithful and at the same time sufficiently
> alienated from their own people.[16]

As his quarrel with Tito developed, Stalin was (perhaps luckily for Tito) enmeshed in the Berlin crisis. The western powers were merging their zones perceptibly into a three-power entity. The Soviet zone stood apart. Economic conditions were diverging. A measure of prosperity was restored to the western zones as American aid was pumped into them. The Soviet zone, stripped for reparations, remained prostrate. Deep in the Soviet zone lay the old capital Berlin, itself divided into zones, which it had been intended should be the capital of a unified four-power administration. Stalin feared the re-emergence of a strong Germany, and was suspicious of any move to this end. When the western powers introduced a currency reform in their zones, the new heavier Mark obviously threatened to make the Soviet-backed currency worthless in the one area where both were traded – Berlin. West Berlin had long been an irritant to Stalin. In June 1948 he initiated a land blockade of the city, as an each-way bet. Either the west would be forced to pull out of the city altogether as it starved, or they would have to abandon currency reform and move towards a united West Germany.

**81 Lifeline to Berlin. The 1948–9 airlift defeated Stalin's blockade.**

It was a miscalculation of western airpower and ability to continue to bring supplies through the recognised air corridor – which he could only shut off by forcing down planes and provoking war. His old caution reasserted itself, the supply planes were not touched and winter for once did not come to Stalin's aid.

His fears about what kind of Germany might emerge from the

unifications of western zones were not unreasonable. What he could not see was the impression that the blockade made on the west. It looked like a crude territorial grab. The last steps on the road to a North Atlantic Treaty specifically aimed at 'containing' the Soviet Union and reintegrating the USA in a European military alliance were taken in the fateful autumn of 1948. Neither side can escape blame. It took two to make the quarrel. Stalin's inflexibility and isolationism intensified – and were in turn intensified by – the west's suspicion of him.

# 8 TWILIGHT OF A GOD

I'm finished. I trust no one, not even myself.[1]

J. V. Stalin to Khrushchev, 1951

The dacha had no park, no garden, no elegantly trimmed bushes or trees. Stalin loved nature as it is, untouched by the hand of man. . . . Not far away stood several hollow, limbless trunks, and houses for birds and squirrels were arranged in them – a veritable birds' kingdom. Stalin would come out nearly every day to feed the birds.[2]

General S. M. Shtemenko:
*The Soviet General Staff at War*

We travelled to Moscow together on the train that November of 1948. . . . As we pulled in at the various stations we'd go for a stroll along the platform. My father walked as far as the engine, giving greeting to the railway workers as he went. You couldn't see a single passenger, it was a special train and no one was allowed on the platform. It was a sinister, sad, depressing sight. Whoever thought such a thing up? Who had contrived all these stratagems? Not he. It was the system of which he himself was a prisoner and in which he was stifling from loneliness, emptiness and lack of human companionship.[3]

Svetlana Alliluyeva: *Twenty Letters to a Friend*

How did Stalin live and work in the last years of his life? Which of these vivid glimpses best conveys the atmosphere in which he lived, and made his decisions? He lived simply. He had no wants, for all was taken care of by his household. His salaries for his various offices were simply stuffed, in their unopened envelopes, into a drawer. In the Generalissimo's circle at least, money had ceased to exist. Train journeys of the kind described by Svetlana were rarities. On them his isolation was total. Gennadi Beglov was on duty on the line through Tula in 1947:

> The most important thing of all was to ensure that at the moment when Stalin's train went through your strip of land there should not be seen a single living person. The brigade was ordered to shoot anybody who appeared at that moment. . . . I suddenly heard a pistol shot. A young lad of fourteen or fifteen had emerged on to the strip to retrieve a blazing coal which had fallen from a passing train . . . My comrade, acting on orders, killed the boy with one shot. Then half an hour later an enormous locomotive thundered past at tremendous speed, with three carriages with lighted windows but the blinds pulled down, and obviously in one of them sat Stalin.

In his villas there were always different bedrooms to choose from at the last moment, cronies to taste the food, limousines to alter direction unexpectedly, but always away from the crowd. Alexander Solzhenitsyn wrote that he disguised the paranoia of these precautions by forcing the rest of the hierarchy to carry out similar evasions.[4]

Nikita Khrushchev's memoirs have an unforgettable picture of the fear and loathing around the lonely old dictator as his key colleagues were summoned out to another long evening of films, feasting and crude horseplay. The rotund Khrushchev was made to dance the 'Gopak' on his haunches. He kept smiling through. 'As I later told Anastas Ivanovich Mikoyan, "When Stalin says dance, a wise man dances."'[5] Stalin was happy to carouse for half the night, knowing that he could sleep it off while the wretched guests were back at their desks. For someone in frail health like Zhdanov, these evenings were a life-shortening experience.

Seeing enemies at home and abroad, Stalin began to behave once more like the Stalin of the 1930s. His Politburo colleagues knew that he had not actually killed any of them for a decade, but the killer instinct was dormant, not dead. In the strained times of 1948 it stirred. 'You come to Stalin's table as a friend,' said Bulganin, 'but you never know if you'll go home by yourself or if you'll be given a ride – to prison.'[6] He played cat-and-mouse with his visitors. In 1948 Marshal Zhukov was summoned back from his obscure command. He found Stalin holding a memorandum from Beria, the long-

**82 Lavrenti Beria, a man of unbridled appetites and ambitions, with terror at his beck and call.**

serving security agency chief, which said that the marshal had been an agent of British intelligence for fifteen years!

> Stalin kept moving about the room. He stopped next to me and put his hand on my shoulder. 'I don't believe this about you. But you can see for yourself – there are two signatures and some typist did this copy. Two or three people on my staff have read it. You yourself can understand it would be awkward to let you stay in Moscow.[7]

On another occasion Khrushchev records him as saying of two wrongly imprisoned aviation officials (one of whom had been denounced by Stalin's alcoholic son Vasili): '"Say, are Shakurin and Novikov still in jail?" "Yes." "Don't you think it might be all right to release them?" '[8] Was he playing a game by asking such a question of Beria, who was in charge of the case against them? Or was it that an old man forgot, and fretted? No one knew. No one could be sure.

Westerners who negotiated with him over the Berlin Blockade in 1948 did not find him forgetful at all. Frank Roberts was impressed. 'He always knew his brief perfectly, knew exactly what he wanted . . . he wouldn't make it an essential issue but he would say: "Don't forget that is my interest." . . . I used to count my fingers when I went to negotiate with Stalin to make sure I'd got them all when I came out.'

Milovan Djilas saw Stalin for the last time in 1948, and could compare him with the self-confident war leader of four years before:

> Stalin had changed completely, physically and mentally. He
> was now the complete opposite of how he had been when I had
> seen him during the war, 1944, 1945. He was a weakened man,
> physically weakened, mentally weakened. . . . Fair enough,
> he would forget names, which for a man of his age isn't
> unusual. But he would mix up states, he would mix up ideas,
> he had no order in his presentation of things. He would jump
> from one subject to another. . . . I had the impression that the
> war had somehow been his last inner mental and physical
> motivation, that in the war he had experienced his physical
> cataclysm; he held on until the end of the war and when it
> ended his physical and spiritual powers ended too. And at
> that time he was at the very peak of his power.

It is the Stalin portrayed in Solzhenitsyn's *The First Circle*, exhausted, brooding, muddled, forever vindictive. He had always had a strong streak of anti-semitism, which came out in tirades to his children about their Jewish spouses or lovers. But he was on the record as saying in 1931 that: 'Communists, as consistent internationalists, cannot but be consistent and sworn enemies of anti-semitism.'[9] In old age he reverted to a casual anti-semitism while still coarsely teasing others for the failing. Djilas fell victim to this on his last visit:

> Stalin expressed this anti-semitism of his in a two-faced way,
> accusing others, apparently in fun, of being anti-semitic.
> For instance, he asked me why there were no Jews on our
> central committee, save one, Pijade, and I told him: 'Force of
> circumstance, because of the way the party developed.' And
> he laughed and said, 'Djilas you're anti-semitic. Can't you see
> he's anti-semitic' – and his staff were proud of the fact that
> Zhdanov had 'cleansed' the Central Committee of Jews.

This 'cleansing' put the Jews in the forefront of the new victims of the regime. They were a convenient scapegoat when things went wrong – Stalin even suggested to Khrushchev that aviation workers' discontent could be diverted if they were issued with 'clubs so they can beat hell out of those Jews at the end of the working day'.[10]

And there was now an international dimension. Russia had been the first state to recognise Israel, but Stalin rapidly came to see Israel as an American stalking-horse, and Zionists as conspirators against him. The enthusiastic reception among the Soviet Jewry for Golda Meir, when she came to Moscow as Israeli foreign minister, must have preyed on Stalin's mind. A vicious press campaign against 'rootless cosmopolitans' began. The members of the Jewish Anti-Fascist Committee, which had worked hard to further the Soviet cause among Jews worldwide, became suspect at once. Solomon Lozovsky was a Party activist trusted with the running of the Committee. He was arrested with his colleagues, and most of them were shot. The great Soviet Yiddish actor, Solomon Mikhoels, was murdered in a fake road accident. Maxim Litvinov would almost certainly have been assassinated in the same way. Lucky to the last, he thwarted Stalin by dying a natural death, murmuring to his wife, 'Englishwoman, go home.'[11]

New 'crimes' made their appearance, including 'praising American democracy' and 'kowtowing to the west'. If Jews were under suspicion for their alleged foreign links, so were all Soviet citizens who belonged to that wider world of culture: Kapitsa the scientist, Pasternak the poet, Eisenstein the film director. The new wave of arrests and purges after 1948 effectively terrorised the population, without needing the boundless numbers of the 1930s purges.

Harrison Salisbury came to Moscow as a journalist in 1949. He knew the city well from wartime, and thought he had many friends there:

> I'd first gone to Moscow in 1944, during the war. At that time
> of course we were all allies, the Russians, the English, the
> Americans. And despite many difficulties there was a certain
> camaraderie and a feeling of being together. Five years later,
> when I returned in 1949, all of that was gone. . . . I had many
> friends in Moscow, that I had met during the war. I telephoned
> several of them. Either the telephone didn't answer, or when
> they heard my voice they hung up. . . . As I walked down Gorky
> Street, not infrequently I would meet someone whom I had met
> during the war. At first I tried to speak to them, but they would
> look right through me and go straight ahead without speaking.

> I quickly understood it was too dangerous to talk to me. I
> was regarded by that time by the police and the government, I
> suppose, as a dangerous espionage agent. Every foreign
> correspondent, in fact I suppose every foreigner in Moscow,
> was so regarded. And for any Russian to have a contact with
> me was equivalent almost certainly to arrest and possibly a
> one-way ticket to Siberia.

Zhdanov had done Stalin's bidding all his days. Now the Leningrad
Party chief and hammer of the intelligentsia died in his turn – a rare
natural death which inevitably became shrouded in rumour. Stalin
turned on the Leningrad Party. He had never liked the second city of
the USSR, with its pretensions and its proximity to the west. It had
been in Leningrad that Zhdanov had launched his campaign against
the writers Akhmatova and Zoshchenko and the journals which
published them in 1946. Now there were secondary cells of this
cancer.

The Party leaders had taken Leningrad through the terrible days
of the great siege. They were innocent of the conspiracies of which
they were now accused. It did not save them. The Leningrad Party
secretary A. A. Kuznetsov and all his principal aides were shot. So
was the Prime Minister of the Russian Federal Republic, and the
Chairman of State Planning, Nikolai Voznesensky, the most talented
of the generation pushing into Stalin's inner circle, and deeply
resented for it. After a decade without arbitrary death touching
them, that circle saw people of almost equivalent rank first isolated
and cowed, then arrested and shot. (The death penalty, formally
abolished, was restored for treason, and so these judicial murders
could take place.) Beria's hand was in it, Khrushchev alleges. But
Beria, the sinister police chief and paedophile, whose Georgians had
long surrounded Stalin, was himself under a cloud. Was Molotov's
wife a foreign agent, or Voroshilov? If that was what the *Vozhd*
thought of these oldest of Old Bolsheviks, loyal to him through every
purge and plot, who was safe? As the great purges got under way in
Eastern Europe in 1949 they must have had even more troubled
hours.

In 1949, Stalin had his wife's sisters arrested. They were harmless
and apolitical, but one had produced a chatty memoir with a
down-to-earth portrait of Stalin. Svetlana asked him why: 'He said,

"They knew too much and they talked too much. That is helping our enemies." In these later times he was completely mistrustful of everybody, including myself. Those were the last years of his life, which were very dark times for the whole country.'

Stalin could not lay his hands on the man who most vexed him now – at least since one of his creatures had sunk an ice-pick into Trotsky's skull. He had, by his own standards, wooed and flattered Tito. Belgrade had housed the Cominform. There had been talk of a Balkan federation, the sly disingenuous advice to 'swallow' Albania. But Tito was no puppet. He would not let the Russians operate without restraint in his territory. When reproved he answered back. Solzhenitsyn's fiction comes close to the fact of Stalin's rage.

> How could they have been so mistaken about this snake in the grass? Those were great days in 'thirty-six and 'thirty-seven when they had chopped off so many heads – yet they had let Tito go . . . Joseph Stalin had met his match in Joseph Broz-Tito. The fact that Kerensky was alive somewhere had never worried Stalin. He would not have cared if Nicholas II or Kolchak had come back from the grave – he had nothing against them personally: they had been avowed enemies, they had never had the impertinence to offer their own brand of a new and better socialism. Better socialism! . . . In other words different from Stalin's! The little guttersnipe! How could you have socialism without Stalin?[12]

Elsewhere in what was now called the socialist camp those who perhaps wanted socialism without Stalinism were going to their deaths. Sometimes they had wanted to slow collectivisation, to discuss Marshall Aid, or to reach a concordat with the Church. Or perhaps they had a sneaking sympathy for Tito.

In Bulgaria Kostov, in Hungary Rajk, in Czechoslovakia Clementis – all were sacrificed to the Stalinist Moloch. Only in the newest and largest member of the fraternal communist world was there a party which could say, like Tito's, that it owed Stalin very little and had come to power by itself. The People's Republic of China had surprised Stalin, its shifty step-parent, by being born so swiftly. He had not anticipated it, had assumed and argued that a truce with the Kuomintang government should be achieved. It would have left a weakened China, split for the immediate future between Chiang and Mao. Mao Tse-tung, however, pressed on to

**83 The heretic denounced.** *Krokodil* presents the new official view of Tito, after Yugoslavia's break with the Cominform. 'I have only to lift my little finger,' Stalin told Khrushchev, 'and there will be no more Tito.'

take the whole country, and the people's republic thus proclaimed in October 1949 was seen in the United States as a Soviet rook to add to the pawns of Eastern Europe. The concerns of the Cold War shifted from containment in Europe to global confrontation with communism, and in the USA a new anti-communist frenzy developed, with a paranoia matching Stalin's own. Mao and the North Korean leader, Kim Il Sung, followed their own roads, committed to the complete removal of right-wing forces from their countries, whether Stalin wanted it or not.

84  Laszlo Rajk on trial for his life in Budapest, September 1949. This was one of a series of show trials of national communists throughout Eastern Europe, who were thought to be insufficiently accommodating to Stalin's needs.

In the west these distinctions were rarely made. Stalin's isolation, and the grotesque purges of Eastern Europe, were seen as the threatening shape of revolution for export, not as a spasm within the 'revolution from above' that Stalin had imposed. Internationally, the old man moved with a caution which contrasted with the mounting fury of his attacks on enemies within. Stalin signalled his willingness to end the Berlin Blockade in May 1949, and the land route was opened with a unified western German state more likely than ever to be brought into being. The Russians finally accepted that the best they would get would be one of two German states with the proclamation of the German Democratic Republic (DDR) in the same year.

For all his rhetoric, he did not send the Red Army into Yugoslavia after the Cominform called for Tito's overthrow. And when Kim Il Sung came to Moscow in March 1949, Soviet forces having been withdrawn from Korea ahead of the American troops in the south, he did not conclude a defence treaty with Kim, although he must have known that Kim intended to try a pre-emptive strike in what Moscow would see as a Korean civil war. Mao, Kim and the Vietnamese Ho Chi Minh were Asian nationalists, not open to the control which Stalin exercised over the vassal states of Eastern Europe. In the United States, however, they were seen as his puppets by the Republican opposition, and by some in the Truman adminis- tration. The Soviet explosion of an atomic bomb in September 1949, breaking the west's monopoly, also increased pressure in the west for a new arms race, although it had been obvious from 1945 onwards that Stalin would get his hands on nuclear technology, and redress the one balance that conspicuously stood in the west's favour.

The arrival of Mao Tse-tung for Stalin's seventieth birthday celebrations might have provided a clue. The Generalissimo was drenched in adulation. At the Bolshoi Theatre he sat with the Moscow Party chief Khrushchev on his left and a bewildered Mao on his right, as schoolchildren fluted their praise and his aides vied with each other in sycophancy. Khrushchev's own unctuous effort de- serves resurrection:

> Like a careful gardener, Comrade Stalin cultivates and trains
> his personnel in a spirit of ardent Soviet patriotism. He has
> taught and is teaching them the Bolshevist mode of work and
> sharp implacability towards the slightest manifestation of
> alien bourgeois ideology towards the ideology of bourgeois
> nationalism, rootless cosmopolitanism and servility before
> decadent bourgeois culture.[13]

85  Stalin, flanked by
Mao, Voroshilov, Ulbricht
and Khrushchev, listens to
birthday tributes in the
Bolshoi Theatre.

86  Stalin's seventieth
birthday extravaganza in
Moscow, December 1949.

The display of presents took over the Museum of the Revolution. (Mao, in his gnomic way, had arrived with a bag of onions; a rare variety, he explained, which would make your enemy think well of you!) *Pravda* took two years to publish all the greetings. Stalin's daughter, who believes that he himself had despised and disliked the more grotesque aspects of the Cult, was angered by its falsification.

> All those terrible statues and portraits made from some kind of idea that the man was great and big and had huge shoulders and looked like a massive rock of granite. . . . In fact he had a very unathletic figure, with drooping shoulders and quite stooped in his later years, not that mighty at all. A figure of an intellectual, you know, who never did sports.

But by now, the old man in the Kremlin, surrounded only by yes-men, had come to believe his own myth in the bloated terms in which it was purveyed. The Cult was now at its highest point. No one, young or old, escaped it. Pavel Litvinov (grandson of Maxim) was a schoolboy then:

> Stalin was like God for us. We just believed he was an absolutely perfect individual, and he lived somewhere in the Kremlin, a light always in his window, and he was thinking about us, about each of us. That was how we felt. For example, somebody told me that Stalin could be the best surgeon. He could perform a brain operation better than anyone else, and I believed it. I knew that he was busy with other things, but if he wanted to do it he would be better.

Mao ungraciously stayed on in Moscow for a further two months until he got the economic assistance agreement he needed, but on such harsh terms that he made no attempt to hide his dismay when he was filmed at its signature alongside the grinning, shuffling Stalin. His reflections on his two months in Moscow have not been recorded, but his face on the visual record tells its own story.

Stalin and Mao both had wind of what might happen in Korea that year, but events were to take a turn which they may not have anticipated, and which forced further decisions from them through a bitter war. Stalin, who bitterly resented the pro-western majority which the Americans could command at the United Nations, had ordered his delegation to boycott the Security Council in protest at the UN's failure to seat the Chinese communist government and eject Chiang's rump regime now entrenched on Formosa. When Kim Il Sung staged his blitzkreig against the rickety, corrupt South Korean government the Russians seemed to be taken by surprise. The Security Council met, and condemned North Korean aggression. South Korea had been set up on the legitimacy of a UN-sponsored election. The Americans, with Berlin fresh in their minds, thought the invasion was a Soviet probe by proxy. They pushed through a Security Council resolution calling for UN action to repel the aggressors. The chair of the Soviet delegate, Jacob Malik, remained empty. There was no Russian veto. Andrei Gromyko claimed in his memoirs that Stalin specifically overruled the Soviet foreign ministry, and the Soviet absence was on his direct orders.

It is possible to see this as another example of the paralysis of an administration in an old man's faltering hands. It is equally possible that Stalin was glad to see the USA embroiled, at no cost to himself,

**87 The empty chair of the Soviet delegate during the UN Security Council debate on Korea, June 1950.**

and reasoned that if they lost their prestige everywhere would suffer, whilst if they looked like winning, the Chinese would be forced into the war before there was any threat to the Chinese (and Russian) borders of North Korea. Whether planned or not, this was the course of events. The Chinese were drawn in, with terrible losses including Mao's own son, before they and the American-led UN forces fought each other to a bloody standstill. Soviet advisers had been pulled back when the war began, but Soviet and Eastern European volunteers fought on the side of the North Koreans. How much did Stalin plan events, and how much was he helplessly carried along by them? The question parallels the one asked about him by his aides in the Soviet Union itself. Did he know what he was doing, or not? As long as either hypothesis could be argued, the fear he inspired, and the power he held, remained vast.

This was the more so because by 1950 Stalinist reconstruction envisaged in the fourth Five Year Plan was coming into effect. Prices were cut and wages rose from 1948 until Stalin's death to give 'a sharp and striking increase in living standards'.[14] These improvements had been brought about by immense toil and further sacrifice on the part of the Soviet population. Armaments expenditure had been reduced until 1949, although the Soviet Union had retained large conventional forces. After 1950 it was the dramatic acceleration of US rearmament which helped to push the Soviet Union into a new and costly arms race, actually giving it the offensive capacity it had not had at the outset.[15]

Heavy industry and the transport system were rebuilt. A series of grandiose public works – the Volga–Don Canal, the Turkmenian Canal, the huge 'wedding cake' public buildings of Moscow – were put under construction. All across the Soviet Union the great empire of the Gulag supplied a captive labour force. The camps had filled after the war. Prisoners-of-war, 'Vlasovites', deported Balts from occupied Latvia, Lithuania and Estonia, and the 'politicals' sentenced for anti-Soviet activities were jumbled in with every kind of common criminal.

The futility of the Gulag in Stalin's last years has been bitterly summed up by two Soviet authors:

> In the most extreme and cruel forms which the administrative system took in the Stalin period, it represented a 'labour camp

**88  Korea. Cold War turned hot.** *Krokodil*'s view of Churchill discarding the club of
General MacArthur for the axe of his replacement, General Ridgway.

economy'. According to some estimates, at various times there were in the camps from 10 to 15 million prisoners, and in fact at the time of Stalin's death 12 million – i.e. between a fifth and a quarter of those engaged in material production.

If you add to this about 35 million peasants who had been attached to the land, whose conditions of work differed little from those of the camps, then one could say that in Stalin's time close to four-fifths of the entire economy was based on a form of non-economic compulsion, the least effective method of organising the economy known to history.[16]

It was slave labour which toiled on projects like the Salekhard-Igarka Railway. At section 501 one of the many prison revolts took place in 1951.

These Arctic camps remain today, a ghostly presence among the encroaching birches, their watch-towers memorials to untold suffering. The Salekhard journalist Alexander Khersonsky has begun to write about the futility of the work on section 501:

> What on earth was it for? This was a question that was frequently asked, and the answer that was given was that the railway was started for the sake of doing something with the prisoners. . . . They decided to build a railway. Of course all this was a little bit erroneous. The whole of our country was, practically speaking, a camp. This was the way that the Dnepropetrovsk and Magnitka electric schemes on the Amur River and virtually all the colossal building projects of the time were done. This was considered to be a cheap labour force.

The railway led nowhere, achieved nothing and was never finished.

As so often under Stalin, the peasants in the countryside suffered for the system's sake. The collective farms were being merged in the belief that bigger meant better. Huge afforestation schemes were lauded on the principle that Stalin could even change the landscape. The theories of Lysenko, endorsed by Stalin, were used to bludgeon plant geneticists who might have been able to improve Soviet agriculture. One favoured reform – associated with Khrushchev – would have removed the peasants from their villages altogether, to resettle them in agro-towns, eliminating their small private plots at the same time.

**89** Abandoned labour camp. Salekhard on the Arctic Circle. From here thousands toiled on a railway which went nowhere and was never finished.

In making these proposals Khrushchev overreached himself. The contenders for power trod carefully in their contest for Stalin's ear. Zhdanov was gone. His Leningrad associates had been liquidated. Molotov was under a cloud, his wife exiled to the camps. Malenkov and Beria often made common cause, the better to ensure their survival. Beria was now the object of Stalin's suspicion. Challenged to purge the Georgian party, in his own power base, Beria had no alternative but to do so. A new Commissar for State Security, Ignatiev, was appointed to run the MGB (a forerunner of the KGB); he was not Beria's man, and embarked on a purge of the security forces.

Beria had reason to be fearful. No one could read Stalin's mind at this time. He emerged less and less from the Kremlin and the Kuntsevo villa. His only publication for many years had been an obscure polemic on the development of language, against the theories of a long-dead scholar N. Y. Marr. It was reverentially analysed by those in the field of linguistics, who confessed that only now had their eyes been opened. Then, in 1952, Stalin stirred. He was persuaded to call a new Party Congress – the Nineteenth, and the

**90  Stalin, isolated and silent, listens to the report presented by Malenkov at the Nineteenth Party Congress, 1952.**

first for thirteen years. And he produced a new theoretical work on economics for the delegates to study and agonise over the correct line to take on it.

At the Nineteenth Congress Stalin spoke for only seven minutes. He sat in brooding isolation while Khrushchev and Malenkov, rivals to succeed him, delivered their reports to the Congress, with barbed remarks about each other, and fulsome ones about him. It was decided that the new Central Committee and Presidium would be twice their previous size. Why was Stalin proposing this? Men who held power fretted at its dilution, and the possibility of a new and terrible purge. In January 1953 they received an unmistakable sign. Nine Kremlin doctors were arrested as agents of western intelligence, and charged with murdering Zhdanov and other party luminaries. Most of the doctors were Jewish. Some were tortured and two of them died at the hands of their jailors. Professor Yakov Rapaport was arrested when he arrived back at his flat:

> It was like a dying man finally coming face to face with death, which relieved him of the fear . . . so I got into the car with the [KGB] colonel and we drove off to the Lubyanka. After a wait of about half an hour, I was shown into an office where a young man in the uniform of a KGB officer was sitting. He introduced himself as an investigator and accused me of being a Jewish, bourgeois nationalist, which was tantamount to saying I was a terrorist because I was an enemy of the people.

Rapaport refused to sign a confession, although he was told that it was his only chance to stay in the Lubyanka.

> My head was completely shaved, I was given a cold shower, and then I was bundled into a black maria and taken away, somewhere far away. . . . [There] they said to me point blank: 'You realise you were arrested on 12 January on the ground that you doctors were murderers and refused to confess your crimes.'

Stalin told his security chief Ignatiev that he would be 'shortened by a head' if he did not extract confessions. They were duly forthcoming. Was this, as his drinking partners came to believe and fear, a premeditated attempt to set them up as the instigators of a general plot? Stalin was more obsessed than ever with his personal safety. He

**91** The 'doctors' plot', obligingly presented in *Krokodil* with the necessary amount of paranoia.

had recently sacked his own head of security after thirty years' service, together with his secretary – men who had given their lives to his every whim. As his health declined and his powers faded, he worried, as all old men do. Shooting the Kremlin doctors might have been an end in itself, but all Moscow feared otherwise.

Was Stalin going mad in 1952? The consensus is that he was not, as Stephen Cohen puts it:

> There is no hard evidence I know of dysfunctional madness. All we can say with certainty is that he continued to be Stalin, that the Stalin of the 1930s was still present. After all, he was preparing a new terror. It's even conceivable to me that at the end of his life Stalin was preparing to replay his great triumphs of the 1930s when he became Stalin. That is, he now wanted to force even the collective farm peasants into state farms. He wanted a new terror against the survivors of the old terror like Molotov.

There was to be a different end, however. On 1 March 1953 Stalin was recovering from a heavy night carousing with his circle. For the whole of that Sunday, to their surprise, they did not hear from him. Then, according to Khrushchev, Malenkov came on the telephone. The rivals spoke cautiously. Something had happened at Stalin's villa. He was unconscious. None of them could afford not to be at his bedside, to watch him, and to watch each other. The last act had come.

# 9 THE FALLEN IDOL

That name didn't know a smaller measure
Than that of a deity
Given by people of deep religious faith.

Just try and find the man who
Didn't praise and glorify him,
Just try and find him!
Alexander Tvardovsky: 'Horizon Beyond Horizon',[1]
*Poems*, 1963

We must state that after the war the situation became even
more complicated. Stalin became even more capricious,
irritable, and brutal; in particular his suspicions grew. His
persecution mania reached unbelievable dimensions. Many
workers were becoming enemies before his very eyes. After the
war Stalin separated himself from the collective even more.
Everything was decided by him alone without any
consideration for anyone or anything. This unbelievable
suspicion was cleverly taken advantage of by the abject
provocateur and vile enemy, Beria, who had murdered
thousands of Communists and loyal Soviet people.[2]
N. S. Khrushchev: Secret Speech to the
Twentieth Party Congress, 1956

There is a mystery about what had happened to Stalin. His guards
had become alarmed when he had not asked for his evening snack at
11 p.m., but had not initially gone into his locked bedroom. When
his maid Matryona Petrovna did so, she found him on the floor. He
had already lost the power of speech but seemed to be gesturing for
help. The security men picked him up and put him on a sofa, but
doctors were not summoned until the morning. Stalin's Soviet

biographer, General Volkogonov, claims that this was the fault of Beria. 'Everyone said, "You need to apply to Beria," but for a long time Beria couldn't be found. Finally Beria arrived drunk, and saw Stalin croaking and dying. And Beria said, "What's all this panic for. Comrade Stalin is sleeping peacefully!" He sent everyone away until the morning and drove away himself.' According to Khrushchev, the inner group (Malenkov, Beria, Bulganin and himself) had gone out during the night but had not called a doctor. Only on the following day did they return with a doctor who diagnosed a stroke. Thus the autocrat of all the Russias lay helpless and untreated for the better part of a day, making recuperative treatment much harder. For Volkogonov this was the final irony:

> Stalin ended up as the hostage of his own system. In any civilised country any leader would get help within minutes. It would be too bad if it took as long as an hour. But here was a man who was able to shift millions of people from one end of the country to the other, a man who possessed limitless power, colossal power. At the moment he was struck down nobody could come to him . . . a god on earth couldn't receive the simplest medical help because everything was so boxed in by a variety of bureaucratic institutions.

Why did the Party leaders prolong the delay? Some historians see evidence of premeditated murder. Abdurakhman Avtorkhanov sees the cause in Stalin's visible preparation of a purge to rival those of the thirties. And the Politburo had a long memory.

**92 Stalin dead at last. Calculating their chances are (*left to right*) Khrushchev, Beria, Malenkov, Bulganin, Voroshilov and Kaganovich.**

> Either Stalin would make another great purge . . . the
> annihilation of the majority of the Politburo, the General Staff
> and the intelligentsia and afterwards even of the KGB itself,
> because Stalin was very fond, after his crimes, of liquidating
> those people who had participated, so that no witnesses should
> remain. And the Politburo understood only too well that this
> dilemma could be solved in only one of two ways: either by the
> liquidation of Stalin himself, and his consequent removal from
> power, or Stalin, as a result of his new purge, would liquidate
> them.

On this theory it would have been Beria, out of favour and nervous
of the new security chief Ignatiev, who would have thought that it
was either him or Stalin – kill or be killed. The guards, some of whom
later 'committed suicide' could have been briefed to help Stalin out of
the world if he became incapacitated. No one knows what Beria did
or said when he first arrived at Kuntsevo. At the very least he delayed
treatment. His behaviour at the bedside was certainly bizarre. He
spoke roughly to the doctors and, according to Khrushchev, 'spewed
out hatred' of the unconscious dictator. Then he got a rude shock, in
Khrushchev's vivid description:

> Once, during the day, [Stalin] actually returned to
> consciousness. Even though he still couldn't speak, his face
> started to move. They had been spoon-feeding him soup and
> sweet tea. He raised his left hand and started to point to
> something on the wall. His lips formed something like a smile.
> I realised what he was trying to say and called for attention.[3]

At this point, to the disgust of his fellow-watchers, Beria grovelled at
the old man's side.

There was one terrible moment when Stalin in his death throes
opened his eyes and threw out an accusatory left arm at the crowd
around him. Later, Beria departed in high good humour for his car.
Was it in fact more than the relief of a man who must have felt that
now he was safe?

Stalin died on 5 March 1953. There is no evidence that his death
was not the result of a massive cerebral haemorrhage. 'The Kremlin
mountaineer'[4] had scaled his last peak. His son Vasili accused both
his doctors and his Politburo colleagues of murder in the course of

drunken rantings around Moscow in the following month. But Vasili was a chronic alcoholic, whom the Soviet government eventually locked up. His sister is more circumspect:

> Although the cause was natural, a stroke, because this old man in his seventies was deprived of medical help for a considerable time, more than twelve hours, and of proper diagnosis, that is what I call helping him to die, instead of helping him to recover, and it's quite clear to me that the Politburo had this in mind. . . . It was clear in much more detail to my brother, who talked about it more than I did.

Much as she disliked him, she does not accuse Beria. And when he in his turn was arrested and shot, this was not among the many real or fanciful crimes of which he was accused.

Stalin was dead, but in no sense was he buried. The body was carried through the streets of Moscow on a bitterly cold March day by Malenkov, Beria, Khrushchev, Molotov, Voroshilov and Vasili. Stalin was mummified and placed in the Lenin Mausoleum. All over the country people wept, at the removal of this strong unyielding symbol in a cold and cheerless world. In Moscow there were hysterical scenes as people mourned, with many crushed to death. The American correspondent Harrison Salisbury went out expecting to see expressions of relief and joy, but found the opposite: 'They cried. I saw women crying in the streets of Moscow although the man they were crying for may very well have murdered their husband, or sent relatives to a concentration camp. . . . A more common reaction was, "What's coming next? Will it be something worse?" As it might well be.'

Lev Kopelev, imprisoned in a labour camp, was moved despite himself:

> At that point I still thought that for all his shortcomings maybe he was the last Communist in the Politburo – he really wanted something good – and I even cried in secret. I'm not ashamed to admit it, but when they were burying him and the horns were blowing I went into an empty hut where there was nobody, so that I shouldn't be seen either by my comrade prisoners or by the guards, and I cried, because I knew that when my brother had perished he was shouting for the Motherland and for Stalin.

**93 Stalin's funeral in
Moscow, 9 March 1953.
Behind Malenkov as chief
pallbearer is Stalin's
alcoholic son Vasili. Stalin
was placed beside Lenin
in the Mausoleum on Red
Square.**

**94 Weeping Muscovites mourn their loss.**

Even in the depths of the Gulag some wept, without knowing why. Other victims of the Gulag had a less complex response. Alice Mulkigian, aged eighteen and an American citizen, had been arrested for alleged spying during a visit to Armenia. She spent five years in appalling conditions in a labour camp – Karaganda in Kazakhstan. When the news reached her camp:

> There were actually women there that cried, but 99 per cent
> just jumped up and said, 'Today is a holiday!' . . . We all had a
> cup of cider and we celebrated that Stalin died, and we said,
> 'None too soon'. It was one of the happiest moments and we
> had a feeling that something good was going to happen,
> because it just couldn't continue in this way.

But what was to follow? The nervous and frightened men who carried Stalin's bier knew that his legacy weighed even more heavily on them. Would there be a continuance of terror? A change of this magnitude might be washed in the blood of the losers. The Stalinist system, so identified now with terror, had no easy way to settle intra-Party disputes and successions without it. There was the dangerous international scene, with the Korean War dragging on and the United States now talking in the bellicose language of John Foster Dulles as well as of Senator McCarthy. And there was the economic stagnation of a command economy that could find no room for individual initiative in its copious blueprints and Five Year Plans.

It did not take long for the system which Stalin had created to produce its own bloody resolution to the problem of there being no heir apparent. There were three possible contenders for power from the older generation; Molotov, for all his seniority, the incompetent Voroshilov, and Kaganovich were disqualified. All three had depended on Stalin, and done his bidding without question, but neither their position nor their Party following were substantial enough for them to aim for the top. There was Malenkov, the Michelin man of the Party bureaucracy, only fifty but long at the centre of government. There was the Georgian security chief, Beria, with whom Malenkov had made common cause in the past – so much so that they were often seen walking arm-in-arm. And there was Khrushchev, the shrewd Party man from the country, who had twice feared that Stalin might destroy him. Khrushchev did not stand higher than fifth in the formal order of seniority in the Politburo, but he had assets in hand: good links with the military dating back to his war service, and supporters in the Ukraine and Moscow districts which he had run.

Initially, Malenkov seemed to be presented as a successor, having the senior government and Party posts. Beria was placated with the first deputy premiership, ranked second in the hierarchy, with control over internal affairs, including security. It was Beria's security troops, observers noted, who thronged Moscow during Stalin's funeral. But Beria had to be cautious in recalling his own supporters to key positions. Khrushchev too bided his time, strengthening his hold on the Party secretariat when Malenkov was compelled to give up his Party posts to concentrate on the government. It seems to have been Beria's strategy to win himself a certain popularity by liberal gestures. He was thought to court the nationalities. The 'doctors' plot' was declared to be a fake and a provocation. Some eminent victims of denunciation were released. There was a general amnesty for prisoners sentenced for up to five years – unless they were political prisoners. The amnesty backfired on Beria. As brilliantly portrayed in Alexander Proshkin's film *The Cold Summer of 1953*, the criminals who had been amnestied brought about a reign of terror in town and country alike. In the film the villagers are terrified when the hoodlums who have occupied their settlement accuse them, in mock-Stalin language, of being 'enemies of the people'.

In fact, one of the worst nightmares of the Gulag for the political prisoners was that it had to be shared with 'apaches', as the common criminals were sometimes called. As the political prisoners tried to organise themselves camp authorities often turned the criminals loose on them. The journalist Alexander Khersonsky describes what happened in the camps along section 501 of the Salekhard-Igarka Railway:

> If anyone tried to demonstrate that something was unfair,
> gathering a group around him, they would quickly be sent
> under armed guard to the adjacent camp to the thieves. And
> the very next morning the severed heads of these people were
> already lying on the ground by the checkpoint. The thieves
> knew why they'd been sent along there.

To turn such people loose won Beria no friends, but he may have calculated that the unease which they provoked would make it easier for an incoming strong man to preach discipline and repression once more.

Ironically it may have been the need for repression abroad which enabled Beria's opponents to move against him. In the early summer of 1953, with the heavy hand of Stalin removed and the new Soviet government apparently embarked upon a conciliatory policy towards the west – soon to lead to a cease-fire in Korea – the Eastern European satellites began to stir against their neo-Stalinist masters. Ulbricht in East Germany, Gottwald in Czechoslovakia, Rakosi in Hungary – these had been Stalin's most devoted creatures. Demonstrations were mounted against them, and the Soviet leadership acquiesced in the removal of Rakosi. But matters soon got out of hand. There was a workers' uprising in East Berlin, crushed by Soviet tanks on 17 June. The uprising had taken the Soviet Union by surprise. Beria had failed to forecast it. On 28 June *Pravda* omitted Beria's name from the list of the Party hierarchy, in ranking order, attending *The Decembrists* at the Bolshoi Theatre.

Two days previously he had been confronted by his colleagues in the Politburo. Khrushchev, who portrayed himself later as the principal conspirator, seems to have been able to win over Malenkov – not least because he had the ear of the army and at least one of

**95 Soviet tanks in East Berlin quell a popular uprising, 18 June 1953.**

Beria's deputies who was ready to betray him, General Ivan Serov. Khrushchev opened the indictment, accusing Beria of anti-Soviet activities in the interests of foreign powers since 1920! He reports his own concluding words: 'As a result of my observations of Beria's activities, I have formed the impression that he is no Communist. He is a careerist who has wormed his way into the Party for self-seeking reasons. His arrogance is intolerable. No honest communist would ever behave the way he does in the Party.'[5]

Beria, who could remember Stalin's similar public dismissal of the wretched Yezhov,[6] would have known by the time his colleagues had finished that he would suffer his predecessor's fate. He was arrested there and then by Marshal Zhukov, and his close collaborators joined him in the cells. What happened to him there is uncertain, but it cannot have been worse than the fate he had meted out to countless thousands. The announcement of a condign punishment for Beria and seven of his associates did not appear in *Pravda* until Christmas Day 1953. They had been shot, after a trial, it was said.

Although other security chiefs were executed in 1954, and there were purges of Beria's supporters, there was no return to mass terror. Like the Jacobins, Beria and his unsavoury henchmen sated the appetite for blood which they had helped to create. The Ministry of State Security was reorganised as a committee answerable to the Party – the KGB. The KGB in its time also came to stand for repression, surveillance and autocratic rule. But it never replicated the arbitrary killing and state terrorism of the Stalin years. In that respect one important aspect of Stalinism died not with Stalin, but with the execution of Beria, who had been so ostentatiously distancing himself from it. Stalin's heirs were to disagree fundamentally time and time again, not least about their attitude to Stalin's record, but the losing side did not lose everything. As Hélène Carrère d'Encausse puts it: 'No matter how widely they differed, nor how great their ambitions were, the leaders no longer killed each other. And although to give up power meant certain political death, this political death did not lead to physical death.'[7]

It was against the background of these rivalries that the next stage of the deconstruction of the Stalin cult was played out. Malenkov remained chairman of the Council of Ministers for two years. He announced a switch of priorities from heavy industry to consumer needs, accompanied by a fall in prices. The western powers were conciliated by the 1953 Korean armistice and the 1955 treaty granting Austria full independence – clear signs that the expansionism the West had attributed to Stalin was over. Meanwhile Khrushchev consolidated the power that came with his appointment as General Secretary of the Party in September 1953. Stalin had treated the Party with contempt, and had ruled through agencies of government which acted on his whim. Khrushchev now flattered the Party cadres by restoring their authority. Those traditionalists and military men who felt threatened by Malenkov's apparent downgrading of heavy industry and military priorities – two cherished concerns of the Stalin Five Year Plans – found Khrushchev a sympathetic voice. Even his vast plan to plough up the virgin lands, from the Volga to Siberia, unveiled in 1954, had the right combination of Party ideals and Stalinist gargantuanism.

Malenkov now faltered. His price cuts had led to further short-term consumer shortages. Agriculture was in disarray. He was removed from his post in February 1955, making no public defence

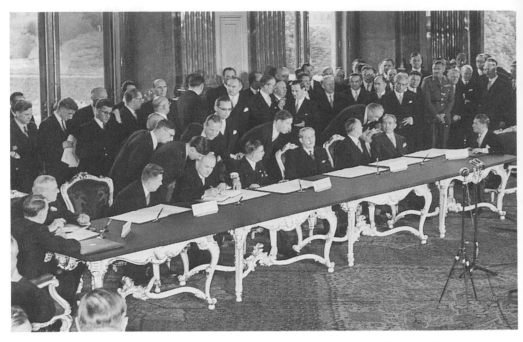

**96 A thaw begins. Molotov signs the Austrian State Treaty in the Belvedere Palace, Vienna, 16 May 1955.**

**97 Rivals. Khrushchev and Malenkov, 1955.**

but the traditional self-criticism of the fallen. However, he remained an influential member of the Politburo for two further years, and was even allowed to travel abroad. His successor, Marshal Bulganin, was a far less assertive character than Khrushchev, happy to have nominal pre-eminence whilst real power remained with the General Secretary.

Khrushchev was shrewd. He had a mixture of raw courage and blundering insensitivity which made him the right man to tackle that part of the Stalin legacy which could be seen as an excrescence of Marxism–Leninism. Within the communist bloc the dispute with Yugoslavia still festered. Foreign Minister Molotov adamantly defended the correctness of the Stalin line on Tito. Khrushchev now effected a public reconciliation in spectacular style, by making a pilgrimage to the heretic's headquarters. Often explosive, sometimes drunk, Khrushchev nevertheless succeeded in his basic mission. He

**98 Khrushchev demonstrates his desire to make it up with the Yugoslavs during a visit in March 1956.**

accepted, as Stalin never could, that each communist state must have its own road to socialism. Many who watched in the Soviet Union must have wondered what Khrushchev would say on his return about those who had been disgraced, imprisoned and executed as 'Titoists' during the Stalin years. Some redemption had already been made to other eminent post-war victims. The Leningrad purge of 1949 had been disowned in 1954, and its principal executor Abakumov tried and executed – as an accomplice of Beria, but with no mention of Stalin. But what was now stirring was the whole Gulag itself, where the victims of Stalin still rotted in their millions.

There had been camp uprisings before, right across the system. With the death of Stalin and the release of amnestied criminals, the political prisoners asserted themselves. Back home their relatives, who had hardly dared acknowledge their existence, began to petition for clemency and rehabilitation. Some of those released in 1953, like the Old Bolshevik A. V. Snegov, were able to press for a reform of the Gulag from within its administration. For the 7 to 10 million inhabitants of the camps it was not soon enough. Sometimes the response was a violent one. At Alice Mulkigian's camp in Kazakhstan, the May 1954 uprising had begun with the prisoners barricading themselves in and sending out balloons laden with leaflets. It ended with the arrival of tanks: 'They opened fire with the machine guns, and 600 people were killed right here like that. . . . There was a Ukrainian girl who had been just sixteen when they arrested her. She had been there nine and a half years and only had six more months. She fell under a tank and the tank just smashed right over her.'

In other camps the authorities held back from such atrocities. The writer Mikhail Bartalsky was in one of the Karaganda camps around Vorkuta when the prisoners struck for the right of review which they had been promised.

> In the summer of 1955, unexpectedly and quite spontaneously, a strike broke out in our mine too. A convoy guard provoked it when he shot down an old prisoner for no reason at all, only because the man had sat down on the ground. But he picked the wrong year for shooting people. The prisoners began to shout; the convoy guards got scared and raised their weapons. Then someone shouted, 'We won't march with a convoy like this.' Everyone rushed back through the gates and the convoy

guards were left to themselves. . . . A general meeting of
prisoners was permitted, and many spoke. A former Soviet
army pilot by the name of Dobroshtan, who had spent
twenty-five years at hard labour, spoke the most daringly and
effectively. He was taken off to Moscow and after a little while
returned [to negotiate for the other prisoners], rehabilitated.
He was the first swallow of spring in our subsection.[8]

Many such swallows flitted between the camps and the Central
Committee in 1955. Khrushchev received personal letters from
many old Party loyalists, wrongfully jailed, setting out their grievances. The decision was taken to release millions of victims; not just
framed Party bosses, but the prisoners-of-war, 'collaborators',
'wreckers' and 'anti-social' peasants and dissidents and luckless
victims of mistaken identity who had kept the Gulag full. Their
formal rehabilitation still left them in spiritual darkness and mental
torment. There were those, like the returning army officer in
Proshkin's film, who sought out the relatives of the friends who had
died at his side, only to be told by one dead man's son: 'He told us to
renounce him. We could do nothing.'

For others there were personal scars. The writer Lev Razgon spent
eighteen years in the camps. He noted there how fast the peasants
died, and that the young peasant girls, sentenced to five years for
stealing a potato on the kolkhoz, survived only through prostitution
and degradation: 'Those who lived until the death of the tyrant, and
who were freed during Khrushchev's time, could never be normal
people. . . . Our society was not only wounded by these camps,
through which millions of people passed, but those wounds have not
healed to this day.'

All were changed, but the stronger characters among the former
inmates returned steeled by their experience and determined to clear
their names and expose those who had sent them on their dreadful
journey. So did the relatives of those who had been sent on that
dreadful journey. 'Enemies of the people', unpersoned, had no
rights. Nor did their descendants and dependants. Thus the need for
rehabilitation was both moral and practical. A series of commissions
of inquiry into the more obviously rigged prosecutions had been set
up, but Khrushchev sensed that an explanation had to be made, to
the Party itself. Punctilious now about calling meetings of the
Central Committee and the Party Congress, he intended the Twen-

tieth Congress in 1956 to entrench his position, after which he would make an explanation of the Stalinist times. The formal meetings of the Congress both downgraded the status and memory of Stalin and struck out in new directions itself. In open sessions Anastas Mikoyan had attacked the 'cult of personality' but Khrushchev wanted more. He told his colleagues that he proposed to use the evidence so far gathered by the commissions to denounce the crimes of Stalin, in a closed session. There was consternation, as he later told his son Sergei:

> Everyone around him was categorically against this speech of his. . . . Voroshilov and Kaganovich said, 'But what will happen to us, what will become of us? You can't do that!' So Khrushchev replied that everyone must be responsible for what he'd done and that he would bear his own part in all this. Some people would be guilty. Others less so. He concluded: 'I was a member of the Seventeenth Congress and the Eighteenth, am prepared to take responsibility vis-à-vis the Party, and if it decides to hold me responsible then so be it.' When nobody agreed he said that he would give the speech in his capacity as an ordinary member of the Congress. It was only after that that the others gave their agreement. Remember there could have been another scenario where members were simply arrested. Times then were different.

Khrushchev was in fact taking a risk of a different kind. The Congress was packed with his supporters. It was Mikoyan, not he, who had made the running in remarks which by implication criticised the whole leadership. The 20,000-word speech Khrushchev eventually delivered was not extempore: it had been written in advance; if it was not communicated the leadership would seem guilty of suppression; if it was, the chance of a new cult around a single leader was much diminished. Much as they protested, some of the old guard must have seen that if these things had to be said there were advantages in having Khrushchev say them, and take that responsibility. And they knew, better than any, that the report was the truth – if not the whole truth. Mikoyan showed Stalin's daughter Svetlana the text before Khrushchev spoke:

> A lot of what I read there was true. I didn't feel that I'm going to jump up and say: 'Oh this isn't true.' Because it was the

history of our family, how it was happening there, and I knew it was true. I felt right away that it would be difficult for those who won the war together with him to take it . . . but it was the need of the time.

Khrushchev was heard in silence, disturbed only by rumbles of unease and cries of indignation. What he said was crucial to the later development of the Soviet Union. So was what he omitted. He denounced Stalin as 'despotic' and 'sickly-suspicious', and derided the Generalissimo's war record. Stalin's errors in the dispute with Tito, and some but not all of his crimes against the deported Soviet nationalities were listed. He described how 70 per cent of the members of the Central Committee elected at the Seventeenth Congress in 1934 had been shot by Stalin, together with more than half the delegates. And he went into extended personal detail on the torture and false confessions of Party faithful like Kedrov and Eikhe during the Terror. It was suggested that Kirov's murder should be investigated to see if the clue led back to Stalin. The effect of the speech on those who heard it was devastating.

General Volkogonov remembers:

> Until the Twentieth Congress, despite the fact that I lost my father during Stalin's terror, and my mother was in exile dying there, I was stunned because I was a Stalinist. I thought that Stalin had nothing to do with the misfortunes of my family and other people. But here I was, a member of the Party . . . for several hours there was a silence of the grave reigning in the hall. It was as if there were two people standing on the stage, Khrushchev, and the ghost of a familiar man with a very familiar profile. When Khrushchev spoke, it was as though he was threading beads on to a string and adding more and more new facts, more and more criminal acts. Sometimes the hall buzzed with indignation, sometimes there were shouts of outrage and sometimes the hall was as silent as a block of ice, because everyone was stunned by what they heard.

Khrushchev's speech at the Twentieth Congress ensured that there could be no return to crude mass terror as an instrument of policy within the Party, perhaps not even in the country. That most powerful weapon of Stalinism had been neutralised. Yet the speech was also an exercise in damage-limitation. Its omissions are striking.

**99 A speech that shook the world. Khrushchev at the Twentieth Party Congress.**

There was no reference to errors before 1934, no mention of the millions of peasants and non-Party or oppositionist victims of the Bolsheviks who had been slaughtered in this period. Khrushchev's extended periods of responsibility in the Ukraine meant that he knew better than most what had gone on. The Party, in this version, had no need to rehabilitate Trotskyites, Zinovievites and Bukharinites. This was very comforting for the Party cadres who had to digest the speech. The Party had been found not guilty. Stalin and his clique had strayed away from 'holy Leninist principles',[9] but the Party had been right on course in 1934 and could now resume its leading role in every aspect of society shorn of Stalinist brutality.

For all its bravery, therefore, Khrushchev's speech has all the limitations of the man who made it and his times. The question of why and how Stalin had emerged to do these terrible things was not addressed. Svetlana Alliluyeva still feels betrayed that the speech stopped short: 'The Party found the scapegoat and stopped there, and what have we improved? Well, we have improved one thing. We have returned many of those people still in Siberia back to life. What else have we done? Well, not much. The KGB is still there. Everything else is much as it used to be.'

One thing was certain. Khrushchev in 1956 destroyed the myth of Stalin, the omnipotent godhead of the revolution, although it was to be a further five years before his body was taken out of the Mausoleum in Red Square. What he did not do was to eliminate the other elements of the Stalin system. He was bone of their bone. He could not do it. That is why the Stalin question still has such force in the modern Soviet Union, thirty-seven years after his death.

# 10 **THE STALIN LEGACY**

One day Lara went out and did not come back. She must have been arrested in the street, as so often happened in those days, and she died or vanished somewhere, forgotten as a nameless number on a list which was afterwards mislaid, in one of the innumerable mixed or women's concentration camps in the north.[1]
Boris Pasternak: Nobel Prize for Literature, 1958

The letter that I one day held in my hand was painful. It came from a family deported from one of the Baltic states to Siberia in 1949, and was addressed to relatives in Poland. The family consisted of a mother and two daughters. The letter was a terse account of their life on a kolkhoz. The last letters of every line were slightly stressed, and reading vertically one made out the words 'Eternal Slave'. If such a letter happened to fall into my hands, then how many other, similarly disguised expressions of despair must have found their way to people who could not make any use of them? And, calculating the possibilities, how many such letters remained unwritten; how many of those who might have written them died of hunger and overwork, repeating those hopeless words, 'Eternal Slave'?[2]
Czeslaw Milosz: Nobel Prize for Literature, 1980

We are not dealing with the tyranny of an individual but with the tyranny of a Party that simply has put the production of tyrants on an industrial footing.[3]
Joseph Brodsky: Nobel Prize for Literature, 1987

Our country has started on the path of cleansing away the foulness of Stalinism. 'We are squeezing the slave out of ourselves drop by drop' [an expression of Anton Chekhov]. We are learning to express our opinion, without taking a lead from the bosses, and without fearing for our lives.[4]
Andrei Sakharov: Nobel Peace Prizewinner, 1975

The legacy of Stalin is first of all personal pain, bequeathed to countless millions. On it have been built everything from enduring bureaucracies to great works of art. The four men whose words head this chapter come from different generations. The youngest of them was only a boy when Stalin died. Yet all of them lived their lives (as long as they were permitted to do so) dominated by the spectre of Stalin. The international acclaim they and many like them have achieved was accompanied by vilification in their own countries, but they have all expressed the moral core of the Soviet and Eastern European intelligentsia, hardened by the cold Stalin years, and what happened afterwards. Irrational mass terror ceased to be an internal instrument of policy after Stalin's death. Overwhelming force was identified with the measures his successors took to keep his empire intact, and even, it might be argued in the case of Afghanistan, to expand it.

With the end of the cult of personality came the restoration of the cult of the Party. The vast apparatus of a centralised bureaucracy – the Nomenklatura – was freed from being one of the targets of the despot, and became despotic in its turn, with a stagnation in whose muddy shallows neo-Stalinism was spawned. And on all these phenomena the artists and writers of Russia cast a continuously critical eye.

The contradictions of the post-Stalin Soviet Union were vividly evident in the outsize personality of Khrushchev. The economic depredation of Eastern Europe caused its most volatile nations to erupt in protests and riots in the autumn after the Twentieth Congress speech. Khrushchev, the affable debunker of Stalin, was able to handle Polish discontent without more than the hint of force and with some judicious concessions. With the Hungarian uprising in 1956, however, matters got out of hand. The Soviets had acquiesced in the removal of the Stalinist Matyas Rakosi and the rehabilitation of Laszlo Rajk. The new government of Imre Nagy was carried along on a tidal wave of popular emotion. Secret policemen were hunted and lynched. The huge statue of Stalin in Budapest was destroyed. Initially Soviet troops were withdrawn from the capital. Then, after Khrushchev had secured the formal agreement of his other allies in the Warsaw Pact, they returned in overwhelming force. The Nagy government, which had declared its neutrality, protested, and finally appealed to world opinion.

100, 101, 102 Images of Hungary, 1956: a) Stalin overthrown, b) Resistance fighter and murdered AVO (Hungarian Secret Police) man, c) The Red Army returns.

With the west fatally divided over the concurrent invasion of Egypt by Britain, France and Israel, nothing more than moral indignation came to the help of the Hungarians. The Nagy government was overthrown by force, after prolonged fighting. He and his defence minister Pal Maleter were separately arrested as a result of treachery, and later shot after a secret trial. At the very end of his life Khrushchev still wrote of the Hungarian events as a counter-revolution, which would have spilled 'proletarian blood' without the intervention of the Red Army. (In fact Nagy's strongest supporters had all called for the retention of 'socialist gains' in Hungary.[5]) With unconscious irony he wrote that he had rectified the wrong done to the Hungarians in 1848: 'In that year there was a successful revolution in Budapest, but Nicholas I threw in his legions, crushed the revolution, and helped restore the rule of the Austrian monarchy in Hungary. That was a disgrace.'[6]

The situation in Hungary aroused strong protests among the western Left. Coming so soon after Khrushchev's revelations about Stalin it further eroded the position of western communist parties, which suffered many defections. In the Soviet Union the Hungarian affair, which did not interrupt Khrushchev's programme of domestic reform, was less traumatic than the invasion of Czechoslovakia ordered by Leonid Brezhnev twelve years later.

Khrushchev had started with immense goodwill. He was not Stalin. He was not a killer. And he was transparently sincere in his beliefs. How did he go wrong? At home he had massively consolidated his position after 1956. He had been outvoted in the Presidium (as the Politburo was now called) and had then used his majority on the Central Committee to purge it and send the Stalinist old guard packing – demoted, but not sent to death camps. Then he got rid of premier Bulganin and ran both Party and government with a concentration of power which recalled Stalin's heyday. His policies, however, did not. He was a loud, even vociferous, believer in the superior virtues of the communist system, and in the age of Sputnik and Soviet heavy industrial advance that was not fanciful. He was a meritocrat and an egalitarian, with an Old Bolshevik's dislike of organised religion.

He understood that there had to be a wider freedom of expression in the Soviet Union, yet could explode in paroxysms of rage when this took forms he feared or disliked, in books or paintings. In 'the thaw' of the late fifties these were bumping up against the limits of the permissible. Artists like Boris Birger had been freed from the worst compulsions of Stalinism: 'This was the first time I'd taken part in an exhibition [with] a portrait of a girl I knew . . . it was a major change that you could paint ordinary people. You no longer had to paint Stalin with the people and some well-known worker that no one had ever clapped eyes on.' But when Khrushchev later saw one of Birger's paintings on exhibition, 'he had probably hit a hundred grammes of vodka before he came, and he was very excited, swearing and ranting and raving'.

Birger declined to grovel in self-criticism and he was removed from the Union of Artists. When it came to the crunch the Union of Writers was to prove equally craven. A variety of novelists, including some repentant former time-servers, had addressed the theme of personal responsibility in the face of injustice. But in 1957 the novel *Dr Zhivago* by the writer and poet Boris Pasternak was published in Italy after being turned down by Soviet publishers. Within a year it had become a world sensation, and he was offered the Nobel Prize for his life's work. He was forced to reject it, and had to watch his fellow-writers demanding that he should lose his citizenship. Within two years he was dead. When his friends came to bury him at Peredelkino the pall-bearers included two young writers, Yuli Daniel and Andrei Sinyavsky, who would later make the struggle for free expression their own.

This struggle took many forms. Young people had taken advantage of the 1957 Youth Festival and the 1958 American Exhibition (scene of a memorable eyeballing between Khrushchev and the then Vice-President Nixon about the comparative virtues of communism and capitalism) to expand their foreign contacts. Jazz helped. So did greater freedom to visit the USSR. Impromptu poetry readings under the impressive new statue of Mayakovsky, celebrated poet and suicide, in the square named after him, led to police provocations and arrests. One of those arrested was Vladimir Bukovsky:

> Some were expelled from universities for attending or taking
> part in it. Later they started beating us up, waiting to . . .
> drive us to some obscure cellar and beat us for several hours.
> Finally when that failed to produce any impact on our
> behaviour then five people were arrested. . . . We knew for

103 Pasternak's funeral, 1960. His coffin was carried by Sinyavsky and Daniel.

104 The Moscow Youth Festival, 1957.

sure that the treatment we got [in jail] was much milder than
anything our people could have got in Stalin's time.

Important as these things were to the participants, the real struggle
was being waged within the Party and the Nomenklatura. Khrushchev had offered a respite from killing and a scapegoat in Stalin. Now
at the Twenty-Second Congress in 1961 he seemed to be challenging
present privilege as well as past excesses. Stalin's crimes against the
nation as a whole were excoriated. His mummy was removed from
the Mausoleum and his name removed from Soviet towns and public
works. With the 1962 publication of Solzhenitsyn's *One Day In the
Life of Ivan Denisovich* in *Novy Mir* it seemed that open season had
arrived for a debate on the camps. That would have meant that the
jailer and the signer of the routine detention order would have to
justify themselves and their blind acceptance of monstrous orders.
There were millions of such 'apparatchiks'. Worse, Khrushchev had
proposed at the Twenty-Second Congress that the offices in the gift
of the Party should be rotated. Sinecures would be limited in time.
The historian Abdurakhman Avtorkhanov believes that this was
Khrushchev's cardinal error: 'What he should have done was as
follows: first of all to annihilate the system, and then to annihilate
Stalin. Because in fact a dead Stalin didn't really represent a great
deal of danger for Khrushchev. What was dangerous was his system,
the system he had created.'

The system could always hit back. Khrushchev had appointed a
commission to inquire into the Kirov murder (see Chapter 5). Its
report was suppressed, to the bitter frustration of its surviving
member Olga Shatunovskaya:

> [Khrushchev] was afraid. He was surrounded by Stalinists who
> in the end removed him. They convinced him that [the report]
> was dangerous, that the people wouldn't understand it, and
> that it would affect the authority of the Party. He took it and
> placed it in the archives, covered it up. By this he gave them
> the opportunity of falsifying and destroying [the evidence] and
> making forgeries.

In Khrushchev's last years in power he made an abundance of
bullets for his enemies in the Party bureaucracy to fire. He wanted
the command system to work, when it could not without an effective

market mechanism. He wanted the Party to supervise, but could not devise a way to harness efficiency in such a system of nomination and responsibility. His virgin lands were eroded by over-cultivation. The harvest failed in 1963. His quarrels with Mao and his climb-down in the Cuban missile crisis portrayed him (unfairly) as a clumsy buffoon. In fact he was, as the writer Anatoli Strelyany describes him, 'a romantic, the last romantic because he so blindly believed in the system that he posed many impossible tasks for it. And he really did in all seriousness try to mend the country from all its ills.'

In this he failed. The last romantic was removed in October 1964, whilst he was on vacation. His colleagues did not kill him, or even exile him. Those days were over. But a recrudescence of Stalinism was about to begin.

In Leonid Brezhnev, whose personal power soon eclipsed the collective arrangements made after Khrushchev's fall, there was the perfect example of that tyrant from the production line described by Brodsky. A political officer in the war, he had been a minor satrap in Moldavia and Kazakhstan and on the brink of the Politburo when Stalin died. His career had advanced solidly under Khrushchev but it retained a greyness which matched his dour personality. It was said that if there was ever to be a cult around him (and there were some risible attempts) it would be a cult without a personality.

Censorship was intensified, great writers like Solzhenitsyn silenced and eventually driven into exile, rising stars like Brodsky sent to prison for 'parasitism', and historians like Alexander Nekrich expelled from the Party for relating the facts about Stalin's errors in 1941. The trial of Sinyavsky and Daniel in 1966 for 'agitation or propaganda seeking to weaken the Soviet power' by publishing their work abroad under pseudonyms ended with them being sentenced to forced-labour camps. They were tried in open court, but with limited access, and cross-examined at length on the treasonable implications of what they had written. Thus the judge demanded of Sinyavsky:

> Do you really think your article on socialist realism isn't covered by Article 70 of the Criminal Code? 'So that there should be no more prisons, we built new prisons; so that not one drop of blood should be shed we killed and killed and killed.' What connection does this have with the study of literature?[7]

105 Yuli Daniel after his sentence to labour camp.

106 Prague, 1968. Russian tanks in the streets after the 20 August Warsaw Pact invasion.

The defendants remained patiently unrepentant, and in marked contrast to the Stalin years some Soviet literary opinion dared to rally to their support, though the Union of Writers played its usual role, and the venerable novelist Sholokhov appeared at the Twenty-Third Party Congress calling for rougher justice for the miscreants:

> If these fellows with the black consciences had been caught in the memorable 'twenties, when people were tried but not on the basis of closely defined articles of the criminal code, but in accordance with revolutionary justice, then, my goodness, they would have got something quite different, these turncoats! But now, if you please, people talk about these sentences being too harsh.[8]

Sinyavsky, from his very different standpoint, also notes the difference: 'Daniel and I were not physically tortured or beaten, and therefore we did not confess to being guilty. . . . In Stalin's time we would have been shot.' He now sees the Brezhnev period in its context: 'Khrushchev was three steps forward with the exposure of Stalin and two steps back with the Hungarian invasion. . . . During Brezhnev's time two more backward steps were taken and history wavered on the edge of returning us to full Stalinism . . . but stopped short.'

In fact, the text of the Sinyavsky–Daniel trial was widely circulated in the *samizdat* medium of unofficial manuscript and photocopy. The arguments of the defendants were thus widely known, despite their scurrilous defamation in the official media. Protests and petitions in their defence brought a further wave of reprisals and the trial of Alexander Ginzburg and others for the 'anti-Soviet' activity of distributing *samizdat* material. This trial was in turn protested against by over a thousand people, and a petition 'To World Opinion' was drawn up by Pavel Litvinov and Larisa Bogoraz Daniel (the then wife of Yuli Daniel). It was these two who, in August 1968, determined that, whatever the cost, the world should be told of internal Soviet opposition to the invasion of Czechoslovakia. Litvinov remembers:

> We brought some primitive banners. My slogan was 'For your and our freedom' . . . and we decided to sit right across the

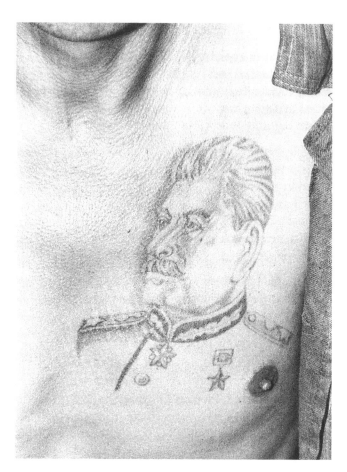

107 Stalin as totem – a prisoner's tattoo.

108 Stagnation and neo-Stalinism. Brezhnev, Kosygin and Podgorny accept the plaudits of the toiling masses.

groomed, and his hair style is not too modish either. There is
no anarchical disorder on the one hand or bourgeois smartness
on the other; everything is in the semi-modern, bureaucratic
style. In the old days he (or his predecessor) affected the
representative-of-the-proletariat style, ostentatiously untidy,
rude and energetic. This gave way to a recent, austere style, to
behaving like a block of icy determination. . . . His real
passion is sitting at his desk, with the government telephone
(the 'vertushka') within reach, scanning Central Committee
resolutions that will become tomorrow's laws, making
sovereign decisions that will affect the life of millions, saying
into the telephone, 'Think it over carefully, but to me it seems
advisable to do it this way,' then settling back in his chair
knowing his 'suggestion' will be carried out.[10]

Of such was the kingdom of Stalin, under his successors. It could
behave with state violence, as in Czechoslovakia and later Afghanistan. It could misuse psychiatry as an arm of the secret police. It could
and did send individual dissidents to the camps, where some of them
died. It wielded a heavy and repressive censorship of the arts and
literature. It doggedly pursued the expansion of the Soviet military-
industrial complex to the detriment of consumer welfare. But was it
Stalinism? That, according to Anatoli Strelyany, depends on how
you define the term:

> Does Stalinism exist any more? . . . If one were to understand
> Stalinism as the ideology and putting into practice of the
> official command of violence and of compulsion, then of course
> Stalinism is still flourishing in our day. But if you perceive it as
> the reign of terror, red terror then of course there aren't even
> traces of it any more. If you could see it as a schizophrenic faith
> in the things that could be constructed in a non-materialist way
> – that would be more acceptable to mankind than your
> imperfect materialistic economy – then Stalinism is very much
> alive in the minds of our ideologists and of ordinary people.
> What is Stalinism? It depends what you read into it.

Just as Brezhnev presided over a cult without a personality, so the
Soviet command system slithered into the eighties as an ideology
without a target. In Party headquarters throughout the land paper
was shuffled from one desk to another by the Nomenklatura whose

main aim was to hold on to their privileges, mouthing the Party slogans of the radiant future.[11] The intelligentsia held the regime in open contempt. The workforce chafed without motivation. The imperative of terror had been withdrawn, but the incentive of self-advancement seemed not to be on offer. There was corruption on high, and a debilitated social contract between ruled and rulers summed up in the quip: 'You pretend to pay us and we'll pretend to work.' As the Brezhnev generation grew old and senile in power the state funeral – of Brezhnev, Andropov, Ustinov, Chernenko – became in the early 1980s as much a part of the rotation of the seasons as the anniversary of the October Revolution.

Eventually change could not be postponed. The ablest of a fresh generation, Mikhail Gorbachev was born in 1931 on one of the new kolkhoz settlements when Stalin was already about his terrible work of collectivisation. He became the new General Secretary in 1985, nominated by the veteran Gromyko. The peasant's son who had taken a law degree at Moscow University during the last paranoid years of Stalin's terror had been friendly with a young Czech communist student, Zdenek Mlynar. Mlynar remembers his scepticism about 'enemies of the people':

> In 1952 . . . we were led to believe that any ideas that differed even slightly from the rigid party line were anti-party, and that any person who held such views should be tried, executed, taken out of the history books. . . . It was then that Gorbachev said to me: 'Lenin did not have Martov arrested, he allowed him to leave the country'. . . . To confide an opinion of this sort to a foreigner, even to a friend, was unusual in those days.[12]

Mlynar later became a leader of the reform faction in Czechoslovakia, a country Gorbachev visited in the wake of the Warsaw Pact invasion, drawing his own conclusions about how Stalin's legacy in Eastern Europe should be handled. He also travelled in the west, and his Party posts in Soviet agriculture taught him the deficiencies of the planning structure in the hardest way – by personal failure.

Gorbachev is a convinced Leninist. Where Khrushchev had

109 Mikhail Gorbachev at the Congress of Deputies, 1989.

drawn one line at the Twentieth Congress, after which there were 'crimes', so the new policy was to go back beyond Stalin altogether to return to a purified, generous Lenin, the Lenin of NEP. He exists, like other Lenins. But even this Lenin put the leading role of the Party, and the preservation of its unity, above democracy either within it or in civil society as a whole. The Gorbachev keynote themes, *glasnost* (openness) and *perestroika* (restructuring) were intended to make Soviet society engage in dialogue with itself, and to begin the painful transformation to dismantle the Soviet state, and somehow start afresh.

Nevertheless, almost the whole of the Stalin inheritance has been dumped. *Glasnost* and the removal of overt repression have set off an unprecedented debate about Stalin. The Soviet press has become a humming information exchange, rather than a monotonous loud-speaker of official views. Journals like *Ogonyok* and *Moscow News* take the lead, but others follow. The banned classics of Bulgakov, Pasternak and Solzhenitsyn are published in their homeland, along-side powerful new works like Rybakov's *Children of the Arbat*, in which Stalin is shown brooding over the elimination of Kirov. Kopelev, Sinyavsky and the director Lyubimov have been welcomed back with honour. Stalin, Lenin and Trotsky have been portrayed on stage in the plays of Shatrov, engaged in real debate about the course of the revolution. The organisation Memorial, with offshoots throughout the Soviet Union, has dedicated itself to producing an ineradicable monument to the victims of Stalin's terror, 'to give the country back its past, its history', in the words of its joint organiser Alexander Daniel: 'Without repossessing the past, we shall have no future.' This has caused great unease in the Party apparatus, as the Byelorussian writer Ales Adamovich (now an elected member of the Congress) points out:

> The goal of the organisation was so obviously a sacred national
> one that nobody wanted to reveal himself as a fully fledged
> Stalinist who would want to forbid it. But resistance there was,
> because if you go along that path of absolute frankness and
> truth people will ask the question who is to blame. Where are
> those who perpetrated these deeds? . . . What were the social
> and political structures responsible for these goings-on?

**110 On the shelf. A store of redundant Stalin busts.**

The leadership has alarmed the functionaries by allowing Memorial to organise openly. But this has won it an ally. Sir Fitzroy Maclean, after more than fifty years of watching the Soviet Union, believes that 'for the first time in Russian history, and I say advisedly Russian history, the government have the intelligentsia on their side'.

The new openness has had a profound effect on Stalin's heirs, the 18 million or more members of the 'partocracy' and the military. They have seen their shortcomings ruthlessly publicised, when once they could be hushed up. Where there is a scandal, be it the explosion at Chernobyl or the massacre in Tbilisi, Georgia, the media now want to report it and, worse, to apportion blame. A new constitution will enshrine rights under the law, not in the gift of the administrative class. The elections to the 1989 Congress allowed multiple choice for many seats, and a negative vote in others where the Party boss was the sole permitted nominee. Thirty Party secretaries were defeated. The debates of the Congress, of the Supreme Soviet selected from its ranks, and the Party Plenum on Nationalities, were carried at length on Soviet television, where programmes like *Pyatoe Koleso* (Fifth

Wheel) in Leningrad and *Do i posle polunochi* (Both Sides of Midnight) in Moscow also operate in their own right according to classic journalistic criteria. Millions watch, enthralled.

But can it last? Can Gorbachev get away with his gamble? Some distinguished dissidents, like Vladimir Bukovsky, sent involuntarily into western exile in 1976, think not. He believes that the reform programme incubates its own antibodies in the displaced and displeased Nomenklatura.

> The reversal of the current trend of liberalisation will inevitably be forthcoming. That is the nature of the Soviet system. It couldn't be otherwise. There is nothing in between. There is no known political system in between totalitarianism and democracy. . . . There are 18 million members of the Communist Party; the new class which will not give up its own role, its privileges, its position of power. What do you propose to do with these 18 million people?

Apart from free speech, Gorbachev clashes with the ghost of Stalin in four key areas. First, he can be charged with the destruction of Party infallibility, that casket in which the jewel of ideology is held. Secondly, his economic model is not succeeding for the mass of the people, who are keener on sausage on the table than *glasnost* on television. Thirdly, his tolerance of the break-up of Stalin's Eastern European monolith gives security worries – of different kinds – to both the Soviet Party and the military. Finally, the nationalities question within the Soviet Union, for which Stalin had a brusque and brutal answer, has re-emerged to haunt the Russians.

First, on ideology the Stalinists grumble that the old master is being scapegoated for all the ills of Soviet society, including those for which the present regime is responsible, without the opportunity for reply. On 13 March 1988, the newspaper *Sovetskaya Rossiya* published a full-page letter from Nina Andreyeva, a Leningrad chemistry lecturer in her early fifties, which protested bitterly at the presentation of Soviet history as one of unrelieved terror and coercion. Andreyeva lamented a lost asceticism, and the questioning of 'collectivisation, industrialisation, the cultural revolution, which brought our country up to great power status'. She went on to argue that: 'These attacks on the state of the dictatorship of the proletariat and on the then leaders of our country have not only political, ideological and moral causes, but also their social basis.'[13]

This she identified with the social classes overthrown by the October Revolution, and those whom it had subsequently vanquished, a motley crew of kulaks, NEP men, Trotskyists, Social Democrats and national deviationists. In the pause before *Pravda* published a reply to this attack the Moscow intelligentsia wondered who had inspired it, and grew profoundly uneasy. There is no doubt that Andreyeva speaks for an enraged section of the older generation. More letters of this kind are written to the Soviet press than is suggested by the tiny number which are published. These people want the old certainties back, and a leader whose use of power was based on the Party's historic claim to monopolise it for ever.

How might this minority, which is shut out from most media, but never intimidated by terror in the manner it would reserve for its own opponents, become a majority? Not by reinvoking what the masses see as an exhausted ideology. There is substantial evidence that the masses will use their power in the ballot box against the Party as a whole if they get the chance, and for reformers within like the flawed but vigorous Yeltsin. An August 1989 opinion poll showed Gorbachev approved as a popular choice for President by 46 per cent of Soviet citizens, and by a further 29 per cent 'with reservations', as against 14 per cent opposed.[14]

Popularity vanishes with hunger and hardship. *Perestroika* is not yet working on the economic front. Its challenge might come from economic discontent. The painful transition from centralised allocated and heavy subsidy to enterprises which have to succeed in a social market has not been made. And *glasnost* allows this point to be made openly in the Soviet media, fanning the flames of discontent. Pollution, alcoholism and high rates of infant mortality are now the subject of critical and comparative analysis as much as the economy.

In 1987 Nikolai Shmelev wrote in *Novy Mir*:

> Today we have an economy characterised by shortages, imbalances, in many respects unmanageable and, if we were to be honest, almost unplannable. . . . Through the years of stagnation the working masses have reached a state of almost total disinterestedness in freely committed and honest labour. . . . Apathy, indifference, thieving have become mass

phenomena, with at the same time aggressive envy towards high earners.[15]

To which the apathetic masses reply: 'What have you done for us?' A worker from Nizhny Tagil put it for them at the 1988 Party Congress: 'The workers ask, where is *perestroika*? Food supply was bad, it is still bad, and now they have introduced ration coupons for sugar. There was no meat, there is no meat. Industrial consumer goods seem to have vanished.'[16] The new co-operatives are widely disliked for profiteering. As Alec Nove remarks: 'There are so many shortages that you get a possibility of enrichment akin to allowing people freedom of trade during the war. Clearly, there's no war on, but Soviet popular psychology accustomed to state prices resents the high prices charged by the co-ops.' And among the general grumbling at this situation, as bad or worse in Moscow as on the Soviet periphery, there is the submerged aside that things were not like this in Stalin's time.

At the unofficial private Stalin museum in Tbilisi run by Ushangi Davitashvili, the exhibit which attracts most attention is a simple display of the decrees reducing prices during Stalin's last years, and the percentages by which they came down. The point is not lost. Davitashvili tells his many visitors:

> After the war ration cards were abolished. Stalin abolished them, and every year the general material welfare of the people got better and better, but now everything's going back. Everyone says this. We've already had four years of *perestroika* and no one can see any benefits. And the well-ordered state which Stalin built with his own merciless right hand is falling apart.

One Soviet journalist felt moved to write, in September 1989, to a British newspaper in confirmation of this mood:

> Many in the Soviet Union certainly yearn for a 'strong hand' and blame *perestroika* for all our economic and other ills. These sentiments are prevalent among the apparatchiks who are nostalgic about 'the good old days'. But they are not alone in clinging to the past. Many workers, farmers, and intellectuals also complain, but for other reasons. One popular grievance is

that under Stalin there was enough soap, whereas now it is rationed. Democracy, it is said, has spoiled the people.[17]

Thirdly, there is the unease which goes beyond the Party at the acquiescence of the Soviet leadership in what has happened in Eastern Europe, and the concessions to the United States in disarmament negotiations. The parents of young conscripts brought home from Afghanistan rejoiced at that skilful disengagement. The conscripts still on garrison duty in Eastern Europe will shed no tears if they go home. But a substantial part of the security system which Stalin created and which his successors upheld by force of arms has gone. There are multi-party systems in Hungary and Poland, where fulsome apologies have been made for the 1968 invasion of Czechoslovakia. The 'counter-revolutionary Nagy' has been rehabilitated. The Czech quislings have been swept contemptuously aside. Worst of all, Stalin's second-best solution to the German problem – permanent partition – now appears to be tottering. The Berlin Wall is down, and East Germans can look to the West. An Anschluss in the heart of Europe would have incalculable consequences. That Soviet generation which lost more than 25 million war dead looks askance at these changes, to which there seems no limit. The ostentatious visit by Gorbachev's principal critic Yegor Ligachev to East Berlin, as refugees began to flood out of the disintegrating DDR to the west, marks the agonised debate in the Soviet leadership and the military.

This is replicated within the Soviet Union itself by the problem of the nationalities. The tsarist empire (with the exception of most of Poland and Finland) was reabsorbed by the Soviet Union between 1920 and 1945. Stalin, the Georgian turned Great Russian, used deportation, suppression and terror against the nationalities. They were cowed, but not tamed. Now nationalism has re-emerged as the strongest motor force of more than 100 million Soviet citizens. In the Baltic, in Georgia, and in the Ukraine, they taunt and tug at Moscow's control. Elsewhere, as in the bloody dispute between Armenia and Azerbaijan over the disputed enclave of Nagorny Karabakh, they fight each other and the Russian military power imposed to keep the peace. The Baltic states are moving towards separatism, to the alarm of their substantial Russian minorities, declaring the 1940 decision under compulsion to enter the Soviet Union to be null and void. Despite the hostility to the idea of the 1989

Plenum on Nationalities, the Lithuanian Communist Party has declared that it will 'become a political force in the creation of an independent Lithuanian state based on law [by] itself seeking independence in the course of *perestroika*'. Georgia, forcibly incorporated in 1921, itches to follow. And Gorbachev's need to reform the power structure of the Soviet Union means that he has to continue to remove the strong Stalinists who remain in power in the Soviet republics, like Shcherbitsky in the Ukraine, who kept the iron hand of repression on this nation of 60 million for so long. Now the Ukraine and Byelorussia are stirring too. Memories of massacre and famine feed national sentiment. In Byelorussia the relentless exhumation of the Kuropaty killing fields by Zenon Pozniak has fused with the mood of national separatism.

All this arouses unease among the Russians, who remain a precarious majority in the Soviet Union. Even crusading journalists like Lyudmila Saraskina feel it.

> The Russian empire still exists, although it is called the Union of Soviet Socialist Republics. But to put right a historic injustice by giving back all the territories of the Soviet Union to their original occupiers – what will be the price? In the Baltic states I heard people say we must divide up the Soviet Union at any cost, and if you ask them at what price they say, well, let there be civil war. If we allow such a thing to happen again in our history it will just destroy us.

Already Great Russian chauvinism has been easily inflamed. The openly anti-semitic and Russian nationalist organisation *Pamyat* (Memory) speaks in paranoid tones that may win a response if the Soviet Union unravels. Exasperation with the nationalities and their claims is growing in the centre. Elements in the Party and the military yearn to follow Stalin's methods with dissenters. Some see the test case as the events of 9 April 1989, when an entirely peaceful demonstration in Tbilisi was broken up by tanks and troops armed with poison gas and sharpened spades. More than a score of demonstrators were massacred. This provocation, organised in Gorbachev's absence in Britain by a Politburo chaired by Ligachev, has been widely seen as a dress rehearsal for tougher action, if the signal comes.

So the stake has not yet been driven through the heart of the sleeping Stalin. He may rise again. Even in his native Georgia, co-existing with nationalist sentiments, it is not difficult to find this fervour. The huge official museum at Gori may be closed for 'reorganisation', leaving the visitor to gape at the house where he was born, reconstructed under its grotesque marble canopy in 1936. The staff peer out, and do what they dare to show off their treasures to the Russian tourists who come down to this illicit shrine. In Tbilisi the private museum which Davitashvili began in angry response to Khrushchev's denunciation draws thousands of visitors. There are eighteen bound volumes of their signatures, including Svetlana Alliluyeva and the head of the local KGB, signing himself as such. Davitashvili and many like him appear in Tofik Shakhverdiev's 1989 film *Stalin is With Us*. Schoolteachers, soldiers, ex-jailers, ordinary workers. They remain believers. Things were better then. There was order, not crime. Prices went down, not up. Speculators were shot. There was a class war to be fought. The verdicts against the enemies of the people were just and fair – why, they confessed in open court! Nowhere do you feel this brooding presence of an unappeased ghost more than in Gori itself, a forlorn embittered place where morose drunks congregate in the shattered cemetery on the slopes that lead up to the citadel, and the back streets can explode in sudden, violent quarrels. A crowd gathers, a worker offers his view. Stalin will return. What is being said about him now is a tissue of lies spread by Zionists and wreckers. The Moscow government is afraid to tell the truth.

This bitterness exploded in a Moscow courtroom when the lawyer Ivan Shekhovtsov brought an action against Ales Adamovich for allegedly defaming the dead Stalin. His rage is manifest:

> The situation is unpredictable. It is explosive. I'm talking about this as a veteran of the Second World War and as a communist with grief in my heart. People are saying that we are like the Fascists. If we are Stalinists it is in the sense that we are very sensitive to the pain which our country is suffering today. We're worried to death because we defended this state and we can see that what we defended is crumbling, and that hurts. Do you understand? That's the sense in which we are Stalinists. We're defending what Stalin made of our people. But we are considered as enemies of the people, and hung with these tags. . . . It's disgraceful and dishonourable, and not a

single Stalinist has been given the opportunity in the press to explain what it means to be a Stalinist.

Feelings like these could merge with those of the deposed, the deprived, and the nostalgic, if Stalin's apologists acquire the lure of forbidden fruit. Akaki Bakradze, President of the Rustaveli Society in Stalin's native Georgia, a literary critic turned politician, put it this way:

> 'Stalin was born to be two legends. They created one for him as a living god, flattered by everyone, glorified by everyone. After his death they created another legend, namely that he was Satan. In my opinion he was neither God nor Satan. We can see him best as a strong man of politics.'

And so he was, a consummate politician, who waged what he thought was the class struggle against an ever-widening circle of enemies and faint hearts. He could use both the Cult and the terror to shape the masses to his will, yet be mordantly cynical about both. He goes down in history, against formidable opposition, as the greatest mass killer of the twentieth century. But it would be wrong to see him as a criminal psychopath, without acknowledging his skills of manipulation, persuasion, endurance and – in extremis – self-correction. If his creation now falls apart, nostalgia for this successor of Ivan and Peter may reappear as the last cries of the last victims die away.

An open debate on Stalin, in which his detractors and supporters alike have their say, is the best guarantee that there will be no furtive Stalin cult in the Soviet Union. This book is intended as a modest contribution to that debate, and the wider debate about the Leninist state with which it is now joined. It portrays Stalin the man, not the monster, but its dedication none the less must be to the nameless millions of his victims, whose sufferings have scarred a whole society.

**111**

# NOTES

## Introduction

1 Mikhail Gorbachev, Report to the CPSU, Central Committee and the USSR Supreme Soviet on the 70th Anniversary of the Great October Socialist Revolution, 2 Nov. 1987. Quoted in Robert V. Daniels, *A Documentary History of Communism*, vol. 1, *Communism in Russia*, p. 441, (University Press of New England, Hanover and London, 1988 edn)

2 ibid., p. 441

3 ibid., p. 438

4 Moshe Lewin in a paper presented to the Cortona Conference, 'Il Mito dell'URSS nella Cultura Occidentale', April 1989

## Chapter One

1 Quoted by Robert C. Tucker, *Stalin as Revolutionary: 1879–1929*. p. 72 (Chatto & Windus, London, 1974)

2 V. Kaminsky and I. Vereshchagin, 'Detstvo i iunost' vozhdia dokumenty, zapisi, rasskazy' *Molodaia gvardiia*, no. 12 (1939) (Tucker, op. cit., p. 76)

3 Tucker, op. cit., p. 67

4 ibid., p. 10

5 Kaminsky and Vereshchagin, 'Detstvo', (Tucker, op. cit., p. 84)

6 Stalin, *Works*, 1955 edn, vol. 13, p. 115 (Lawrence & Wishart, London, 1955)

7 ibid., vol. 8, p. 183

8 Isaac Deutscher, *Stalin*, p. 44 (Pelican Books, London, revised edn, 1966)

9 Lenin, 'What is to Be Done?' from Daniels, *A Documentary History of Communism*, vol. 1, p. 8

10 Daniels, op. cit., vol. 1, p. *xx*

11 Quoted by John Keep in *The Blackwell Encyclopedia of the Russian*

*Revolution*, Harold Shukman, ed., p. 357 (Basil Blackwell, Oxford, 1988)

12  Stalin, op. cit., vol. 1, p. 135
13  ibid., p. 136
14  Quoted by Roy Medvedev in *Let History Judge*, pp. 582–3 (Columbia University Press, New York, revised edn, 1989)
15  Tucker, op. cit., pp. 102, 113
16  Quoted by Tucker, op. cit., p. 108


### Chapter Two

1  Stalin, *Works*, vol. 6, p. 56
2  ibid., p. 57
3  Robert Service, 'Stalin before Stalinism', paper presented to the Urbino Conference on *L'Eta Dello Stalinismo*, 1989, p. 4
4  Quoted by Tucker, *Stalin as Revolutionary*, p. 150
5  ibid., p. 149
6  Service, op. cit., p. 5
7  Deutscher, *Stalin*, pp. 119, 120
8  ibid., p. 120
9  Quoted by Tucker, op. cit., p. 152
10  Stalin, op. cit., vol. 2, p. 375
11  Lenin, 'Two Tactics of Social Democracy in the Democratic Revolution', July 1905, extract in Daniels, *A Documentary History of Communism*, vol. 1, p. 29
12  Central Party Archive, Institute of Marxism–Leninism, collection 17, list 1, item 385, sheet 11, quoted in Medvedev, *Let History Judge*, p. 41
13  Medvedev, op. cit., pp. 42, 43
14  Stalin, op. cit., vol. 3, p. 37
15  Lenin, *Works*, vol. 25, p. 281 (Progress Publishers, Moscow, 1964)
16  John Reed, *Ten Days That Shook The World* pp. 265–7 (Penguin Books, London, 1977 edn)
17  Lenin, op. cit., quoted by Robert Conquest, *The Harvest of Sorrow*, pp. 43–4 (Oxford University Press, New York, 1989)
18  Deutscher, op. cit., p. 174


### Chapter Three

1  Quoted by Alec Nove in 'Stalinism, Marxism, Leninism', paper presented to the Cortona Conference on 'Il Mito dell' URSS nella Cultura Occidentale', April 1989, pp. 2, 3

2 Lenin writing in *Pravda* on 15 Nov. 1917, quoted by Reed, *Ten Days That Shook The World*, p. 242

3 Lenin, *Works*, vol. 25, p. 404

4 Lenin, op. cit., vol. 26, p. 435

5 Medvedev, *Let History Judge*, pp. 56, 57

6 Lenin, *Pravda*, 22 Nov. 1917

7 Jan Meijer, ed., *The Trotsky Papers 1917–22*, vol. 1, pp. 717–19 (Mouton & Co., The Hague, 1964)

8 ibid., vol. 2, p. 279

9 Letter from Lenin to the Politburo, 19 March 1922. This is not in Lenin's Published Works, but has circulated in private in the Soviet Union and was published in *Vestnik Russkogo Studencheskogo Khristianskogo Dvizheniya*, no. 98, 1970, pp. 54–63. There is, however, a direct reference to the letter in Lenin's *Works*, 5th edn, vol. 45, pp. 666–7 (Moscow, 1964)

10 Quoted in Alec Nove, *An Economic History of the USSR*, pp. 62–3 (Penguin Books, London, 1984)

11 Lenin, op. cit., vol. 32, p. 215

12 Lenin, op. cit., quoted by Moshe Lewin in *Lenin's Last Struggle* (Faber & Faber, London, 1969)

13 Lenin, op. cit., vol. 32, p. 200

14 Moshe Lewin, *The Making of the Soviet System*, p. 23 (Methuen, London, 1985)

15 Michael Voslensky, *Nomenklatura: Anatomy of the Soviet Ruling Class*, p. 47 (Bodley Head, London, 1984)

16 Quoted by Alec Nove in 'Stalinism, Marxism, Leninism', p. 6

17 Lenin, op. cit., quoted in Tucker, *Stalin as Revolutionary*, p. 234

18 Lenin, op. cit., vol. 33, p. 358

19 Quoted in Medvedev, op. cit., p. 80

20 ibid., p. 81

21 ibid., p. 84

22 Lewin, op. cit., p. 205

23 Stalin, *Works*, vol. 6, p. 47

24 Stalin, *Works*, vol. 7, p. 402

25 John McDonald, *Strategy in Poker, Business and War*, quoted in Tucker, *Stalin as Revolutionary*, p. 300

26 Service, 'Stalin before Stalinism', p. 16

27 Stalin, *Works*, vol. 12, p. 178

28 Leszek Kolakowski, *Main Currents of Marxism*, vol. 3, *The Breakdown*, p. 38 (Clarendon Press, Oxford, 1978)

## Chapter Four

1 Stalin, *Works*, vol. 12, p. 146
2 ibid., p. 173
3 Quoted by Alec Nove in 'Stalinism, Marxism, Leninism', p. 5
4 Lewin, *The Making of the Soviet System*, p. 126
5 Medvedev, *Let History Judge*, p. 234
6 Moshe Lewin, *Russian Peasants and Soviet Power*, p. 508 (George Allen & Unwin, London, 1968)
7 Quoted by Robert Conquest in *The Harvest of Sorrow*, p. 306 (Oxford University Press, New York, 1986)
8 Lev Kopelev, *The Education of a True Believer*, p. 279 (Wildwood House, London, 1981)
9 Quoted in *The Foreign Office and the Famine*, p. 313, ed. Marco Carynnyk, Lubomyr Y. Luciuk and Bohdan S. Kordan (The Limestone Press, Kingston, Ontario, 1988); tour of Mr W. Duranty in North Caucasus and the Ukraine; William Strang (Moscow) to Sir John Simon (Foreign Secretary), 26 Sept. 1933 (FO. 371/17253 N7182)
10 Quoted by Conquest, op. cit., p. 316
11 ibid., p. 317
12 *Manchester Guardian*, 28 March 1933
13 Stalin, op. cit., vol. 11, p. 170
14 Stalin, op. cit., vol. 13, p. 41
15 Quoted by Stephen F. Cohen in *Bukharin and the Bolshevik Revolution*, p. 178 (Wildwood House, London, 1974)
16 Stalin, op. cit., vol. 12, pp. 52, 53
17 Kopelev, op. cit., p. 249
18 Hiroaki Kuromiya, *Stalin's Industrial Revolution: Politics and Workers 1928–1932*, p. 143 (Cambridge University Press, 1988)
19 Stalin, op. cit., vol. 12, p. 241
20 ibid., p. 274
21 Kuromiya, op. cit., p. 316
22 Conquest, op. cit., pp. 170, 171
23 Lenin, *Works*, vol. 26, p. 109
24 Quoted by David J. Dallin and Boris Nicolaevsky, in *Forced Labour in Soviet Russia*, p. 208 (Hollis & Carter, London, 1948)
25 ibid., p. 102
26 Quoted in ibid., p. 90
27 Conquest, op. cit., p. 307
28 Stalin, op. cit., vol. 12, pp. 176–7

### Chapter Five

1 Quoted in *Izvestia TsK KPSS*, no. 6, p. 106, 1989
2 *Ogonyok*, no. 15, April 1989
3 Medvedev, *Let History Judge*, p. 297
4 Cohen, *Bukharin and the Bolshevik Revolution*, p. 344
5 Medvedev, op. cit., p. 303
6 Stalin, *Works*, vol. 13, p. 354
7 Quoted by Robert Conquest, *Stalin and the Kirov Murder*, p. 28 (Hutchinson, London, 1989)
8 Stalin, op. cit., vol. 13, p. 385
9 Medvedev, op. cit., p. 332
10 Anton Antonov-Ovseyenko, *The Time of Stalin: Portrait of a Tyranny*, p. 82 (Harper & Colophon Books, New York, 1983)
11 Conquest, *Stalin and the Kirov Murder*, p. 29
12 Evidence submitted to the 1956 Special Commission of Inquiry into the murder of Kirov, quoted by Nikita Khrushchev in an extract from his memoirs published in *Ogonyok*, no. 28, July 1989
13 Robert Conquest, *The Great Terror*, p. 59 (Macmillan, London, 1968)
14 Medvedev, op. cit., p. 335
15 From Nikita Khrushchev's memoirs, op. cit.
16 Conquest, *The Great Terror*, p. 53
17 Lewin, *The Making of the Soviet System*, p. 45
18 Cohen, op. cit., p. 357
19 Stephen F. Cohen, ed., *An End To Silence*, p. 23 (W. W. Norton & Co., New York, 1982)
20 Lewin, op. cit., p. 309
21 Quoted by Medvedev, op. cit., p. 603
22 Daniels, *A Documentary History of Communism*, vol. 1, p. 272
23 Conquest, *The Great Terror*, p. 146
24 Quoted in Conquest, *The Great Terror*, p. 147
25 From Khrushchev's secret speech as quoted in *Khrushchev Remembers*, comm. Edward Crankshaw (André Deutsch, London, 1971)
26 Daniels, op. cit., p. 261
27 Lewin, op. cit., p. 310
28 Osip Mandelstam, *The Eyesight of Wasps*, poems transl. James Greene (Angel Books, London, 1989)
29 Anna Akhmatova, *Selected Poems*, p. 69, transl. Richard McKane (Penguin Books, London, 1969)
30 Quoted by Antonov-Ovseyenko, op. cit., p. 149
31 Moshe Lewin in a paper presented to the Cortona Conference, April 1989

## Chapter Six

1 Quoted in Alex de Jonge, *Stalin and the Shaping of the Soviet Union*, p. 460 (William Collins, London, 1986)

2 Adam B. Ulam, *Expansion and Co-Existence: A History of Soviet Foreign Policy 1917–1973*, p. 135 (Praeger, New York, 1974)

3 Theses and Resolutions, XII Plenum of Executive Committee of the Comintern, p. 11 (Moscow, 1932)

4 Svetlana Alliluyeva, *Only One Year*, p. 369 (Hutchinson, London, 1969)

5 *Pravda*, 22 June 1989

6 Deutscher, *Stalin*, p. 419

7 Stalin, 'Problems of Leninism', Report to the XVIII Congress of the CPSU

8 *Izvestia*, 1 Sep. 1939

9 Quoted in O. A. Rzheshevsky, *Europe 1939: Was War Inevitable?*, p. 138 (Progress Publishers, Moscow, 1989)

10 *Izvestia*, 1 Nov. 1939

11 *Izvestia*, 25 Dec. 1939

12 During the 17 months of the Pact the Soviet Union supplied Germany with 865,000 tons of oil, 140,000 tons of manganese ore, 14,000 tons of copper, 3,000 tons of nickel, 101,000 tons of raw cotton, 1 million tons of lumber and 1,462,000 tons of grain. Figures from Mikhail Heller and Aleksandr Nekrich, *Utopia in Power*, p. 353 (Hutchinson, London, 1986)

13 Quoted in *Pravda* article by G. Kumanev, 22 June 1989

14 *Izvestia*, 14 June 1941

15 *Foreign Policy of the Soviet Union during the Great Patriotic War*, *Moscow 1946*, vol. 1, p. 29, quoted in Heller and Nekrich, op. cit.

16 *Khrushchev Remembers*, p. 169

17 Czeslaw Milosz, *The Captive Mind*, p. 69 (Vintage Books, New York, 1981)

## Chapter Seven

1 Milovan Djilas, *Conversations with Stalin*, p. 84 (Penguin Books, London, 1963)

2 *The Conferences at Malta and Yalta, 1945*, p. 589 (US Government Publication, 1955), quoted in Heller and Nekrich, *Utopia in Power*, p. 423

3 Lev Kopelev, *No Jail for Thought*, p. 87 (Secker & Warburg, London, 1977)

4  Alexander Solzhenitsyn, *The Gulag Archipelago*, vol. 1, p. 238 (Collins Harvill, London, 1974)

5  Mark Gefter, *Rabochii klass y sovremennyi mir* (The Working Class and the Contemporary World), no. 1, 1988, quoted in Alec Nove, *Glasnost in Action* (Unwin Hyman, London, 1989)

6  B. Sokolov, *Voprosy Istorii*, no. 9, 1988, quoted in Nove, op. cit.

7  Walter Isaacson and Evan Thomas, *The Wise Men*, p. 308 (Faber & Faber, London, 1986)

8  Deutscher, *Stalin*, p. 548

9  Quoted in Averell Harriman and Elie Abel, *Special Envoy to Churchill and Stalin, 1941–6*, p. 518 (Random House, New York, 1975)

10  Isaacson and Thomas, op. cit., p. 352

11  *Izvestia*, 21 May 1988, quoted in Nove, op. cit.

12  Svetlana Alliluyeva, *Only One Year*, p. 387

13  W. Laqueur, *A World of Secrets: The Uses and Limitations of Intelligence*, p. 11 (Basic Books, New York, 1985)

14  Quoted in H. Gordon Skillings, 'Stalinism and Czechoslovak Political Culture' in Robert Tucker, ed., *Stalinism: Essays in Historical Interpretation*, p. 267 (W. W. Norton, New York, 1977)

15  Bevin to Inverchapel, 25 Feb. 1948 (FO 371/71284)

16  Wlodzimierz Brus, 'Stalinism and the "Peoples' Democracies"', in Robert Tucker, ed., *Stalinism: Essays in Historical Interpretation*, p. 249 op. cit.

**Chapter Eight**

1  *Khrushchev Remembers*, p. 307

2  General S. M. Shtemenko, *The Soviet General Staff at War*, vol. 2, p. 45 (Progress Publishers, Moscow, 1986)

3  Svetlana Alliluyeva, *Twenty Letters to a Friend*, p. 205 (World Books, London, 1967, by arrangement with Hutchinson)

4  Alexander Solzhenitsyn, *The First Circle*, p. 112 (Collins Harvill, London, 1968)

5  *Khrushchev Remembers*, p. 301

6  ibid., p. 258

7  Antonov-Ovseyenko, *The Time of Stalin*, p. 292

8  *Khrushchev Remembers*, p. 253

9  Quoted in Medvedev, *Let History Judge*, p. 803

10  *Khrushchev Remembers*, p. 263

11  John Carswell, *The Exile: A Life of Ivy Litvinov*, p. 162 (Faber & Faber, London, 1983)

12  Solzhenitsyn, op. cit., p. 96

13 Thomas P. Whitney, ed., *Khrushchev Speaks*, p. 17 (University of Michigan Press, 1963)
14 Alec Nove, *An Economic History of the USSR*, p. 311
15 See tables in Paul Kennedy, *The Rise and Fall of Great Powers*, pp. 384–5 (Unwin Hyman, London, 1988)
16 Nikolai Shmelev and Vladimir Popov, *Na Perelome* (At the Watershed), pp. 88–9 (Novosti Press Agency, Moscow, 1989)

## Chapter Nine

1 A. Tvardovsky, 'Horizon Beyond Horizon', transl. by Vera Dunham, quoted in Cohen, ed., *An End to Silence*
2 'Khrushchev's Secret Speech', appendix to *Khrushchev Remembers*
3 *Khrushchev Remembers*, p. 318
4 Mandelstam's poem no. 286 in James Greene's transl. *The Eyesight of Wasps*
5 *Khrushchev Remembers*, p. 337
6 The style of the sudden denunciation was perfected by Stalin. His destruction of Yezhov at a committee of the Eighteenth Congress is recorded in Medvedev, *Let History Judge*, p. 459
7 Hélène Carrère d'Encausse, *Stalin: Order Through Terror*, p. 194 (Longman, London, 1981)
8 Mikhail Bartalsky, 'Rebellion in the Northern Camps', quoted in Cohen, op. cit., pp. 99–100
9 *Khrushchev Remembers*, p. 571

## Chapter Ten

1 Boris Pasternak, *Dr Zhivago*, transl. Max Hayward and Manya Harari, p. 491 (Fontana Paperbacks edn, London, 1961)
2 Czeslaw Milosz, *The Captive Mind*, p. 232
3 Joseph Brodsky 'On Tyranny' in *Less Than One*, p. 120 (Viking, London, 1986)
4 Andrei Sakharov, 'Progress, Coexistence and Intellectual Freedom' in *Sakharov Speaks*, p. 72 (Fontana Paperbacks edn., London, 1975)
5 Tibor Meray, *Thirteen Days That Shook the Kremlin*, p. 212 (Thames & Hudson, London, 1958). Thirty years later Meray was invited back to Hungary to give the commemorative oration at the re-burial of Imre Nagy.
6 *Khrushchev Remembers*, p. 429. In fact the Russian troops were sent into Hungary in 1849, not 1848

7   Leopold Labedz and Max Hayward, ed., *On Trial: The Case of Sinyavsky and Daniel*, p. 215 (Collins Harvill, London, 1967)

8   Labedz and Hayward, op. cit., p. 292. Quoted back to Sholokhov in a letter of protest by Lidia Chukovskaya

9   Boris Chichibabin, 'Stalin is not Dead', transl. by Vera Dunham, in Cohen ed., *An End to Silence*, pp. 183–4

10  Michael Voslensky, *Nomenklatura*, p. 73 (Bodley Head, London, 1984)

11  See Alexander Zinoviev, *The Radiant Future* (Bodley Head, London, 1981) for a brilliant evocation of party sterility

12  Zhores Medvedev, *Gorbachev*, p. 38 (Basil Blackwell, Oxford, revised edn, 1988)

13  *Sovetskaya Rossiya*, 13 March 1988, quoted in Nove *Glasnost in Action*, p. 60

14  *Ogonyok*, no. 34, August 1989

15  *Novy Mir*, no. 6, 1987, quoted in Alec Nove, *Stalinism and After*, p. 177 (Unwin Hyman, London, 3rd edn, 1989)

16  Quoted in Nove, *Glasnost in Action*, p. 200

17  Vladimir Mikhailov, political correspondent *Sovetskaya Rossiya*, letter to the *Independent*, dated 6 Sep. 1989

# APPENDIX: LIST OF INTERVIEWEES

APPENDIX: List of Interviewees

The following people kindly gave interviews for the Thames Television series *Stalin* upon which much of the material in this book is based. Not all the interviewees were seen in the series or quoted in the book, but each made an invaluable contribution to our understanding of the complex history of the Soviet Union under Stalin.

**Adamovich, Ales** Byelorussian writer, active in Memorial, People's Deputy, 1989.

**Aichenwald, Yuri** Writer, son of Alexander Aichenwald, Bukharinite who was shot as an 'enemy of the people'.

**Alexeyev, Vasili** NKVD officer, courtroom guard for Bukharin and other defendants in show trial.

**Alliluyev, Vladimir** Stalin's nephew, journalist.

**Alliluyeva, Kira** Stalin's niece, herself a camp victim.

**Alliluyeva, Svetlana** Stalin's daughter, writer.

**Antonov-Ovseyenko, Anton** Soviet independent historian and camp victim, son of Vladimir Antonov-Ovseyenko, Old Bolshevik shot in 1937.

**Astrov, Valentin** Graduate of Institute of Red Professors, close colleague of Bukharin, secret agent of the NKVD.

**Avdeyenko, Alexander** Writer, former builder of Magnitogorsk.

**Avtorkhanov, Abdurakhman** Historian, graduate of Institute of Red Professors.

**Babyonyshev, Sarra** Writer. Her husband was arrested and later died in a labour camp during the purges of the 1930s.

**Bakradze, Akaki** Georgian political activist, writer, President of the Rustaveli Society.

**Beglov, Gennadi** Writer and film director. Former MGB agent and camp inmate.

**Berberova, Nina** Writer and poet, left Russia in 1922.

**Berezhkov, Valentin** Stalin's interpreter.

**Berg, Revekka** Daughter of convicted Socialist Revolutionary, herself a camp victim.

**Birger, Boris** Fought at Stalingrad, artist who fell foul of the authorities during the Khrushchev period. Painter of several dissidents.

**Bukhrikidze, Tevdora** Veteran of the Great Patriotic War, Georgian.

**Bukovsky, Vladimir** Soviet dissident and Human Rights activist, forcibly exiled in 1976.

**Buziashvili, Georgi** Caretaker at the Stalin Museum in Gori, Georgia.

**Cherkezishvili, Nodar** Proprietor of private Stalin Museum in Osiauri, Georgia.

**Chernik, Nikolai** Army conscript who trained camp guards on Section 501 of the Salekhard-Igarka Railway.

**Chernyshov, Viktor** Member of a nine-man leasehold farm in the Ukraine.

**Chukhin, Ivan** Lieutenant-Colonel in the MVD in Petrozavodsk, has had access to the archives concerning the construction of the Belomor Canal.

**Cohen, Stephen F.** Historian, Professor of Politics and Director of the Russian Studies Program at Princeton University. Author: *Bukharin and the Bolshevik Revolution; Rethinking the Soviet Experience.*

**Daniel, Alexander** Member of the Memorial Steering Committee.

**Davitashvili, Ushangi** Proprietor of private Stalin Museum in Tbilisi, Georgia.

**Djilas, Milovan** Yugoslav dissident, former Vice-President of Yugoslavia under Tito, author: *The New Class; Conversations With Stalin.*

**Drach, Ivan** Ukrainian writer, political opposition spokesman.

**Gamsakhurdia, Zviad** Georgian political activist, instrumental in organising protest which preceded the massacre of 9 April 1989 in Tbilisi.

**Goldovskaya, Marina** Director of *Vlast Solovetskaya*, pioneering Soviet film about Solovki prison camp.

**Golofast, Valeri** Professor of Sociology, Leningrad.

**Grigoryants, Sergei** Editor of unofficial, *samizdat* journal *Glasnost.*

**Hazard, John N.** Nash Professor Emeritus of Law, Columbia University, Student Moscow Juridical Institute 1935–7.

**Ioffe, Nadezhda** Daughter of Adolf Ioffe, herself a Trotskyite who went to prison and camp for her beliefs.

**Itskov, Iosif** A lawyer in Moscow in the 1920s, member of the party apparatus 1924–7.

**Ivanyura, Vasili** Chairman of a collective farm in the Ukraine.

**Kalachev, Alexei** Deputy Chairman of the Bukharin Club, Naberezhnye Chelny.

**Kavtaradze, Maya** Daughter of Georgian revolutionary, Sergo Kavtaradze.

**Khailov, Alexander** Worker who participated in the events of the October Revolution in Moscow.

**Khersonsky, Alexander** Journalist on the newspaper *Krasny Sever*, Salekhard. He walked the length of the railway at Section 501.

**Khrushchev, Sergei** Scientist, son of Nikita Khrushchev.

**Kim, Yuli** Singer-songwriter, composed a song-cycle about dissidents and Soviet martyrs.

**Klyashtornaya, Maya** Spent her childhood in the camps, now believes her father is buried at Kuropaty Forest.

**Kopelev, Lev** Party activist in the Ukraine in the 1920s and '30s, arrested after the war, writer and memoirist.

**Kvachadze, Valerian** Georgian actor who played Stalin on the stage.

**Larina, Anna** Widow of Bukharin, camp victim, charged with being wife of an 'enemy of the people'.

**Leschiner, Vyacheslav** History teacher in Moscow secondary school.

**Lewin, Moshe** Professor of History, University of Pennsylvania, expert on social and political structures of the USSR. Author: *Russian Peasants and Soviet Power; The Making of the Soviet System*.

**Litvinov, Pavel** Grandson of Maxim, Red Square demonstrator in 1968, Human Rights activist.

**Luriye, Samuil** Literary editor of *Neva* magazine in Leningrad which published Robert Conquest's *The Great Terror*.

**Maclean, Sir Fitzroy** Former MP, Second Secretary, British Embassy, Moscow 1937–9. Author: *Eastern Approaches*.

**Martynov, Viktor** Lorry driver, Kamaz factory, Naberezhnye Chelny.

**Martyukhin, Lev** Worked as a prisoner on the Belomor Canal, 1935–6.

**Maslo, Alisa** Witness to the 1933 famine in the Ukraine.

**Matusevich, Tatyana** Witness who heard the shots and saw the activity during the massacres at Kuropaty Forest, while on guard at her state farm.

**Meshko, Oksana** Ukrainian dissident, twice a camp victim, active in Ukrainian Helsinki Watch.

**Metter, Israel** Leningrad writer, lived through the Blockade, was present at the meeting when Zhdanov denounced the writers Akhmatova and Zoshchenko.

**Mitchison, Naomi** Writer. In 1932 went to Soviet Union on visit organised by Society for Socialist Inquiry and Propaganda (part of Fabian Society).

**Moiseyev, Semyon** NKVD officer in charge of section 8 on the Belomor Canal.

**Muggeridge, Malcolm** Writer and broadcaster. Correspondent for the *Manchester Guardian* in Moscow, 1932–3. Reported his own eyewitness account of the famine in the Ukraine, 1933.

**Muggeridge, Kitty** Wife of Malcolm Muggeridge, in Moscow, 1932.

**Mulkigian, Alice** American citizen, was arrested on a false charge during a visit to Armenia and spent 5 years in a Soviet labour camp.

**Nove, Alec** Professor Emeritus of Economics at Glasgow University, expert on the Soviet economy. Author: *An Economic History of the USSR; Was Stalin Really Necessary?; Glasnost in Action.*

**Ovdiuk, Alexandra** Retired schoolteacher in the Ukraine, she witnessed the famine, 1933.

**Papava, Alexander** Georgian party member, worked with Beria in the 1930s, arrested and sent to the camps under Stalin.

**Pishy, Mykola** Ukrainian war veteran, as a small boy he witnessed the famine in his village.

**Polyakov, Yuri** Soviet Academician, historian.

**Pozniak, Zenon** Byelorussian historian and archaeologist who disclosed the mass graves and supervised the exhumations at Kuropaty Forest.

**Rapoport, Yakov** Doctor arrested in the Doctors' plot.

**Razgon, Lev** Writer, spent many years in the camps, active in Memorial.

**Roberts, Sir Frank** Retired diplomat and former Ambassador to USSR, served in the British Embassy, Moscow 1945–7.

**Rodionova, Natalya** Widow of Nikolai Rodionov, delegate to the Seventeenth Party Congress, 1934.

**Roginsky, Arseni** Member of Memorial Steering Committee.

**Rybin, Alexei** NKVD officer, member of Stalin's personal bodyguard from 1932–53.

**Rzheshevsky, Oleg** Institute of General History, Moscow. Specialist in diplomatic and military history.

**Salikhov, Romil** Komsomol leader. Founder member 'Avangard' co-operative in Naberezhnye Chelny. Member Bukharin Club.

**Salisbury, Harrison E.** Writer and historian. Moscow correspondent for the *New York Times*, 1949–54. Author: *The 900 Days: The Siege of Leningrad; Black Night, White Snow – Russia's Revolutions 1905–1917.*

**Samoilenko, Mikhail** NKVD officer in charge of re-education on Section 501 of the Salekhard-Igarka Railway.

**Samsonov, Alexander** Soviet Academician and military historian. Made public criticism of Stalin as war leader.

**Saraskina, Lyudmila** Soviet writer and journalist on *Moscow News*.

**Seldes, George** Writer and journalist. Moscow correspondent for the *Chicago Tribune*, 1922–3.

**Shekhovtsov, Ivan** Retired lawyer, filed a lawsuit against Adamovich in defence of Stalin.

**Shapiro, Henry** Moscow correspondent *New York Herald Tribune*, 1933, Reuters 1935, UP 1936 Bureau Chief UPI 1939–73.

**Shapiro, Ludmilla** Journalist. Russian-born wife of Henry Shapiro.

**Shatunovskaya, Olga** Member of Khrushchev Commission of Inquiry into the murder of Kirov.

**Shengelaya, Eldar** President of the Georgian Film-makers' Union and a People's Deputy.

**Shereshevsky, Lazar** Former prison-labourer on Section 501 of the Salekhard-Igarka Railway.

**Shirkov, Dima** Founder member of 'Avangard' co-operative, Naberezhnye Chelny, member Bukharin Club.

**Shkapa, Ilya** Veteran of the October Revolution, camp victim, writer.

**Sinyavsky, Andrei** Literary historian and writer, put on trial in 1966 with Yuli Daniel.

**Slavutskaya, Wilhelmina** Worked for Comintern, arrested and sent to the camps in the 1930s, served 20 years.

**Sliozberg, Olga** Arrested in the 1930s, sent to the camps.

**Strelyany, Anatoli** Writer and journalist.

**Sturua, Melor** Senior political correspondent on *Izvestia*, son of Georgi Sturua, the Georgian revolutionary who became President of Georgian SSR.

**Sverstiuk, Yevgen** Ukrainian writer, arrested for 'bourgeois nationalism' in the 1970s.

**Ter-Yegiazarova, Tamara** Tenant in the 'House on the Embankment', Moscow, since 1931.

**Tron, Alexander** Astrophysicist, leader of independent university, Leningrad.

**Tsipko, Alexander** Soviet philosopher, former Central Committee advisor, author: *Istoki Stalinisma* (Sources of Stalinism).

**Tsurkov, Arkadi** Former camp inmate, released 1987.

**Tsurkova, Irina** Wife of Arkadi, imprisoned for collecting political jokes and aiding dissidents.

**Tucker, Robert C.** Professor at Princeton University. Biographer of Stalin; author of *Stalin as Revolutionary 1879–1929*

**Tyomkina, Yelizaveta** Leningrad Party activist, her husband, General Jung, was arrested during the purge of the military, 1938.

**Ulyanova, Olga** Lenin's niece.

**Volkogonov, Dmitri** Red Army General, Stalin's official Soviet biographer.

**Volkov, Esteban (Seva)** Trotsky's grandson in Mexico, saw Trotsky dying.

**Volkov, Oleg** Writer, arrested in 1928, spent 27 years in the camps.

**Voslensky, Michael** Former member of Soviet *apparat*, defector. Author: *Nomenklatura*.

**Whitney, Thomas P.** Writer and translator, Chief Economic Section, US Embassy, Moscow 1944–7; correspondent for the Associated Press, 1947–53.

**Yelizarova, Alexandra** Pro-Stalin resident of Salekhard.

**Yevtushenko, Yevgeni** Poet, active in Memorial, People's Deputy, 1989.

**Young, Harry** Member of the British Young Communist League, in Moscow in the early '20s.

**Yurasov, Dmitri** Young independent historian, compiler of lists of those repressed under Stalin.

**Yushina, Valentina** Saw the unloading of bodies into unmarked pits, near the edges of a Moscow cemetery in late 1930s.

**Zakharova, Valentina** Retired librarian. Cultivates private plot, Naberezhnye Chelny.

**Zhigulin, Anatoli** Poet and writer, spent many years in Kolyma camps.

# GUIDE TO FURTHER READING

Few Soviet historical works are quoted in this list, since few are in English, and until very recently historians were not in the forefront of the quest for truths that did not match 'scientific socialism'. This omission is now being rectified by the Institute of General History. Meanwhile, the most up-to-date writing on Stalin is to be found in the weekly newspaper *Moscow News* and, for readers of the Russian language, in the publications *Ogonyok*, *Voprosi Istorii* and *Argumenty i Fakty*.

Unless otherwise stated, London is the place of publication.

Akhmatova, Anna, *Selected Poems* (Penguin Modern European Poets, 1969)

Akhmatova, Anna, *Selected Poems*, ed., Stanley Kunitz with Max Hayward (Collins Harvill, 1989)

Alexeyeva, Ludmilla, *Soviet Dissent: Contemporary Movements for National, Religious, and Human Rights* (Wesleyan University Press, Middletown, Connecticut, 1985)

Alliluyeva, Svetlana, *Twenty Letters to a Friend* (Hutchinson, 1967)
——, *Only One Year* (Hutchinson, 1969)

Antonov-Ovseyenko, Anton, *The Time of Stalin: Portrait of a Tyranny* (Harper & Row, New York, 1981)

Avdeyenko, Alexander, *I Love* (Cooperative Publishing Society of Foreign Workers in the USSR, Moscow, Leningrad, 1934)

Avtorkhanov, Abdurakhman, *Stalin and the Communist Party* (Institute for the Study of the USSR, Munich, 1959)

Bassow, Whitman, *The Moscow Correspondents: Reporting on Russia from the Revolution to Glasnost* (William Morrow & Co., New York, 1988)

Berberova, Nina, *The Italics are Mine* (Longmans, Green & Co., 1969)

Bergson, Abram and Levine, Herbert, *The Soviet Economy: Toward the Year 2000* (George Allen & Unwin, 1983)

Bethell, Nicholas, *The Last Secret* (André Deutsch, 1974)

Brodsky, Joseph, *Less Than One* (Viking, 1986)

Bulgakov, Mikhail, *The Master and Margarita* (Harvill Press, 1967)

Bukovsky, Vladimir, *To Build A Castle* (André Deutsch, 1978)

Carr, Edward Hallett, *A History of Soviet Russia: The Bolshevik Revolution 1917–1923*, 3 vols (Macmillan, 1950, 1951, 1953)

——, *A History of Soviet Russia: The Interregnum 1923–1924* (Macmillan, 1954)

——, *A History of Soviet Russia: Socialism in One Country 1924–1926*, 3 vols (Macmillan, 1958, 1959, 1964)

——, *A History of Soviet Russia: Foundations of a Planned Economy 1926–1929*, 3 vols, vol. 1 with Davies, R. W. (Macmillan, 1969; vol. 2, 1971; vol. 3, 1978)

——, *The Twilight of the Comintern* (Macmillan, 1986)

Carrère d'Encausse, Hélène, *Stalin – Order Through Terror* (Longman, 1981)

Carswell, John, *The Exile: A Life of Ivy Litvinov* (Faber & Faber, 1983)

Carynnyk, Marco; Luciuk, Lubomyr Y.; Kordan, Bohdan S., eds., *The Foreign Office and the Famine* (The Limestone Press, Kingston, Ontario, 1988)

Chamberlin, William H., *The Russian Revolution 1917–1921*, 2 vols (Macmillan, 1935)

Cohen, Stephen F., *Bukharin and the Bolshevik Revolution* (Wildwood House, London, 1974)

——, ed., *An End To Silence* (W. W. Norton & Co., New York, 1982)

——, *Sovieticus: American Perceptions and Soviet Realities* (W. W. Norton & Co., New York, 1986)

——, with vanden Heuvel, Katrina, *Voices of Glasnost: Interviews with Gorbachev's Reformers* (W. W. Norton & Co., New York, 1989)

Commission of the CC of CPSU, ed., *History of the Communist Party of the Soviet Union (Short Course)* (Foreign Languages Publishing House, Moscow, 1943)

Commission on the Ukraine Famine, *Investigation of the Ukrainian Famine, 1932–1933*, First Interim Report (US Government Printing Office, Washington, 1987)

——, *Investigation of the Ukrainian Famine 1932–1933*, Second Interim Report (US Government Printing Office, Washington, 1988)

——, *Investigation of the Ukrainian Famine 1932–1933*, Report to Congress (US Government Printing Office, Washington, 1988)

Conquest, Robert, *The Great Terror* (Macmillan, 1968)

——, *The Harvest of Sorrow* (Oxford University Press, New York, 1986)

——, *Stalin and the Kirov Murder* (Hutchinson, 1989)

Dallin, David J. and Nicolaevsky, Boris I., *Forced Labour in Soviet Russia* (Hollis & Carter, 1948)

Daniels, Robert V., *The Conscience of the Revolution* (Harvard University Press, 1960)

——, *A Documentary History of Communism*, vol. 1 (University Press of New England, Hanover and London, 1984)

Danilov, V. P., *Rural Russia under the New Regime* (Hutchinson Education, 1988)

De Jonge, Alex, *Stalin and the Shaping of the Soviet Union* (Fontana Paperbacks, 1987)

Deriabin, Peter and Gibney, Frank, *The Secret World* (Arthur Barker, 1960)

Deutscher, Isaac, *The Prophet Armed: Trotsky 1879–1921* (Oxford University Press, 1954)

——, *The Prophet Unarmed: Trotsky 1921–1929* (Oxford University Press, 1959)

——, *The Prophet Outcast: Trotsky 1929–1940* (Oxford University Press, 1963)

——, *Stalin: A Political Biography* (Pelican Books, revised edn, 1966)

Djilas, Milovan, *The New Class* (Thames & Hudson, 1957)

——, *Conversations with Stalin* (Penguin Books, 1963)

Erickson, John, *The Soviet High Command 1918–1941* (Macmillan, 1962)

——, *The Road to Stalingrad, Stalin's War with Germany* (Weidenfeld & Nicolson, 1975)

——, *The Road to Berlin, Stalin's War with Germany* (Weidenfeld & Nicolson, 1983)

Fainsod, Merle, *Smolensk under Soviet Rule* (Macmillan, 1959)

Fülöp-Miller, René, *The Mind and Face of Bolshevism* (G. P. Putnam's Sons, New York, 1927)

Ginsburg, Evgenia, *Into the Whirlwind* (Collins Harvill, 1967)

——, *Within the Whirlwind* (Collins Harvill, 1981)

Grigorenko, Petro G., *Memoirs* (Harvill Press, 1983)

Gromyko, Andrei, *Memories* (Century Hutchinson, 1989)

Grossman, Vasily, *Forever Flowing* (Harper & Row, New York, 1972)

——, *Life and Fate* (Collins Harvill, 1985)

Harriman, Averell and Abel, Elie, *Special Envoy to Churchill and Stalin, 1941–1946* (Random House, New York, 1975)

Heller, Mikhail and Nekrich, Aleksandr, *Utopia in Power: The History of the Soviet Union from 1917 to the Present* (Hutchinson, 1986)

Herling, Gustav, *A World Apart* (Heinemann, 1951)

Hingley, Ronald, *The Russian Secret Police* (Hutchinson, 1970)

Hosking, Geoffrey, *A History of the Soviet Union* (Fontana Books and William Collins, 1985)

Isaacson, Walter and Thomas, Evan, *The Wise Men* (Faber & Faber, 1986)

Janzen, Marc, *A Show Trial under Lenin* (Martinus Nijhoff, The Hague, 1982)

Kaminskaya, Dina, *Final Judgement: My Life as a Soviet Defence Lawyer* (Harvill Press, 1983)

Kennedy, Paul, *The Rise and Fall of Great Powers* (Unwin Hyman, 1988)

Khrushchev, Nikita, *Khrushchev Remembers*, 2 vols (André Deutsch, 1971, 1974)

Kislitsyn, Nikolia and Zubakov Vassily, *Leningrad does not surrender* (Progress Publishers, Moscow, 1989)

Knight, Amy W., *The KGB: Police and Politics in the Soviet Union* (Unwin Hyman, 1988)

Koestler, Arthur, *Darkness at Noon* (Jonathan Cape, 1940)

Kolakowski, Leszek, *Main Currents of Marxism:* vol. 1, *The Founders;* vol. 2, *The Golden Age*; vol. 3, *The Breakdown* (Clarendon Press, Oxford, 1978)

Kopelev, Lev, *No Jail for Thought* (Secker & Warburg, 1977)

——, *The Education of a True Believer* (Wildwood House, 1981)

Kostiuk, Hryhory, *Stalinist Rule in the Ukraine* (Stevens & Sons, 1960)

Krasnov, Vladislav, *Soviet Defectors: The KGB Wanted List* (Hoover Institution Press, Stanford University, California, 1985)

Kuromiya, Hiroaki, *Stalin's Industrial Revolution: Politics and Workers 1928–1932* (Cambridge University Press, 1988)

Laqueur, Walter, *A World of Secrets: The Uses and Limitations of Intelligence* (Basic Books, New York, 1985)

Labedz, Leopold and Hayward, Max, eds, *On Trial, The Case of Sinyavsky and Daniel* (Collins Harvill, London, 1967)

Leggett, George, *The Cheka: Lenin's Political Police* (Clarendon Press, Oxford, 1981)

Lenin, *Works*, vols 1–37 (Progress Publishers, Moscow, 1964)

Lewin, Moshe, *The Making of the Soviet System* (Methuen, 1985)

——, *Russian Peasants and Soviet Power* (George Allen & Unwin, 1968)

——, *Lenin's Last Struggle* (Faber & Faber, 1969)

——, *The Gorbachev Phenomenon* (Radius, 1988)

Maclean, Fitzroy, *Eastern Approaches* (Jonathan Cape, 1949)

McNeal, Robert H., *Stalin: Man and Ruler* (Macmillan Press in association with St Antony's College, Oxford, 1988)

Malsagoff, S. A., *An Island Hell: A Soviet Prison in the Far North* (A. M. Philpot Ltd, 1926)

Mandelstam, Nadezhda, *Hope against Hope* (Collins Harvill, 1971)

——, *Hope Abandoned* (Harvill Press, 1974)

Mandelstam, Osip, *The Eyesight of Wasps*, poems trans. James Greene (Angel Books, 1989)

Medvedev, Roy, *Let History Judge* (Columbia University Press, New York, revised edn, 1989)

Medvedev, Zhores, *Gorbachev* (Basil Blackwell, Oxford, revised edn, 1988)

Meijer, Jan M., *The Trotsky Papers 1917–22* (Mouton & Co., The Hague, 1964)

Mellor, Roy E. H., *The Soviet Union and its Geographical Problems* (Macmillan, 1982)

Meray, Tibor, *Thirteen Days That Shook the Kremlin* (Thames & Hudson, 1958)

Milosz, Czeslaw, *The Captive Mind* (Vintage, New York, 1981)

Muggeridge, Malcolm, *Chronicles of Wasted Time*, Part I *The Green Stick* (Collins, 1972)

——, *Winter in Moscow* (Eyre & Spottiswoode, 1934)

Nicolaevsky, Boris, *Power and the Soviet Elite* (published for the Hoover Institution on War, Revolution and Peace by Frederick A. Praeger, New York, 1965)

Nove, Alec, *An Economic History of the USSR* (Allen Lane, Penguin Books edn, 1984)

——, *Glasnost in Action* (Unwin Hyman, 1989)

——, *Stalinism and After* (Unwin Hyman, 3rd edn, 1989)

——, *Was Stalin Really Necessary?* (George Allen & Unwin, 1964)

Pasternak, Boris, *Dr Zhivago* trans. Max Hayward and Manya Harari (Collins Harvill, 1958)

Procyk, Oksana; Heretz, Leonid; Mace, James E., *Famine in the Soviet Union 1932–1933* (Harvard University Press, Cambridge, 1986)

Reed, John, *Ten Days That Shook The World* (Penguin Books edn, 1977)

Reiman, Michael, *The Birth of Stalinism: The USSR on the Eve of the "Second Revolution"* (I. B. Tauris & Co., 1987)

Rybakov, Anatoli, *Children of the Arbat* (Hutchinson, 1988)

Rzheshevsky, Oleg, *Europe 1939: Was War Inevitable?* (Progress Publishers, Moscow, 1989)

Sakharov, Andrei, *Sakharov Speaks* (Fontana Books, 1975)

Salisbury, Harrison E., *American in Russia* (Harper & Bros, New York, 1955)

——, *The 900 Days: The Siege of Leningrad* (Harper & Row, New York, 1969)

——, *Black Night, White Snow – Russia's Revolutions 1905–1917* (Doubleday, New York, 1978)

Scott, John, *Behind the Urals* (Martin Secker & Warburg, 1943)

Seldes, George, *Witness to a Century* (Ballantine Books, Random House, New York, 1987)

Service, Robert, *Lenin: A Political Life* (Macmillan, 1985)

Shapiro, Leonard, *Russian Studies* (Collins Harvill, 1986)

Shifrin, Avraham, *The First Guidebook to Prisons and Concentration Camps of the Soviet Union* (Bantam Books, New York, 1982)

Shmelev, Nikolai and Popov, Vladimir, *Na Perelome* (At the Watershed) (Novosti Press Agency, Moscow, 1989)

——, *The Turning Point: Revitalising the Soviet Economy* (Doubleday, New York, 1989)

Sholokhov, Mikhail, *And Quiet Flows the Don* (Penguin Books, 1967)

——, *Virgin Soil Upturned* (Picador Classics, 1988)

Shtemenko, General S. M., *The Soviet General Staff at War*, 2 vols (Progress Publishers, Moscow, 1985–6)

Shukman, Harold, ed., *The Blackwell Encyclopedia of the Russian Revolution* (Basil Blackwell, Oxford, 1988)

Sinyavsky, Andrei (as Abram Tertz), *The Trial Begins* (Fontana Books, 1977)

——, *The Icicle and Other Stories* (Collins Harvill, 1963)

——, *The Makepeace Experiment* (Fontana Books, 1977)

——, *Voice from the Chorus* (Harvill Press, 1976)

Solzhenitsyn, Alexander, vol. 1, *The Gulag Archipelago: 1918–1956* (I–II) (Harper & Row, New York, 1973, 1974)

——, vol. 2, *The Gulag Archipelago: 1918–1956* (III–IV) (Harper & Row, New York, 1975)

——, vol. 3, *The Gulag Archipelago: 1918–1956* (V–VII) (Harper & Row, New York, 1978)

——, *The First Circle* (Collins Harvill, 1968)

Stalin, J. V., *Works*, 1955 edn, vols 1–13 (Lawrence & Wishart, 1955)

Trotsky, L. D., *The Stalin School of Falsification* (Pathfinder Press, New York, 1971)

Tucker, Robert C., *Stalin as Revolutionary 1879–1929* (Chatto & Windus, 1974)

——, ed. *Stalinism – Essays in Historical Interpretation* (W. W. Norton & Co., New York, 1977)

Ulam, Adam B., *Stalin: The Man and his Era* (Allen Lane, 1974)

——, *The Rivals: America and Russia Since World War II* (Viking, New York, 1971)

——, *Expansion and Co-Existence: A History of Soviet Foreign Policy 1917–1973*, 2nd edn (Praeger, New York, 1974)

——, *Dangerous Relations: The Soviet Union in World Politics 1970–1982* (Oxford University Press, New York, Oxford, 1983)

Urban, George, ed., *Stalinism* (Wildwood House, London, 1985)

Valentinov, Nikolay, *Encounters with Lenin* (Oxford University Press, 1968)

Voslensky, Michael, *Nomenklatura: Anatomy of the Soviet Ruling Class* (Bodley Head, 1984)

Whitney, Thomas P., *Russia in My Life* (George Harrap & Co., 1963)

——, ed. *Khrushchev Speaks* (University of Michigan Press, Ann Arbor, 1963)

Wolin, Simon and Slusser, Robert M., eds, *The Soviet Secret Police* (Methuen, 1957)

Wolfe, Bertram, *Three Who Made a Revolution* (Dial Press, New York, 1948)

Zinoviev, Alexander, *The Radiant Future* (Bodley Head, 1981)

——, *Homo Sovieticus* (Victor Gollancz, 1985)

# INDEX

Numbers in italics refer to illustrations